Handbook
of
Educational
Technology

Handbook
of
Educational
Technology

THIRD EDITION

**Henry Ellington,
Fred Percival
and Phil Race**

Kogan Page Ltd, London
Nichols Publishing Company,
New Jersey

First published in 1984 by Kogan Page.
This third edition first published in 1993 by Kogan Page.

Kogan Page Limited
120 Pentonville Road
London N1 9JN

© Fred Percival, Henry Ellington and Phil Race, 1984, 1988, 1993

British Library Cataloguing in Publication Data
A CIP record for this book is available from the British Library.

BN 0 7494 0849 9

Published in the United States of America by Nichols Publishing,
P.O. Box 6036, East Brunswick, New Jersey 08816

ISBN (US) 0-89397-389-0

Library of Congress Cataloging-in-Publication Data
Percival, Fred.
    A handbook of educational technology / Fred Percival, Henry
Ellington, Phil Race. — 3rd ed.
        p.   cm.
    Includes bibliographical references and index.
    ISBN 0-89397-389-0 : $39.95 (U.S.)
    1. Educational technology–Handbooks, manuals, etc.
I. Ellington, Henry.   II. Race, Philip.   III. Title.
LB1028.3.P39   1993
371.3'078–dc20   93-8129 CIP

Typeset by DP Photosetting, Aylesbury, Bucks
Printed and bound by Biddles Ltd, Guildford and King's Lynn

Contents

Acknowledgements   *viii*

Introduction   **ix**

Chapter 1 The Nature of Educational Technology   **1**
Introduction   1
Technology *in* Education and Training   2
The Technology *of* Education and Training   3
The Systems Approach   4
Definitions of Educational Technology   9
Development of the Main Concerns of Educational   10
    Technology: the Elton Model
Other Areas in which Educational Technology has Developed   21
A Fresh Look at Learning   22
Conclusions   27

Chapter 2 Basic Educational Strategies   **28**
Introduction   28
The Teacher/Institution-centred Approach   28
The Student-centred Approach   34
Mix and Match – the Strategy for the Future?   44

Chapter 3 Educational Objectives and Competence   **46**
              Descriptors
Introduction   46
An Objectives-based Approach to Learning Design   47
Aims and Objectives   47
Formulating and Writing Objectives   49
Skills Analysis   52
Types of Objectives   53
Advantages and Disadvantages of Using Objectives   57
A Fresh Look at Objectives   58
Competence: 'Can Do' Statements   59
Conclusions   62

Chapter 4 Mass Instruction Techniques   63
Introduction   63
The Main Mass Instruction Methods   63
Audiovisual Media Used in Mass Instruction   71

Chapter 5 Individualized Learning Techniques   84
Introduction   84
Three Different Approaches to Individualized Learning   84
Media Used in Individualized Learning   91

Chapter 6 Group Learning Techniques   103
Introduction   103
General Features of Group Learning Methods   103
The Main Group Learning Techniques   109

Chapter 7 Assessment   121
Introduction   121
Educational Technology and Assessment   121
Desirable Characteristics of Assessment Procedures   122
Criterion-referenced and Norm-referenced Assessment   124
Test Construction   125
A Review of Assessment Methods   127
Learning and Assessment: a Critical Overview   135
Self- and Peer-assessment – Learning by Assessing   140
Conclusions   146

Chapter 8 Evaluation   148
Introduction   148
Instructional Development by Error Elimination – A   149
  'Popperian' Approach
Two Contrasting Paradigms of Evaluation   152
A Review of Evaluation Techniques   154
Evaluation of Cost-effectiveness   161
Summary   162

Chapter 9 Resources Centres   163
Introduction   163
Resources, Resources Centres and Resource-based Learning   163
The Role of Resources Centres in Different Educational   166
  Systems
The Planning, Organization and Operation of a Resources   167
  Centre

Chapter 10 Computers in Education and Training   **177**
Introduction   177
What can Computers Do?   178
How do People Interact with Computers?   178
How can Computers Help People to Learn?   179
Mainframe Computers and Terminals   180
Computers as Substitute Tutors   182
Conclusions   191

Chapter 11 A Glimpse into the Future   **193**
Introduction   193
Current Trends in Educational Technology   193
Pre-school, Primary, Secondary, Tertiary, Continuing   201
    Education and Training
Final Word   202

Glossary   *203*

Bibliography   *253*

Keyword Index   *261*

Acknowledgements

We would like to acknowledge the help that we have received from the following people in producing this book:

- Eric Addinall and Barry Murton for advice and constructive criticism of the earlier editions;
- Bill Black, for taking all the photographs;
- Kogan Page staff Dolores Black, Helen Carley and Robert Jones for their support and encouragement in the work of putting together this third edition;
- Colleagues and students at our respective universities, for comments and reactions to our ideas.

Introduction

Educational technology first emerged as a discipline in its own right in the 1950s, since when a great number of books and journal articles about it have appeared. It has always been a rapidly changing field, with new technological advances making older technologies obsolete very quickly. This book was originally written to meet the need for a 'primer' giving a broad picture of the main aspects of educational and training technology. The book aims to help educators and trainers to employ the various techniques which make up educational technology, and so bring increased effectiveness and interest to education courses and training programmes. The book is also intended for use as an introductory text for students of educational technology, and for new trainers in commerce and industry.

Since our book is not based on any particular educational system, and covers educational technology in broad terms, it should be equally suitable for use by practitioners in the UK, North America, Australasia and other English-speaking countries.

The main text of the book consists of 11 chapters, each addressing a different aspect of educational and training technology.

Chapter 1 provides a broad introduction to educational and training technology, explaining what such terms mean, and providing a brief account of the development of the discipline. For this edition we have added a section giving a down-to-earth model of how people learn, and we have linked this model to discussions about specific aspects of educational technology throughout the book.

Chapter 2 describes two contrasting approaches to education and training: the 'teacher-centred' (or 'institution-centred') approach, and the now prevalent 'learner-centred' approach.

Chapter 3 has been largely rewritten for this edition, introducing a discussion of the uses of competence descriptors in education and training. We have, however, retained much of our previous discussion of behavioural objectives, as this provides the origin for most of the contemporary developments of competence-based education and training.

Chapters 4, 5 and 6 have been updated, and respectively discuss the roles of educational and training technology in mass-instruction (for example, lectures), individualized learning (including open and flexible learning), and group-based learning (including simulations and games).

Chapter 7, 'Assessment', has been considerably expanded. Looking closely at the increasing use of self-assessment and peer-assessment in education and training, it examines in particular the benefits which such assessment processes can bring in terms of enhancing the depth of learning and alerting learners in advance to the nature of assessment criteria and assessment processes.

Chapter 8, 'Evaluation', has been updated, and some new ideas on the advantages and disadvantages of using questionnaires has been included.

Chapter 9, dealing with resource centres, is largely unchanged, apart from some additional comments about the trend towards extended hours of opening of university facilities, and the need to cater for group work in such centres, as well as silent, individual work.

Chapter 10, 'Computers in Education and Training', has been completely rewritten. It is in this area that changes have been most dramatic, and it is true that the rate of change is likely to continue to accelerate. We have therefore restricted our discussion to a broad overview of the field, and have provided an extended bibliography for the chapter, with an additional list of some of the most relevant journals covering developments in the field.

Chapter 11 retains the same title as in the previous edition: 'A Glimpse into the Future'. However, many of the speculations proffered in that edition came to fruition even more rapidly than we could have anticipated. In the present edition, we have chosen to identify a dozen of the 'trends' in educational and training technology today, and offer speculation on how these trends may manifest themselves during the next few years. We have also used this chapter to draw together the connections between the anticipated developments in educational and training technology and the general process where-by people learn, as introduced at the end of Chapter 1.

The book also contains three useful reference sections. The first is a comprehensive glossary of terms, giving explanations of around 1000 words and phrases used by trainers and educators. We have added many more terms which have come into vogue since we wrote the previous edition, but we have chosen to retain some which have slipped into the background somewhat since then, as they are still to be found in the older parts of the literature on educational and training technology.

The second reference section is a wide-ranging bibliography. This has been completely updated to include modern reference texts and articles linked to the respective chapters. While most of the references are recent, we have retained a few of the most important from earlier editions. Some of these are now out of print, but may still be tracked down in large libraries.

The third reference section is a keyword index to the material covered in the 11 chapters of the book.

We decided *not* to replace or print our previous four-page country-by-country list of professional bodies, associations and other organizations involved in the field of educational and training technology. This is mainly because there is a great state of 'flux' in the status of such organisations, many of them being involved in mergers, changes of name and so on. A further reason for dropping this section from our book is that this information is already published in a meticulously updated form every two years in the *International Yearbook of Educational and Training Technology* (also published by Kogan Page) edited by Chris Osborne. The 1992 edition gives a very detailed review of organizations, professional bodies and contact addresses for educational and training technology throughout the world.

Chapter 1

The Nature of Educational Technology

INTRODUCTION

To most people, the term 'educational technology' is, at best, confusing, and, at worst, downright off-putting. To some, the term is associated solely with the technical equipment and media of education – such as overhead projectors, television, tape-slide programmes, computers, etc. Others take the view that educational technology involves a clinical, systematic analysis of the entire teaching/learning process in an attempt to maximize its effectiveness. Indeed, extreme proponents of the latter view have sometimes been accused of treating learners more like 'impersonalized battery hens' than as 'people with inquiring minds who thrive on intellectual stimulation and human contact' – a view with which we have some sympathy.

Largely because of this confusion over its meaning, there can be little doubt that educational technology has for some years been a rather unhelpful jargon expression. Indeed, many practitioners working in the field are embarrassed by it, and, in some cases, have even made an attempt to disown it; several former 'educational technology units' in colleges and universities have, for example, been re-named 'educational development units', 'learning units', or something similar. No one has so far managed to come up with an alternative, universally-acceptable name, however, so we appear to be stuck with it for the time being, and, for this reason, we will continue to use the term 'educational technology' throughout this book.

The perceptions of what constitutes 'educational technology' have evolved over a period of about 30 years, and its exact nature is not easily explained. Indeed Kenneth Richmond, in his excellent book *The Concept of Educational Technology* (1970), devoted the first 70 pages to a discussion of what educational technology is, and of the different connotations of the word 'technology'.

In this chapter, we will describe some of the general 'aspects' of educational technology, and trace its historical development. We will begin by discussing two quite different perceptions of educational technology, namely the idea of the 'technology *in* education and training' and the idea of a 'technology *of* education and training'.

TECHNOLOGY *IN* EDUCATION AND TRAINING

'Technology *in* education and training' embraces every possible means by which information can be presented. It is concerned with the 'gadgetry' of education and training, such as television, language laboratories and the various projected media, or, as someone once said, 'everything from computers to dinner ticket dispensers'. In other words, technology *in* education is basically the popular impression of what educational technology is all about, namely, *audiovisual aids, computer keyboards and monitors.*

The general field of audiovisual aids is itself composed of two related but distinguishable areas, namely, *hardware* and *software*. The hardware side is concerned with the actual equipment – overhead projectors, slide projectors, tape recorders, videocassette recorders, television monitors, microcomputers, etc. The software side, on the other hand, is concerned with the various items that are used in conjunction with this equipment – such as overhead transparencies, slides, audiotapes, videorecordings, computer programs, authoring languages, and so on.

Technology *in* education is obviously one very important aspect of educational technology. Indeed, historically, many of the college-based 'educational technology units' evolved from units which were previously called 'audiovisual aids units'. By making appropriate use of hardware along with suitable software, it is often possible to improve the efficiency or quality of learning in a given situation, and this was the basis of the first developments in educational technology, as we shall see later.

One of the earliest phases in the evolution of educational technology was the 'hardware phase', in which a great deal of work was done in developing effective instructional equipment which was also reliable, serviceable and within the budgets of schools, colleges and training establishments. However, when such hardware eventually became generally available, it was found that there was a shortage of suitable software to use with it; this triggered off a subsequent 'software phase', in which particular attention was paid to the development of suitable learning materials, often based on the contemporary theories of learning and perception. Thus, even within this early development of educational technology, we can identify changes in the interpretation of the term 'technology'.

Initially, this had distinctly engineering connotations, since the main thrust of educational technology was concerned with the development of items of optical and electronic equipment for educational purposes; subsequently, it became much more associated with psychology and learning theory as the main thrust changed to the development of suitable software for use with this equipment.

However, at this stage in the development of educational technology, many people became aware that there was much in education and training which could be improved by thinking more carefully about *all* aspects of the design of teaching/learning situations. Such considerations led to a new, broader interpretation of 'educational technology' as the entire technology *of* education and training rather than merely as the use of technology *in* education, with the latter being regarded as merely a part of the former rather than the whole field as had previously been the case. Let us now examine this new interpretation in more detail.

THE TECHNOLOGY *OF* EDUCATION AND TRAINING

It could be argued that the principal role of educational technology is to help improve the overall efficiency of the teaching/learning process. In education and training, improved efficiency can manifest itself in many ways, for example:

(a) increasing the quality of learning, or the degree of mastery;
(b) decreasing the time taken for learners to attain desired goals;
(c) increasing the efficiency of teachers in terms of numbers of learners taught, without reducing the quality of learning;
(d) reducing costs, without affecting quality
(e) increasing the independence of learners, and the flexibility of education and training provision.

It is a value judgement as to which of the above interpretations are more important, and, indeed, such a judgement must be made in terms of the educational, financial and political aspects of individual situations. They are not necessarily mutually exclusive, but (to quote a hypothetical example) it might be found that certain measures that could well improve the quality of learning in a particular situation would also involve an increase in expenditure, so that a decision based on the likely cost-effectiveness of the measures would have to be made.

However, given well-defined criteria by which an improvement in the efficiency of an educational system, situation or process can be gauged, then decisions regarding the exact measures by which this can best be achieved can often be reached by applying a 'technology *of* education' approach. Recommendations for improvement are thus based on a study of the particular system *as a whole*, together with knowledge of appropriate educational research findings and theories and models of learning. In many cases, ideas and practices drawn from such diverse fields as psychology, sociology, business management and systems analysis are combined with developments in more technical fields such as optics, reprography, acoustics and microelectronics in order to produce the optimum learning or teaching system.

These aspects, which are all part of the technology *of* education, are sometimes called the 'intangible' aspects (or the 'underware', as opposed to the hardware and software already described). In this case, the emphasis is on the *techniques* of teaching and learning rather than on audiovisual aids *per se*. Although the 'intangible' aspects of educational technology are, by definition, less obvious than the 'hardware' and 'software' aspects, they are, nevertheless, just as important (indeed, most educational technologists would say *more* important) when it comes to solving a particular problem.

A 'technology *of* education' approach to educational technology thus involves a systematic, scientific approach to a problem, together with the application of appropriate scientific research, both from 'hard' sciences such as physics and electronics and from social sciences such as psychology and sociology. In applying a technology *of* education approach, changes are not made to a system for their own sake, but only for good educational reasons that are generally based on research findings. Such changes may not always work as intended, but even unexpected outcomes may prove useful to the people involved (and to others) when future developments are being planned.

It is as a technology *of* education and training that most practitioners view educational technology today. Within this concept, technology *in* education is seen mainly as one of the possible means to an end, with appropriate hardware and software being selected or designed to back up the particular strategy that it is decided to adopt in order to achieve a given set of educational aims or objectives. In some cases, this may involve the use of sophisticated equipment such as video or computers; in others, duplicated worksheets may be all that are required. Here it is important that the educational development or innovation has been *systematically* and *scientifically* planned and executed. It is this 'systems approach' to educational technology which is at the heart of the technology *of* education and training.

The relationships between the various aspects of educational technology discussed so far are shown in schematic form in Figure 1.1.

THE SYSTEMS APPROACH

The systems approach to the design and analysis of teaching/training situations is the basis of the great majority of modern educational technology-related developments. However, the terms 'system' (which we have already used in a number of contexts) and 'systems approach' are jargon terms and can have a variety of interpretations. Let us therefore first take a look at these terms in order to define the way in which we are to use them.

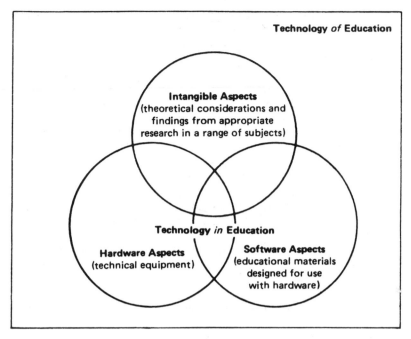

Figure 1.1 **The relationships between the different aspects of educational technology**

In an educational technology context, a *system* is any collection of interrelated parts that together constitute a larger whole. These component parts, or *elements*, of the system are intimately linked with one another, either directly or indirectly, and any change in one or more elements may affect the overall performance of the system, either beneficially or adversely. A simple system is illustrated schematically in Figure 1.2.

In Figure 1.2 the system consists of four distinct elements A, B, C, D which are related to or dependent upon each other as indicated. Note that some interrelationships may be two-way, while others may be one-way only. These elements may themselves be capable of further breakdown into other smaller components, and may thus be regarded as *sub-systems* of the overall system.

The processes of education and learning can be considered to be very complex systems indeed. The input to a given educational or learning system consists of people, resources and information, and the output consists of people whose performance has (it is to be hoped) improved in some desired way. A schematic representation of systems of this type is shown in Figure 1.3.

In such a system, the educational or learning process may be so complex that it can only be considered as a 'black box' whose

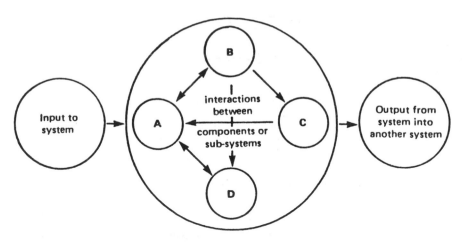

Figure 1.2 **A typical system**

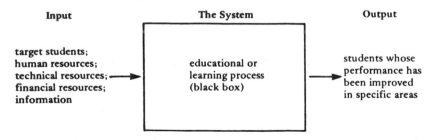

Figure 1.3 **The 'systems' model of the educational or learning process**

mechanisms are not fully understood. However, research into the nature of the learning process has thrown *some* light on what happens inside the 'black box'. This has enabled educational technologists to structure the input to systems of this type in such a way as to try to improve the output through increasing the efficiency of the learning process, thus leading to a systems approach to course design based on existing knowledge of how people learn. Such a systems approach attempts to mould the input to a course in such a way as to enable the optimum assimilation of knowledge and skills to take place during the learning process and hence maximize the quality of the output. It is to the various elements of such a systems approach to the design of courses, lessons and training programmes that we will be paying particular attention in later chapters of this book.

A simple system for the design of teaching/learning situations is given in Figure 1.4. We have deliberately chosen an extremely basic example of a systems approach to course design. Other writers (for

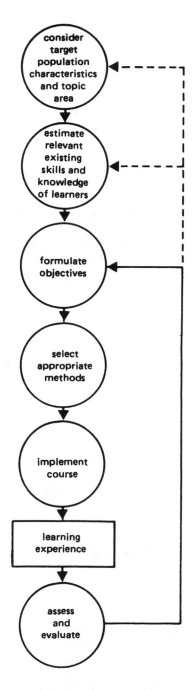

Figure 1.4 **A simplified systems approach to course design**

example, Romiszowski, in his books *The Selection and Use of Instructional Media: a Systems Approach* (1988) and *Designing Instructional Systems* (1988) have described more sophisticated systems, but we feel that these would be unnecessarily complicated for our present purposes. The components of the system all have sub-elements, which we will discuss in detail in later chapters.

In this simple model, having first taken into account the type of learners and relevant levels of skills and pre-knowledge which the potential learners should possess, we start with the formulation of the objectives, or desired learning outcomes of the course, for a given target population of students. It is useful to express such outcomes in terms of the competence which successful learners will be able demonstrate. We will look in detail at the nature and role of objectives and competence descriptors in Chapter 3. Having specified the objectives (that is, exactly what we are trying to achieve in the course) we are then in a better position to select appropriate teaching/learning methods by which the objectives have a reasonable chance of being achieved. There are far more teaching methods available to choose from than most people realize – indeed a book by Andrej Huczynski lists descriptions of no less than 303 different educational and training methods! The exercise of attempting to match appropriate methods to given objectives is normally done on the basis of a combination of research and experience. The strengths and weaknesses of a range of different teaching methods will be discussed in detail in Chapters 2, 4, 5 and 6.

The next element in the system is the actual implementation of the course. This involves all the logistical arrangements associated with running a course, including structuring and pacing, teaching strategies, selecting appropriate media, and ensuring that all aspects of the course run as smoothly as possible. Alternatively, when resource-based learning is being used as part of an open learning or flexible learning approach, it is more usual to talk of a learning programme rather than a course. Indeed, with increasing emphasis on flexibility and learner-centred approaches, the word 'programme' is becoming more common than 'course' in general.

The combined result of these first three steps is that a *learning experience* is provided for the target students. How efficient and useful the pre-planning has been can be measured by studying student performance in course-related *assessments*. These assessments should be closely related to the original specified course objectives. Poorly-achieved course objectives should lead the course designers to examine the entire system in order to identify places where improvements can be made. This could involve a change in the original objectives, a revised assessment of students' pre-knowledge, a critical review of the teaching methods used, an examination of the course structure and organization, a consideration of the assessment methods used, or a combination of some or all of these.

These deliberations, together with feedback on the course from staff, students, employers, etc can lead to an *evaluation* of the entire concept of the course, which should, in turn, form the basis of an on-going cyclical *course development* process. The topics of assessment and evaluation will be discussed in Chapter 7 and Chapter 8 respectively.

The systems approach to course design is therefore no more mysterious than an attempt to tackle course design through a process of logical development and on-going monitoring and evaluation in order to allow continuous evolution of the course to take place. As indicated earlier, more complicated systems approaches to course design do exist, but these all contain the core elements indicated in Figure 1.4.

DEFINITIONS OF EDUCATIONAL TECHNOLOGY

We have so far discussed the perception of educational technology from a number of different stances, namely, technology *in* education and training, technology *of* education and training, and the systems approach. A number of definitions of educational technology have been produced over the years by different bodies and organizations; three of these are given below, in order of increasing detail.

Definition 1

'Educational technology is the development, application and evaluation of systems, techniques and aids to improve the process of human learning'.

National Council for Educational Technology for the United Kingdom (NCET)

Definition 2

'Educational technology is the application of scientific knowledge about learning, and the conditions of learning, to improve the effectiveness and efficiency of teaching and training. In the absence of scientifically established principles, educational technology implements techniques of empirical testing to improve learning situations'.

National Centre for Programmed Learning, UK

Definition 3

'Educational technology is a systematic way of designing, implementing and evaluating the total process of learning and teaching in terms of specific objectives, based on research in human learning and communication and employing a combination of human and non-human resources to bring about more effective instruction'.

Commission on Instructional Technology, USA

All three definitions are similar in that each emphasizes the primary function of educational technology as *improving the efficiency of the process of learning*. As discussed earlier, this is normally done on the basis of what is known as a result of research into the nature of the learning process. Each of the definitions implies a technology *of* education interpretation of the role of educational technology, involving a cyclical systems approach to the design of teaching/learning situations and the use of whatever methods and techniques are judged to be appropriate in order to achieve one's desired objectives. Note also the strong emphasis on testing and evaluation implicit in each of the definitions.

Educational technology, via the systems approach to course and curriculum design, should therefore be flexible enough to react to new knowledge about the process of human learning, and also to new developments in teaching/learning approaches and methods. Examination of the historical development of the main concerns of educational technology provides an interesting insight into the nature of the subject, so we will now conclude this opening chapter by carrying out such a survey.

DEVELOPMENT OF THE MAIN CONCERNS OF EDUCATIONAL TECHNOLOGY: THE ELTON MODEL

One of the most useful overall pictures of the development of educational technology remains that given by Professor Lewis Elton in 1977. He identifies three broad lines along which the field has evolved, namely, *mass instruction, individualized learning*, and *group learning*. Furthermore, he believes that each of these strands has consisted of successive *research, development* and *use* phases, as shown schematically in Figure 1.5.

In essence, Elton believes that educational technology has undergone a progressive change of emphasis since the end of the Second World War, when it first emerged as a discipline in its own right. Initially, there was a concentration on the techniques of *mass instruction*, then a change to *individualized learning*, and finally, during recent years, a move towards *group learning*. In each case, he identifies three broad, overlapping stages in the development, starting with a *research* phase, in which the basic concepts and techniques are developed, then progressing to a *development* phase, in which these basic concepts and techniques are converted into practical teaching and learning techniques together with their associated support materials, and finally leading to a third phase in which the techniques start to achieve widespread *use*. The combined research and development phases have in each case tended to last for roughly 25 years, after which the on-going 'use' phase continues indefinitely. Let us now look in more detail at the way in which each class of techniques has developed, and see where things stand today.

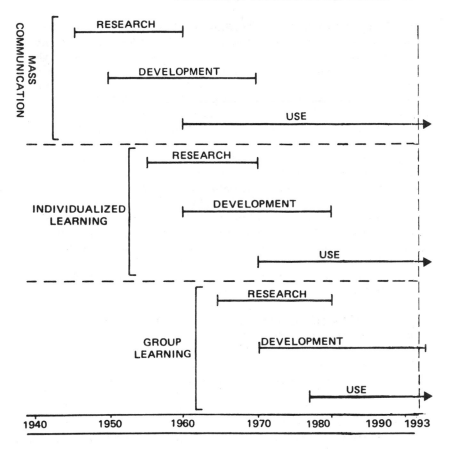

Figure 1.5 **The historical development of the main concerns of educational technology** (after Elton)

Mass Instruction Techniques

Mass instruction is, of course, as old as education itself, with the 'lecture' and 'expository lesson' being the dominant instructional techniques in virtually all sectors of education and training throughout recorded history. It was, however, only in the period following the Second World War that a systematic effort was made to improve the efficiency and cost-effectiveness of the method by using the new types of hardware that were starting to become available. By such means, it was hoped that more people could be educated or trained without necessarily increasing the number of teachers or trainers, and that the overall effectiveness of the teaching process could be improved. Some important outcomes were the development of basic mass instruction tools like the overhead projector and 35mm slide projector, and the increasingly widespread use of 'hardware-based' techniques such as film, radio and television broadcasting and closed-circuit television. Indeed, one manifestation of the 'mass instruction' phase of educational technology was the burgeoning of closed-circuit educational television systems – like the one that linked virtually all schools in Glasgow.

In retrospect, it can be seen that the 'mass instruction' movement failed to live up to its early promise, largely because it soon became apparent that techniques such as mass teaching by closed-circuit television were strictly limited in the type of educational objectives that they could be used to achieve. They were, for example, totally unsuitable for achieving many higher cognitive objectives, and were also almost completely passive, enabling virtually no student involvement to take place. Partly because of these intrinsic limitations (and partly because of the ever-increasing cost of keeping them in operation) many of the large-scale cable educational television networks that were set up during the 'boom' years of the mass instruction phase have now been closed down or drastically reduced in scale. Nevertheless, other mass instruction techniques such as educational broadcasting have continued to grow in importance, and the various techniques and hardware systems that come under the general heading of 'mass instruction' continue to constitute a very important section of the educational armoury available to the modern teacher or lecturer. For example, with the mass availability of video recorders and camcorders, the use of videos as an adjunct to mass instruction has grown enormously. Figure 1.6 lists some of the most important of these techniques, and indicates some of their main educational strengths and weaknesses.

Mass instruction techniques are discussed in much greater detail in Chapter 4.

Individualized Learning Techniques

Although individualized learning, in the form of correspondence courses and similar systems, also has a long tradition of use in education, it was only comparatively recently that it became part of main-stream educational technology. The catalyst for this development was *behavioural psychology*, which was pioneered by B F Skinner and his followers during the 1950s. Skinner's work on the *stimulus/response* mechanism, which represented (in many people's view) the first truly 'scientific' theory of learning, first triggered off the bandwagon *programmed learning* movement that dominated educational thinking during the 1960s. More recently, it led to the development of a wide range of individualized learning techniques (such as tape-slide and the various computer-assisted systems that are now achieving more and more widespread use) as well as to fully integrated individualized instruction systems such as the Keller

Technique	Strengths	Weaknesses
Lectures and similar expository techniques	• Can be very cost-effective in terms of staff/student ratio. • Strong in achieving lower cognitive and *some* affective objectives. • Popular with many teaching staff. • Most students expect lectures (even when not benefiting from them much). • Useful when large numbers of students need to receive the same information at the same time, with explanations and briefings. • Useful for providing large groups of students with a shared experience (eg, dramatic, memorable).	• Highly dependent on skill of lecturer. • Not good for higher cognitive or affective objectives. • Not suitable for psychomotor objectives. • Not useful for developing learners' communication or interpersonal skills. • Little student involvement, therefore little feeling of 'ownership' of learning. • Pace controlled by teacher, therefore does not allow for different learning rates. • Difficult to cater for mixed-ability groups. • Most lectures are much longer than students' concentration spans.
Video and film presentations	• Can be an effective substitute for a lecture if the content and level are suitable. • Particularly useful in short episodes to illustrate particular points. • Can provide illustrative, supportive, background and case-study material. • When professionally produced, can be highly stimulating and memorable (particularly in short bursts). • Can be low-cost or free, for example when educational broadcasts are used directly or recorded off-air (legally!) then used at will.	• Can be viewed quite passively unless level, degree of interest, and content are appropriate. • Much control is delegated to the producer of the video, and teacher using video may feel lack of 'ownership'. • Cannot be used unless suitable playback/projection equipment is present. • Can be expensive to make (particularly in terms of time).
Large-group practical and studio work	• Students learn by doing, and generally enjoy participative learning. • Can help demonstrate the practical relevance of theoretical ideas and concepts. • Can be effective in developing psychomotor objectives, and students' interpersonal and communication skills.	• Can be a waste of time unless the chosen activities are directly relevant to the programme of study. • Generally expensive in terms of time and staffing. • For large groups can be expensive in terms of equipment costs.

Figure 1.6 **Characteristics of some of the main mass instruction techniques**

Plan and open learning systems. However, before we trace these developments and uses, let us first look at the basic tenets of behavioural psychology, so that we can better understand the roots of these developments.

Behavioural psychology, like other branches of educational psychology, attempts to discover how learning takes place, and, consequently, how best to promote learning. It is largely predictive in nature, first attempting to discover which conditions are conducive for certain behaviour to occur, and then attempting to reproduce these conditions in order to bring about the desired behaviour.

Behavioural psychology theory is based on what is commonly referred to as *stimulus and response*, that is, it assumes that learning has occurred when a specific response is elicited from a learner when he or she is placed in a particular situation and given a particular stimulus. Learning of relatively complex behaviour can (it is claimed) be achieved through an appropriate series of stimulus-response situations. At each stage, the learner must actively participate by performing a set task, after which he or she is then supplied with immediate feedback in the form of the correct answer. This is known as *successive reinforcement*. Skinner also argued that each successive stimulus-response step should be small enough to ensure that the learner is almost always correct in his or her response. Use of these small steps, plus successive reinforcement, led to what behavioural psychologists believed was an efficient way of 'shaping behaviour'.

Skinner's original work was with animals, mostly with pigeons. His later work, which evolved from this, was with humans. Many people have since rejected or at least considerably modified Skinner's model, but it is important to remember that his work led to the beginnings of individualized learning, which now exists in many forms in the education and training fields. We shall look at some of these in more detail in Chapters 2 and 5.

The first application of Skinner's research to the classroom situation came in the form of *linear programmed learning*. In this type of programmed learning, the subject matter is broken down into a sequence of small *steps* (or *frames*) logically following upon one another. Each of the steps represents only a very small part of the concept or skill to be taught. In order to reward the learner and so, in turn, reinforce the learning process, each step contains a certain amount of information and requires the student to respond to a question about the information, while the small size of the step practically guarantees the correctness of the desired response. Immediate feedback on the correctness (or otherwise) of the response is designed to provide suitable reinforcement. Ideally, it should be virtually impossible to take a step without having successfully taken the previous ones. There is thus only one possible path which a student can take through the frames; hence the name *linear programmed learning* (see Figure 1.7).

Figure 1.7 **The basic structure of a linear programmed
learning sequence**

Skinner's 'essential' ingredients for programmed learning were the
use of small steps, the high degree of interaction with the programme, and the 'linear' nature of the sequence. The evidence for
the need to use very small steps has subsequently been challenged
from a theoretical standpoint, and, in practice, such an approach can
very often lead to boredom on the part of the learner. It is now
accepted that the optimum step size in any particular learning
programme is governed by a large number of considerations, and,
as a result, large and/or difficult steps are often incorporated into
modern learning programmes, which may also contain a lesser
degree of reinforcement than the early programmes developed by
Skinner and his followers.

In the 1960s, another form of programmed learning known as
branching programmed learning was developed. This involved the use
of several possible paths through the sequence of steps (frames), with
'remedial loops' being included in order to correct misconceptions
identified from student responses to individual steps, which did not
necessarily have to be small. Thus, the topic to be studied was taught
in a number of alternative ways in such a branching programme,
depending on the performance of the learner. Figure 1.8 shows a
simple example of a possible structure for a branching programme of
this type.

The type of branching structure shown in Figure 1.8, only very
much more complex, is the basis of many of the self-instructional
programmes that have been designed for use with the computer
since the 1970s. Use of the computer in this 'substitute tutor' role
allows students to have fast and effective access to what is basically a
branching programmed learning sequence. (A review of the present
role of computers in education and training is given in Chapter 10.)

Later developments in individualized learning have involved a

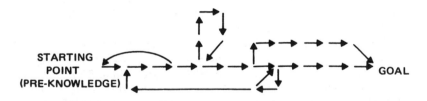

Figure 1.8 **A simple branching programmed learning sequence**

much more flexible approach to programme design than that which was used in the relatively strict early programmed learning procedures. As we shall see in later chapters, much of the present use of individualized learning has evolved and been adapted in order to meet the specific requirements of particular educational or training establishments, or in order to satisfy the special needs of particular students (eg students studying on their own at a distance from the parent institution).

As in the case of the earlier 'mass-instruction' movement, it can, in retrospect, be seen that the individualized learning movement failed to live up fully to its early promise. During the 1960s, programmed learning enthusiasts were predicting the early demise of the traditional classroom teacher or lecturer, claiming that they would be replaced by the new *teaching machines* that they were developing as delivery systems for their programmes. These teaching machines turned out to be the biggest non-event in the history of education, however, partly because of the fact that high-quality software was never produced in the quantities that would have been needed for them to make any real impact, and partly due to the increasing realization that there was much more to education than the teaching of facts and principles.

In particular, the stimulus-response approach to learning has been developed in a much more sophisticated manner in open-learning packages. Open learning is no longer synonymous with distance learning, but is often used in schools, colleges and training centres alongside traditional teaching/learning methods. Suitable elements of a learning programme are turned into learning packages, which learners use at their own pace and in their own ways. Face-to-face sessions can then be used to consolidate the most important learning outcomes of the packages, as well as to deal with any problems that learners have identified in their learning.

Learning packages range from simple print-based materials to highly sophisticated interactive computer-based materials. The factor they have in common is that when learners carry out the tasks built into the materials, they quickly receive a response. For example, when they select an option in a multiple-choice structure, they quickly find out (in a printed response elsewhere in the module, or on the screen with computer-based materials) the answers to the following questions:

Was I right?
If not, *why not*?

Considerably more detail about the design of open learning packages is given in *The Open Learning Handbook* (Race, 1989), *53 Interesting Ways to Write Open Learning Materials* (Race, 1991), *Producing Teaching Materials* (Ellington and Race, 1993) and *Exploring Open and Distance Learning* (Rowntree, 1992).

Technique	Strengths	Weaknesses
Directed study of material in textbooks, literature references	• When texts and references are suitable and relevant, can be a highly effective way for students to learn facts, basic principles, and applications, provided their learning is carefully structured. • Allows learners to work at their own pace. • Does not need specialized facilities.	• Requires careful planning and structuring by teacher. • Dependent on suitable resource materials being available in sufficient numbers for the group. • Unsuitable for achieving higher cognitive and some non-cognitive objectives.
Independent study of handout materials and open-learning materials	• Same advantages as textbooks, and can be more effective if the materials are well prepared. • Learners can work at their own pace, and in their own ways. • Materials are likely to be more relevant and concise than textbooks. • With open-learning materials, learners learn by interacting with the materials, and receiving feedback on their efforts.	• Preparation of open-learning materials is time-consuming and expensive. • Not everyone can write good interactive learning materials! • Learners may feel isolated and lack opportunities to have their questions answered readily. • Learners may lack the opportunity to learn from each other.
Self-instructional packages based on audio-vidual media (audiotapes, videotapes, tape-slide programmes)	• It is possible to address a wide range of learning objectives. • Learners can work at their own pace. • Enable sound, motion, realism to be introduced, increasing stimulation. • Can be useful to save teachers repeating time-consuming demonstrations (for example in laboratory work).	• Ideal ready-made courseware not usually available; preparation of custom-designed courseware can be time-consuming and can require specialist skills. • Requires the availability of playback facilities or hardware. • More expensive to mass produce than open learning packages or books.
Computer-based learning	• A wide range of learning objectives can be addressed. • Learners can work at their own pace. • Highly-interactive approach to learning allows learning by doing, with immediate provision of feedback. • Can provide simulations of otherwise-inaccessible learning experiences.	• Can require learners to be computer-literate, or at least relaxed when using keyboards. • It is not always possible to find relevant, ready-made computer-based materials. • Designing computer-based learning materials requires highly-developed skills.

Figure 1.9 **Characteristics of some of the main individualized learning techniques**

The development of individualized learning did not follow the path of 'teaching machines' but blossomed by placing the emphasis on the processes of *learning*. Individualized learning materials are nowadays more often classified under the broad term 'learning resources' than under any term involving 'teaching'. The various types of learning resource which have developed from individualized learning origins now form essential components of most education and training provision. Some of the most important types of learning resource materials are listed in Figure 1.9, together with some of their main strengths and weaknesses. A more detailed discussion of the design and use of such resources is given in Chapter 5.

Group Learning Techniques

While it can be argued that the 'individualized learning' phase probably had a greater impact on current education and training than the 'mass instruction' phase which preceded it, there are definite limitations to the approach. One of the most obvious stems from the fact that it is, by definition, *individual*, and, as such, cannot enable students to interact with one another and develop group skills such as discussion skills and interpersonal skills. This has led to an increasing realization that the various activities that come under the general heading of *group learning* have a very important part to play in modern education and training.

The theoretical basis for modern developments in group learning is the *humanistic psychology* that was developed by people such as Carl Rogers during the 1960s – a totally different type of psychology from the highly mechanistic behavioural psychology which formed the basis of the programmed learning movement. Humanistic psychology is concerned with how people interact with and learn from one another in small-group situations, and involves the use of the techniques of *group dynamics*.

When used in a learning situation, such techniques generally require no specialized hardware and (in most cases) very little in the way of software other than simple printed sheets and booklets; the emphasis is very much upon the *approach* or *technique* rather than a reliance on specific types of hardware or software.

At the time of writing, group learning is still in the final stages of its 'development phase', although its 'use' phase is now well under way – as evidenced by the widespread use now being made of participative methods such as games, simulations, interactive case studies, and group projects. Some of the more important types of group learning exercises are listed in Figure 1.10, which again identifies their main educational strengths and weaknesses. A much more detailed discussion of all these various techniques is given in Chapter 6, Group Learning Techniques.

Technique	Strengths	Weaknesses
Buzz sessions and similar short small-group exercises	• Constitute an excellent method of introducing variety into a lecture, thus helping to maintain student attention. • Can be used to achieve a wide range of objectives, both cognitive and non-cognitive. • They get students actively involved in a lesson. • They allow feedback to take place.	• They are most useful in a *supportive* role as part of a larger lesson as they are not, by themselves, intended for use as a front-line method of teaching basic facts and principles.
Class discussions, seminars, tutorials, etc	• Same basic advantages as buzz sessions, etc. • In addition, their greater length allows an even wider range of objectives to be achieved, often of a very high level. • Enable relevant topics to be examined in great depth.	• There is a danger that not all the members of a class will take an active part in the exercise unless steps are taken to make sure that they do. • They can cause timetabling problems if a class has to be split up.
Participative exercises of the game/simulation/case study type	• They can be used to achieve a wide range of objectives, both cognitive and non-cognitive, often of a very high level. • High student involvement. • Highly stimulating and motivating if properly designed. • Ideal for cross-disciplinary work.	• Most useful in a supportive or illustrative role rather than as a front-line method of teaching basic facts and principles. • Can be difficult to fit into curriculum, especially in case of long exercises. • Must be *relevant* to course to be of real educational value.
Mediated feedback sessions such as microteaching recorded interviews, or recorded group exercises	• Use of mediated feedback (eg audio or video recording) enables valuable group discussions of student performance to take place. • Can be used to develop a wide range of skills. • High student involvement.	• Some students find method off-putting at first. • Requires suitable hardware and other facilities, often expensive. • Can cause timetabling problems if a class has to be split up.
Group projects	• Suitable for developing a wide range of objectives, both cognitive and non-cognitive, often at a very high level. • Ideal for developing interpersonal and group skills. • Ideal for cross-disciplinary work.	• There is a danger that not all the members of the group will pull their weight unless steps are taken to make sure that they do. • Assessment of contributions made by individual students can be problematic.
Self-help groups	• Can be of considerable help to isolated groups of learners. • Peer teaching extremely valuable.	• Students require to be motivated to form or join such groups.

Figure 1.10 **Characteristics of some of the main group learning techniques**

Summary of the Main Features of Mass Instruction, Individualized Learning and Group Learning

A summary of the main features of the three aspects of educational technology that are included in the Elton model is given in Figure 1.11. As has already been stated, the results of each of these three phases are still very much with us, and will probably continue to develop and evolve as time goes on. Most of the problems associated with their use are now educational rather than technological. The associated equipment will, in all probability, tend to become as cheap, simple and reliable as possible, while the considerations that determine their use in education and training will depend upon the particular criteria that are considered to be most important in a given situation.

	Mass instruction	Individualized learning	Group learning
Theoretical basis	Industrial technology	Behavioural psychology	Humanistic psychology
Model	Economy of scale	Stimulus-response	Group dynamics
Emphasis of methods	Hardware	Software	Techniques
Results	CCTV; broadcasting; video	Open learning plus derivatives; computer-assisted learning	Interpersonal skill sessions; games and simulations

Figure 1.11 **Summary of main features of the three phases of educational technology**

The evolution of emphasis in educational technology from mass instruction through individualized learning to group learning mirrors the progression from a 'hardware' approach through a 'software' approach to the 'technology *of* education and training' approach that was discussed earlier in the chapter. One notable example which Professor Elton believes reflects these changes is the development of the Open University in the UK. This institution, originally conceived during the early 1960s as the 'University of the Air', started offering courses in 1971 using the media of television and radio broadcasts, and there was an extensive period of software development (mainly textual) in order to support students studying on an individualized basis. More recently, there has been a much greater concern with providing situations for closer contact with other students and with tutors, and there has generally been a more human, or group, approach to learning, although such developments have been somewhat restricted owing to financial considerations. Although the Open University has always used all three teaching methods (mass communication, individualized learning and group learning) in its courses, there is no doubt that there has been a gradual change of emphasis over the years, and that first individualized learning, and then, more recently, group learning gradually came to play much more important roles than were originally envisaged. In its evolution, the Open University thus represents a microcosm of educational technology itself.

OTHER AREAS IN WHICH EDUCATIONAL TECHNOLOGY HAS DEVELOPED

Useful as Elton's model is, there are those who correctly criticize it as being incomplete, and taking insufficient account of the evolving social and technological contexts over the timespan charted. For example, it makes no recognition of the development of other important concerns of educational technology such as the management of innovation and the development of student study skills, both of which will now be examined.

The Management of Innovation

Most of the work of the educational technologist is, almost by definition, innovative. Whether the innovation in question is on a small scale (for example, the development of a small open-learning package) or much more ambitious (eg productive of an interactive video package), the success in establishing the innovation as part of the overall educational framework depends on a wide variety of factors (the quality of the innovation, the nature of the potential users, political factors, administrative arrangements etc). Indeed, many highly promising educational innovations have foundered and died because the implementation of the innovation was mismanaged.

As a consequence, the effective management and implementation of innovation has recently been of increasing concern to educational technologists, most of whom have experienced the frustration of seeing many hours of painstaking work failing to realize its potential because of such mismanagement. Indeed, it is not unusual to find educational innovators now spending as much or even more time on fostering an environment in which an innovation can flourish as in developing the actual innovation. This concern is reflected in the literature by a rapidly expanding body of publications on managing educational innovation.

The topic is vast and extremely complex, and, in this book, we do not intend to do more than to underline its undoubted importance in educational technology. For those who want to pursue the subject further, *Open Learning and Open Management* by Ross Paul (1990) makes stimulating reading.

Study Skills Techniques

Another area which has attracted the attention of many educational technologists in recent years is the development of student study skills. Obviously, one way of improving the effectiveness of the teaching/learning process is to increase the efficiency of learners in assimilating the subject matter covered. For this reason, educational technologists and teachers have used the results of educational and psychological research to devise programmes of activities that are specifically designed to assist students in their study technique. Apart from over 100 'how to study' guides that have been written for students, a number have been written for teachers in order to assist them in devising appropriate activities for students. One of the best of these is by Graham Gibbs, entitled *Teaching Students to Learn: A Student Centred Approach* (1981) and interested readers are referred to this. A more recent book intended to help teachers develop in their learners a range of active-learning techniques is *500 Tips for Tutors* by Phil Race and Sally Brown (1993).

The sort of areas covered by study skills include organization of time, effective use of time, reading skills, essay-writing and report-writing skills, note-taking, examination technique, and even job-hunting skills. Also, students in distance-learning schemes may have special study difficulties which have to be coped with. These were addressed in *How to Win as an Open Learner* by Phil Race (1986). More recently, the same author has published *500 Tips for Students* (1992) which addresses a wide range of study skills and learning strategies. Tom Bournen and Phil Race have also written an open-learning book *How to Win as a Part-time Student* (1991).

The growing interest in study skills development is further evidence that educational technology is concerned not only with hardware and software, but also with the less tangible aspects of the teaching/learning process.

A FRESH LOOK AT LEARNING

Whatever sort of training we think about, or whatever sort of educational experience we consider, the one thing they all need to have in common is 'learning'. The human species is unique in its capacity for learning – that is why the species has evolved as much as it has. Human beings have learned ever since the dawn of civilisation (and for quite some time before). Yet much that has been written about *how* we learn tends to have used language which is closer to the ways that educational psychologists think, than to the ways in which the vast majority of human beings learn. Before going into depth on the various teaching, training and learning systems covered in this book, we would like to lead readers through a simple yet powerful model of learning proposed recently by Phil Race in an article in *Training and Development* (1993). We believe that this model of learning can be of direct use to trainers and educators in ways which have eluded some of the more complex models of learning.

Successful Learning and Demonstrable Competence

Getting people to think of something they have learned successfully is a positive start to alerting them to the ways in which they learn. It does not matter what they think of as the successful learning experience of their choice – it can be work-related, or sporting achievement, or any skill. When people are asked to do the following:

Think of something you're good at – something you know you do well;
Write down a few words explaining *how* you became good at it;

their most frequent answers are along the following lines:

- practice
- by doing it
- by trial and error
- by getting it wrong at first and learning from mistakes.

Relatively few people give answers such as 'by being trained' or 'by being taught' or 'by listening to experts' or 'by reading about it'. So one key to learning is 'doing'. There is nothing new about this – it has been called 'experiential learning' for long enough – but let's stay with short words like 'doing' for the present.

Positive Feelings

The matter of *feelings* has not been sufficiently explored by the developers of theories of learning. Feelings are as much about what it is to be human as any other aspect of humanity. Yet a relatively simple question yields a wealth of information about the connection between feelings and successful learning:

Think of something about yourself you *feel* good about – something that gives you a 'glow'.
Explain on what basis you have this positive feeling.

By far the most frequent answers are along the following lines:

- reactions of other people
- feedback

- compliments
- seeing the results.

Relatively few people claim that the origin of their positive feelings comes from within. Most people need to have approval from fellow human beings to develop a really positive feeling about something. Positive feelings are a crucial stepping stone along the way towards successful learning. Indeed, one of the most common things that can prevent successful learning is the absence of positive feedback. Criticism or disapproval can be powerful contributors to unsuccessful learning.

'Doing' + 'Feedback' = Successful Learning?

Though these two elements are essential ingredients of successful learning, there are two further things that need to be in place. These two things are easier to tease out by asking questions about *unsuccessful* learning experiences:

> Think of something you don't do well – as a result perhaps of an unsuccessful learning experience.
> Explain what went wrong.

The answers to these questions are quite complex, but a pattern emerges quite readily. For a start, there are usually some answers which relate to something having gone wrong with the two essentials we've already looked at – 'doing' and 'feedback'. For example:

- lack of opportunity to practise
- bad feedback.

But looking for further factors, the following are often found in people's answers:

- no motivation
- fear of failure
- couldn't see why it was worth doing
- lack of time to make sense of it
- unable to understand it before moving on.

These boil down to two further essentials for successful learning: 'wanting' and 'digesting'. Let's look at each briefly.

'Wanting'

If there is something wrong with one's motivation, it is unlikely that successful learning will happen. However, 'motivation' is a rather 'cold' word – a psychologists' word rather than everyone's word. 'Wanting' is a much more 'human' word. Everyone knows what 'want' means. Also, 'wanting' implies more than just motivation. 'Wanting' goes right to the heart of human urges and feelings. When there is such a powerful feeling at work helping learning to happen, little wonder that the results can be spectacular. We have all been pleasantly surprised at how well people who really want to do something usually manage to do it.

'Digesting'

This is about 'making sense' of the learning experience – and also making sense of feedback received from other people. 'Digesting' is about sorting out what is important in what's been learned. 'Digesting' is about extracting the main ideas from the background information. 'Digesting' is also about discarding what's not important. It is about putting things into perspective. 'Digesting', above all else, is about establishing a sense of *ownership* of what has been learned. It is about *far more* than the nearest word the psychologists come up with – 'reflection'.

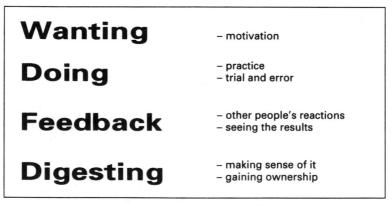

Wanting   – motivation

Doing   – practice
      – trial and error

Feedback   – other people's reactions
      – seeing the results

Digesting   – making sense of it
      – gaining ownership

Figure 1.12 **The four ingredients of successful learning experiences**

Learning Cycles?

Probably the best known 'learning cycle' is that involving the stages 'active experimentation', 'reflective observation', 'concrete experience' and 'abstract conceptualization'. One problem with this cycle is that it is not too clear where on the cycle one should best start – or indeed which way round to go – or even in which order the four steps should be connected. In fact, there are times when one needs to be in two places at once in the cycle. It is tempting to try drawing a cycle with 'wanting', 'doing', 'feedback' and 'digesting'. At least there seems to be an obvious logical order.

However, imposing such an order on learning processes would be, to say the least, a gross oversimplification. In fact, the more that the four processes can be made to overlap, the better. For example:

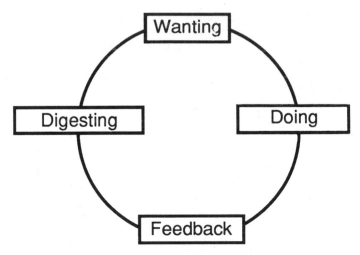

Figure 1.13 **A learning-cycle representation of 'wanting, doing, feedback and digesting'**

- it is important to keep on 'wanting' while 'doing'
- it is useful to be seeking 'feedback' while 'doing' as well as after 'doing'
- it is useful to be continuing to seek 'feedback' while 'digesting'
- it is useful to be continuing the 'doing' while receiving 'feedback' and while 'digesting' and progressively refining the whole process.

The 'wanting' stage needs to pervade throughout, so that 'doing' is wanted, 'feedback' is positively sought, opportunities for 'digesting' are seized, and so on. Perhaps a more sensible model would have 'wanting' at the heart, and 'feedback' coming from the outside, and 'doing' and 'digesting' occurring in an overlapping way. If you look at any successful form of training or education, you will find that, one way or another, all four ingredients of successful learning are addressed. Different training situations and processes attend to each of the four in different ways.

'Wanting' is catered for by the effective face-to-face trainer who generates enthusiasm or by the stimulating lecturer who gives an exciting performance. 'Wanting' is catered for by carefully-worded learning objectives in flexible-learning materials or manuals, which capture learners' wishes to proceed with their learning. Learning by 'doing' is equally at the heart of any good training course, and in any well-designed flexible-learning package. 'Feedback' is provided by tutors or trainers, or by responses in open-learning materials, or by fellow-learners giving feedback to each other. The one that is all too easy to miss out is 'digesting'. However, all experienced tutors and

Figure 1.14 **An 'overlap' model of 'wanting, doing, feedback and digesting' using educational technology to promote 'wanting', 'doing', 'feedback' and 'digesting'**

trainers know how important it is to give learners the time and space to make sense of their learning and to put it into perspective. Similarly, the best learning packages cater for the fact that learners need to be given some opportunity to practise with what they've already learned, before moving on to further learning.

CONCLUSIONS

When looking at the processes of mass instruction, individualized learning and group learning, and the educational technology resources that are used to enhance the effectiveness of the learning which results from these processes, it may be useful to continue to reflect on how 'wanting,' 'doing', 'feedback' and 'digesting' can be accommodated and enhanced.

Chapter 2

Basic Educational Strategies

INTRODUCTION

In Chapter 1 we discussed, in general terms, the nature of educational technology, and gave a brief historical account of the development of the field to date. In this chapter, we will take a look at two broad, contrasting approaches to education and training, within the context of which virtually all important educational technology-related developments have taken place, namely, the traditional *teacher/institution-centred approach* and the more recent *student-centred approach*. In each case, we will first examine the structure of the system that underlies the approach, then discuss its strengths and weaknesses, and finally identify the main teaching/learning methods that it employs.

THE TEACHER/INSTITUTION-CENTRED APPROACH

In the conventional teaching/learning situation, the teacher imparts, to a class of students, subject matter which is laid down in some form of syllabus (or, more often than not, imparts his or her personal interpretation of the syllabus). The classes normally take place at set times and last for a predetermined period, as indicated by a timetable, while the teaching methods are almost invariably of the 'face-to-face' type. The whole system is generally geared towards the smooth operation of the teaching institution, with little or no attempt being made to cater for the different learning styles and particular difficulties of individual students.

The Underlying Structure

A schematic representation of the traditional teacher/institution-centred approach to education and training is given in Figure 2.1.

In such a system, virtually all the decisions as to how a course is to be organized and taught are made either by the institution mounting the course or by the teacher nominated to take the class. The institution decides where and when the class is to meet and how

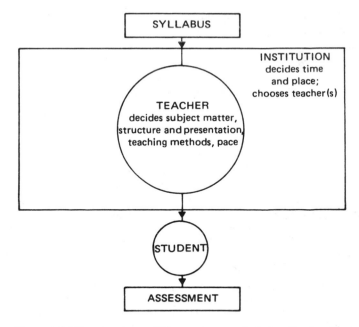

Figure 2.1 **The structure of the system underlying the teacher/ institution-centred approach**

long each session is to last, these arrangements being tailored to fit in with those for all the other courses run by the institution. The institution also decides which particular member (or members) of staff will be responsible for actually teaching the class.

The teacher or instructor makes most of the 'tactical' decisions relating to how the syllabus (which is often laid down by an external body of some sort) should be interpreted, in terms of both the specific subject matter to be covered and the level of sophistication at which this is to be treated. Decisions regarding the structuring, sequencing and presentation of the material are also made by the teacher, as are decisions concerning the teaching methods to be used and the pace of the course.

The students have normally little or no say in any of these decisions, and must try to adapt their learning style to the organizational constraints laid down by the institution and to the educational decisions made by the teacher. Finally, the students' ultimate achievements on the course are normally assessed by an examination of some sort, sometimes set externally, with individual students again having no say regarding how this is done.

Such an approach has its advantages and disadvantages, and these may be viewed from radically different perspectives depending on the level and nature of the course being taught. Let us now examine them in detail.

Advantages

Many of the advantages associated with a teacher/institution-centred strategy stem from the very fact that this represents the traditional approach to teaching and training. Schools, colleges and training establishments are all normally geared to operate via such an approach, and the administrative systems of these institutions are designed to support it. While this administrative convenience is more a reason for the predominance and perpetuation of the teacher/institution-centred than an educational advantage *per se*, it is certainly a very important factor. Indeed, any attempt to adopt a radically different approach will almost certainly fail if it is alien to the teaching staff or administratively awkward for the host institution to implement. Most educational and training establishments have decades of experience in operating this traditional system, and students as well as teachers and administrators have become used to it. Also, the 'certification' of learning is strongly geared to existing teacher/institution-centred learning schemes.

Another important advantage of teacher/institution-centred strategies is that they enable institutions to make relatively efficient use of their accommodation and equipment resources and (in terms of timetabling arrangements) fair and effective use of staff time. A set timetable allows a teacher to tackle a course or syllabus in such a way that the teaching programme fits into the time available, thus making sure that all the material is at least 'covered' – a particularly important consideration when students are being prepared for an externally-set examination. A further advantage of the traditional teacher-centred approach is that it is easier to accommodate increased numbers of learners. Recent expansion of higher education in the UK has to some extent moved institutions back towards such an approach.

Within this type of strategy, a teacher can attempt to provide a range of different learning situations for the students, all designed to match the type of material being covered and the level and sophistication of the learners. Remedial and/or revision exercises can be provided, and a teacher may well know from experience, and from personal knowledge of the class, what will be the most appropriate teaching method to use in given circumstances. This advantage is particularly relevant when one is dealing with young or inexperienced learners (for example, at primary level) where strong leadership is required in order to provide effective pupil learning opportunities. Many learning activities may certainly involve a considerable proportion of individual or small group work, but the teacher remains firmly at the centre, and his or her experience with such learners is vitally important.

Disadvantages

While sound educational cases can often be made for the use of teacher-centred strategies in particular circumstances, there are many cases, particularly at higher levels of education and training, where strong central control of the teaching/learning situation is hard to defend other than in terms of administrative convenience and teacher/student acceptance. While the traditional system can certainly point to many outstanding successes, cynics and critics of the system might argue that these successes have been achieved *despite* the system and not because of it. A number of strong criticisms have been made of the traditional teacher/institution-centred approach to education and training, particularly in circumstances where it is difficult to argue a strong *educational* (as opposed to an *administrative*) case in favour of it. These include many of the situations encountered in further and higher education, industrial and commercial training, and, to a lesser extent, secondary school education.

One of the most obvious limitations of teacher-centred learning is that it is, by its very nature, extremely dependent upon the skill and ability of the teacher. While this can be a distinct advantage if the teacher is talented and experienced, it can also lead to severe problems for the students if this is not the case. The control exercised by teachers is that, amongst other things, they interpret the syllabus, structure the content, select the teaching methods, dictate the pace of coverage, and make decisions regarding the amount of reinforcement material and remedial work to incorporate. Problems may arise in connection with any or all of these factors, and, in many cases, a teacher has only his or her own experience and intuition for guidance.

Many syllabuses are written in very vague terms, and teachers must frequently decide upon the level and content of, say, 10 hours of teaching on the basis of a syllabus entry which may consist of only a few words. If the syllabus is written by an external or central organization, some guidance may be obtained from advisers or past exam papers, but the onus and responsibility is still firmly with the teacher. If the syllabus is written in terms of 'behavioural objectives' or expressed in terms of competences (see Chapter 3), this particular problem is normally not so serious, since this type of syllabus is generally much more detailed and explicit, requiring less interpretation on the part of the teacher.

Structuring the content is again a task for the teacher, and is usually based on a combination of theory, practical experience, and consultation with colleagues. Even with a small class, the structure adopted is unlikely to be exactly suited to the different levels of pre-knowledge and different learning styles of all the individual students, and the problem obviously becomes even greater with large classes; it is, after all, simply not practicable for a teacher to present the same material in all the different ways that would be needed to match students' individual entry skills and learning styles.

Similar problems are likely to arise with regard to the pace adopted by the teacher, since the students in a class (especially a large one) are likely to differ considerably in the degree to which they have mastered earlier work and in the rate at which they can learn new material. The pace dictated by the teacher will (at best) only be appropriate for part of the class, and, even if the teacher manages to match the pace to the needs of the middle-ability majority, it will almost certainly be too fast for the slow learners (who may, incidentally, have high ability) and will probably be too slow for the high fliers, who are liable to become bored or 'switch off' as a consequence.

Another possible drawback of the teacher-centred approach is that the actual teaching methods that are employed may be inappropriate for teaching towards the desired skills and attitudes. At school level, there is scope for a wide range of teaching methods, but school teachers all too often limit themselves to those methods with which they feel comfortable and to which they are accustomed. Teachers at further and higher education levels are often even more limited in their approaches, and it is still fair to say that the lecture continues to dominate teaching practice at these levels, often at the expense of alternative methods which may be more appropriate in certain situations.

The amount of reinforcement and revision to be provided is yet another decision that is left to the teacher. It is well established (from psychological research) that the level of skill in executing a given task, or the amount of recall associated with a subject, is very strongly related to the amount of reinforcement or back-up teaching and learning that is carried out. Once again, a good, experienced teacher will almost certainly try to incorporate a reasonable amount of reinforcement into the teaching scheme, but others may either deliberately leave this to the students to do for themselves or may be under such tight time constraints to 'finish' a course that the reinforcement aspect has to be neglected.

Problems can also arise from the very factors that make the teacher-centred approach administratively convenient from an institution's point of view. Classes, for example, are almost invariably timetabled to fit into standard time slots – normally one hour in length in the case of the lectures that form the 'staple diet' of most students undergoing further and higher education. It has, however, been established that the attention levels of both teacher and student fall off rapidly with time, and that the optimum time for a straight lecture is between 20 and 30 minutes – well below the standard length. While it is true that a good teacher or lecturer will probably take steps to counteract this tendency for attention to decrease by (for example) introducing periodic interactive sessions into a lecture or using a variety of methods within a given teaching period, in many cases the problem is either not recognized or simply ignored.

A further weakness of systems that rely on rigid timetables, at all levels of education and training, is that insufficient attention tends to be given to the problems or difficulties that are faced by individual learners. Even when practice sessions or tutorials are arranged, these cannot hope to deal efficiently with all such problems, particularly if they originated in a class talk or lecture given some time previously and are not related to the topic that is scheduled for revision at the time. The scale of this problem is again obviously greater with large classes in further or higher education, but it does also exist at secondary school level and in training courses.

Teacher/institution-centred systems have also been criticized on the grounds that they tend to encourage spoonfeeding of students, and give little scope for individual investigation and choice of appropriate topics of study related to a student's own interests. While the spoonfeeding practice can be defended in the case of many school courses, and also in the case of core courses in colleges, universities and training establishments, it is less easy to defend if one accepts the view that one of the primary functions of education is to foster the development of an inquiring mind and creative thought. It is generally true that teacher-centred strategies at most levels of education encourage neither intellectual curiosity nor students' responsibility for organizing and planning their learning.

It must be emphasized that many of the above criticisms of the teacher/institution-centred approach can be of greater or lesser importance depending on the level of education involved, the particular institution, and (most important of all) the individual teacher. However, while it is not suggested that any educational or training system could (or should) be 'teacher-proof', it must be pointed out that the success or otherwise of the teacher-centred approach is strongly dependent, in a number of important ways, on the teacher(s) involved. In this lies both its strength and its weakness.

Teaching Methods Used

Within the context of the teacher/institution-centred approach, a wide range of different teaching methods can be used. These range from purely expository methods such as the lecture or talk (see Figure 2.2) to methods which involve a much greater degree of individualized learning or group work. The important point is that all these various activities occur within an educational or training structure which is organized or run by teachers operating within the fairly rigid constraints of the *institution* in which they work.

As mentioned earlier, the almost complete emphasis on the teacher-centred approach at primary school level entails teachers

Figure 2.2 **The 'chalk and talk' lesson – one of the mainstays of the teacher/institution-centred approach to education**

organizing and controlling virtually all pupil learning opportunities; this may involve, amongst other things, short expositions to the class as a whole, individual work and group work.

At secondary school level, expository methods of one form or another are probably the most widely used teaching technique, with set exercises, group discussions, practical work and a certain amount of individualized learning being used to back these up.

At tertiary level, expositions in the form of lectures, videos, broadcasts, etc are by far the most common teaching methods, together with private reading and other individual work, tutorials, seminars and practical work. Tutorials are meant to allow students to discuss individual problems arising from lecture work or private reading, but, if not handled properly, they often tend to become 'mini-lectures'. Seminars that allow discussion of topics within a group and other group learning methods are becoming progressively more popular (see Chapter 6). Practical work commonly takes the form of laboratory and project work in the case of most science and engineering courses, but may involve anything from television production by students to first aid, depending on the course.

THE STUDENT-CENTRED APPROACH

While conventional teaching strategies are strongly dominated by the teacher and by institutional constraints, student-centred strategies are designed to provide the student with a highly flexible system of learning which is geared to individual life and learning styles. In such strategies, the teacher and the institution play supportive, rather than central roles.

A large number of approaches have been developed and used at different levels of education. These vary from systems designed to individualize learning within an existing educational or training environment by extensive use of resource-based learning, to systems where practically all of the conventional barriers to educational opportunity have been removed. With the latter, a potential student can be of any age or background, and can study in places, at times and at a pace which suit the individual rather than the institution. Such systems are called *open learning systems*, and are at present engendering a great deal of interest within the further and higher education and training sectors in the UK and elsewhere.

The Underlying Structure

The basic structure of the system that underlies the student-centred approach can be represented diagrammatically by Figure 2.3, although not all of the factors shown are applicable in every case. In such a structure, the students' requirements are the most important considerations, with all the other components of the system being geared to assist students to achieve their particular learning objectives as effectively as possible.

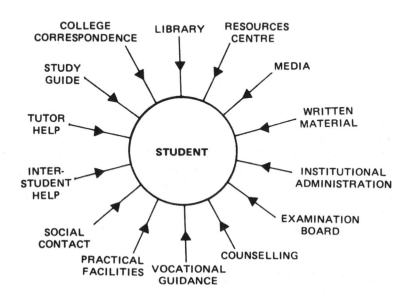

Figure 2.3 **The structure of the system underlying the student-centred approach**

The relationship between the student and the host institution can vary considerably within the context of the student-centred approach, but we can identify at least three basic organizational systems, namely, *institution-based systems, flexible learning systems* and *distance learning systems*. Let us examine these in turn, along with a fourth: *remote learning systems*.

1. *Institution-based systems.* Here, the students work at a particular institution, with learning facilities and tutor help being provided by the institution on an 'open-access' basis, and the students attending the institution for study at times and at a pace which suits them. A popular system of this type is the *Keller Plan*, which will be described in more detail towards the end of this chapter.

2. *Flexible learning systems.* Here, the host institution sets out to offer the student the facilities normally associated with a correspondence course and to back this up with on-the-spot institutional support. Such systems may be aimed specifically at members of the local population whose personal situations render it difficult or impossible for them to conform to the rigid constraints of the formal education system. The student does not have to attend the college on a regular timetabled basis, and may use a range of individualized learning facilities, both in and out of college. As in institution-based systems, college learning facilities are made available on an open-access basis. An example of this type of system is *Flexistudy*, which is becoming increasingly popular in the UK, especially in the field of further education. Figure 2.4 shows part of the 'Learning-by-Appointment' centre in one further education college that offers courses of this type. Flexible learning approaches are increasingly being used for full-time students in traditional sorts of college, where selected parts of the curriculum are devoted to an open-learning approach, with students using specially designed learning resources at their own pace, and at times of their choice. Such students attend traditional lectures from other parts of their curriculum, adding to the variety of the learning strategies they use.

3. *Distance learning systems.* Here, most of the learning takes place away from the host institution. Individualized learning materials are provided for the student, and tutorial help may be made available through correspondence or telephone with the institution or via a local tutor (or both). Self-help groups organized by students in a particular geographical area may also be formed. Probably the best known example of a distance learning system is the *Open University* in the UK.

4. *Remote learning systems.* It is useful to introduce this additional term for various kinds of student-centred learning, where the learners are at some times learning at a distance, and at other times engage in more traditional learning situations, but are kept

Figure 2.4 **A 'Learning-by-Appointment' centre
in a further education college that runs 'Flexistudy' courses**

in regular contact with tutors or trainers using recently introduced technologies such as computer-conferencing and telecon-
ferencing. In this respect, we see 'remote' learning as overlapping
both with institution-centred systems and with student-centred
systems, but in a slightly different way than does flexible
learning which we described earlier (where learners may be
institution-based but learning in different ways for different
subjects). Figure 2.5 shows a representation of the overlaps
between institution-centred systems and learner-centred systems.

The ever-increasing sophistication of educational technology
will result in an increasing proportion of learners being able to
learn in non-traditional ways, not simply being 'distance-learn-
ers' in the accepted sense of the term, nor being 'flexible-
learners' based in an institution, but being able to learn at their
own pace and in their own way, yet also being able to make
contact with an institution in a variety of ways, when they need
or wish to.

In each of the above systems, the students have a high responsibility
for many aspects of learning, so motivation must, of necessity, be
high. Course material is usually broken up into a number of discrete
units, which allow students to master one section before progressing
to the next. As students are permitted to learn at their own rate in

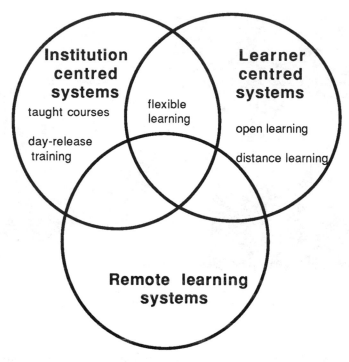

Figure 2.5 **The overlap between institution-centred systems,
learner-centred systems and remote systems**

such systems, the administrative and tutorial support must be
flexible enough to cope with this.

In student-centred courses, the individual course units are often
described in detail in the students' study guide. This document may
also list the behavioural objectives or competence descriptors of each
unit, thus enabling the students to have a clear idea of exactly what is
expected of them (see Chapter 3). Guidance may also be given on
how these objectives may be achieved, and this may (ideally) allow
students to select, from a range of alternative methods and routes,
those particular ones which best suit their personal characteristics.

The learning material that is available in such courses may take
several forms. It may be mainly textual, in the form of set books (or
sections of books), 'custom-designed' material produced by the host
institution, or a combination of the two. Easy access to a library
(either an institutional library or, if this is not possible, a good public
library) is thus more or less essential for students undertaking a
course of this type. Individualized material which has an audiovisual
content (for example, videocassettes, etc) may also be made available,
and so students much also have access to suitable replay equipment,
either at home or through a local college, school or multi-media

resources centre. Practical facilities may also be an important component of the course, and these must be made available either in the host institution (or some other local establishment) or in home-based 'kit' form.

An obvious potential problem in any highly individualized study system is that of student isolation and, in order to prevent this, some mechanism for providing tutorial guidance and remedial help must be built in. In most systems of this type, each student is allocated at least one tutor who can easily be contacted as and when required. Such tutor help may take the form of face-to-face guidance, telephone tutorials or correspondence, depending on the distance between tutor and student and the circumstances of the latter. The role of the tutor is, of course, vital in any student-centred strategy, especially in the early stages, where the student is trying to adapt to a new style of learning. The tutor is in a key position to monitor an individual's progress and to provide strong support in terms of encouragement and counselling. Valuable support for individual students can also be provided through the formation of small local student self-help groups, where common problems can be tackled on a group-discussion basis.

In any student-centred system, the administrative support of the host institution must be geared towards its smooth operation, otherwise the resulting frustration may prove disastrous. This vital area includes making arrangements for recording and monitoring student progress, distributing learning materials, assignments, tutor feedback, etc, handling finance, supporting and training teaching staff in materials production, counselling, etc, and handling publicity. In addition, the institution's student services staff may provide vocational guidance, as well as ensuring that the examination systems (if applicable) are available and familiar to the student.

As with the teacher/institution-centred approach, there are obvious advantages and disadvantages of such strategies. The relative importance of these is again very dependent upon the level of education or training involved, the type of learner, and the specific constraints associated with the institution mounting or hosting the course.

Advantages

In most student-centred learning systems, the material to be learned is much more readily available than in a teacher/institution-centred course. The individual units of study can be learned one at a time, and often in a place which suits the individual's personal circumstances. In addition, students normally have access to well-prepared, well-tested learning materials; hence the quality of the learning material available is less dependent on particular teachers. As the rate of learning is self-paced, students are not rushed past parts of a course they find difficult, nor are they held back on the parts that are easier to master. This aspect makes student-centred learning particularly appropriate for groups that have mixed abilities and/or mixed backgrounds.

Since the course units are normally accompanied by a set of behavioural objectives or competence descriptors which spell out precisely what the student will be expected to do at the end of each unit, both student and tutor know exactly what has to be achieved. Such objectives also help the students to focus their work towards any subsequent test or examination.

Within most individualized learning units, a variety of different media (such as slides, audiotapes, models, videocassettes, practical exercises, computer-based materials and textual material) can readily be incorporated. The characteristics of different media can thus be exploited to the full, and students tend to find such a multi-media approach both stimulating and motivating. Much of the material produced for individualized use is *interactive* in the sense that it involves the student in active participation and in responding to the learning material rather than simply reading, listening or watching in a purely passive manner. This structured interaction facilitates learning and maintains concentration.

The course units are themselves designed to be student-centred and, in many cases, there are several ways in which the same course material may be approached. Ideally, students can select, from a range of options, those methods which best suit their individual needs, interests and personal learning styles. Units may be produced in a number of formats, from which the student chooses the most appropriate 'package' in order to achieve the required objectives. Depending on the subject matter, students may be able to select the order in which they study the units of a course, although the sequence will obviously be partly fixed in that some units will depend and build on more basic units. Also, although some 'core' material is generally compulsory, students may usually select from a range of optional, remedial and enrichment units, depending on their individual needs and progress.

With most student-centred learning strategies, tutor help, counselling and guidance are generally more readily available and relevant than in more traditional courses. The role of the tutor is absolutely vital in supporting the individual students as they progress through a course. The advice and academic assistance given can in this case be geared to *individual* worries and problems rather than to more generalized group needs. Also, in such a system, the weaker students have the opportunity of receiving more attention than stronger or more independent students. Indeed, one of the most useful educational outcomes of such courses is that students learn to study effectively on their own, rather than being spoonfed, as is often the case in more traditional systems. It is one of the roles of the tutor/

counsellor to help students new to this style of learning to adjust in order to get the most out of the system.

Owing to this close relationship between tutor and student, together with the results of tests on each unit, both tutor and student receive regular feedback on the student's progress. Also, as each unit is successfully completed, both the student and the tutor are assured that something definite has been achieved. This provides regular encouragement and motivation for the student.

On a more general note, student-centred learning systems can provide greater educational and training opportunities for those who cannot attend institutions during 'normal' hours. This applies particularly to those in regular day-time employment and those whose personal situations (for example, dependent relatives, physical disability or problems related to distance) make it difficult or impossible for them to attend regular timetabled classes. Thus, at the levels of further, higher and adult education, a completely new market of potential students has been identified, the exploitation of which may even have implications for the long-term viability of some colleges in these sectors of education. There is vast scope for student-centred open learning courses for training, re-training and career updating. Such courses need to be neither long nor certificated, yet can still play a vital role in continuing and community education.

Disadvantages

Since student-centred learning places much more reliance on the active role of the student than does traditional teaching (where the student has a relatively passive role), student commitment and motivation must of necessity be very high. Thus, it may be less appropriate for use with young or inexperienced learners than with older, more mature learners, who have a definite goal to aim for and who enter a student-centred system knowing that they are going to have to work hard and expend effort, not least in organizing their study strategies. Even with a highly motivated group of students, some students may, indeed, never adapt to this style of learning. However, it must also be recognized that many learners who were never at home in traditional teacher-led learning situations return to learning in later life because they find student-centred approaches less threatening and more empowering.

As well as being the producers of learning materials, teachers have another new role in a student-centred learning system. They are no longer the primary conveyors of information, but adopt a more supportive counselling and tutorial role. This function may be difficult for some teachers to fulfil effectively (or even to accept) and, in many cases, it may be necessary to organize in-service courses and other staff development activities in order to help teachers to carry out their new role effectively.

A further disadvantage of student-centred learning is the rather limited range and type of courses to which the strategy is applicable. Because of the generally prescriptive nature of course units (due to the specification of precise objectives or competences), some may consider that this limits breadth and choice of study. Indeed, most applications of the approach to date have been in courses requiring mastery or updating of basic knowledge, mainly in subjects with a strong factual content and structure such as the sciences, engineering, mathematics and medicine, and also in short training courses. In subjects with a high practical component, it is often extremely difficult to build suitable laboratory work, practical demonstrations and skills-related work into essentially self-paced courses.

A student-centred course must obviously have the support of the administrative system of the host institution in terms of funding arrangements and day-to-day operation of the course in matters such as secretarial support, correspondence, telephone calls and access to special facilities (library facilities, computer facilities, laboratories, etc). The host institution must also make appropriate arrangements for student assessment.

All of these can cause administrative problems, especially if the host institution is not geared up to cope with learners in student-centred schemes. All too often, such learners simply do not fit into the system and, as a result, are not given the same priority as 'conventional' students when it comes to allocating resources and facilities. A further potential drawback of student-centred learning schemes is that any qualification gained as a result may be regarded as second-rate or inferior to similar qualifications gained by traditional means. While this may have no foundation in reality, potential students may fear that society, employers or the academic community at large may perceive this to be the case, and so they may be deterred from joining such schemes. However, the quality of graduates of the Open University in the UK is doing much to raise people's opinions of the nature of student-centred learning.

Finally, teachers must realize that student-centred learning is not a soft option on their part, and that it requires a tremendous amount of effort of writing and revising suitable units, together with tutorial and counselling duties, marking tests and assignments, and providing feedback to students.

Teaching Methods Used

The main teaching methods used in the great majority of student-centred courses are individualized methods of one form or another. Many of the materials associated with individualized learning are highly structured and interactive, although this is not necessarily the case. The materials may or may not have an audiovisual element, depending on the topic being covered and the specific design objectives. A review of individualized learning methods and techniques is given in Chapter 5.

As we have seen, tutorial support is a vital feature of all student-centred learning systems, with the precise nature of this support being strongly dependent upon the situation and location of the individual learner. Some courses may require practical work to be incorporated, but this has to be made as accessible as possible for the student, and may involve the development of individualized kits for use at home, or the provision of more organized facilities within the host institution or some other centre.

Expository methods such as lectures have traditionally had little place in such strategies. However, some student-centred courses have always included a certain number of lectures, often on an optional basis, in order to provide an introductory review of a topic or for 'enrichment' purposes. The increasing availability of 'high-tech' delivery systems such as the whiteboard and videophone seems likely to lead to an increase in the use of such methods in student-centred learning systems however, particularly with 'remote learners'.

The Keller Plan Approach

For any readers who have had little or no experience of student-centred strategies, we will now describe the operation of one of the most popular personalized systems of instruction (or PSIs). This system, known as the *Keller Plan*, was developed in the late 1960s by Professor F S Keller of Columbia University in the USA, and is an example of the way in which student-centred learning can be used within a college or similar institution.

In the Keller Plan, the course material is divided into a number of units, each with specified learning objectives, and the students receive a study guide which suggests a number of means of achieving these objectives. Armed with this information, students work largely on their own, using a range of self-instructional materials. The study guide leads through set text books, and contains supplementary notes, worked exercises, assignments, etc. Some units may also incorporate learning aids such as videos, slides, models and other structured learning materials specially prepared for use in the course. Typically, each unit represents roughly one week's work for an 'average' student, but, as students work at their own pace, this is variable. The students are free to discuss problems associated with the unit with their tutors at any time. For this reason, tutors have to be available on a fairly regular basis. Tutors are normally members of the teaching staff, but they may be, in certain circumstances, students who have previously completed the unit successfully. Thus, the possibility of *peer teaching* can be incorporated into a Keller Plan approach. The use of more-advanced students to teach their less-experienced peers is now being extended into higher education as 'Supplemental Instruction'. Here, for example, third year students may be formally employed to help first year students to learn specified parts of the curriculum.

When students feel they have mastered a given unit and have achieved the objectives identified and can demonstrate the competences specified, they present themselves for a test (oral or written). If they pass such a test to a specified standard, they move on to the next unit. With the Keller Plan, a high degree of mastery is often required, and pass marks on tests may be of the order of 80 or 90 per cent. There is, however, no penalty for failing, and students may attempt tests on a given unit as many times as is necessary. After each test, the student and tutor discuss any problems which may have arisen during work on the unit, or during the test itself.

In the Keller Plan, lectures, although not a main element of the teaching, are sometimes used to provide an overview of the course material or to illuminate certain aspects of the topics studied. Laboratory work (if required) is normally carried out under the direct supervision of a laboratory assistant.

The basic Keller Plan approach has been modified and adapted to meet a wide variety of needs. Peer teaching is not always used; tests on groups of units (rather than on single units) may be included; a high level of mastery is not always required; and the final grades can be decided using different methods. Whatever the variations, however, the essential elements of the Keller Plan are *individualized learning, independent study, self-pacing* and *tutor support*. Although the Keller Plan has been used with a wide range of subjects, the most common applications to date have been with medical and science subjects, usually at college or university level.

The distinctive features of other well-known examples of open, student-centred systems of learning (eg 'local' systems such as Flexistudy, and distance learning schemes such as the Open University) are described in Chapter 5.

'MIX AND MATCH' – THE STRATEGY FOR THE FUTURE?

For many years, teacher-centred approaches and learner-centred approaches seemed poles apart, and proponents of each kind of approach seemed sometimes to be at war. However, there is at last evidence that the two kinds of approach are being incorporated into a unified picture. Many colleges, training centres and universities now provide both sorts of approach. Selected topics are offered in traditional face-to-face expository training or lecturing, while learners are enabled to study other topics in a flexible-learning mode, using custom-designed or off-the-shelf learning resource materials. Even in traditional institutions of education and training, the importance of learning resource centres has grown, and the number of hours that learners spend studying in such centres has increased, while the number of hours they spend in traditional classrooms or lecture theatres has decreased.

Teachers and trainers who are brilliant at providing lectures continue to do so, not least because their learners find them valuable and stimulating. Teachers and trainers who are not brilliant at expository techniques (the majority no doubt) are often much more successful as facilitators of learning, providing tutorial support for learners studying open-learning packages, computer-based training materials and self-directed reading.

Learners and trainees have more choice. Some learners enjoy 'passive' learning situations such as lectures, and welcome their trainers taking on the responsibility for guiding them through their studies. Other learners welcome the challenge of taking on for themselves the responsibility for managing their own learning, when necessary using trainers or tutors as a resource. Perhaps the ultimate expression of learner-centredness is for learners to have the choice, so that they can decide for each topic they study whether it is best, in the light of their own personal approaches to learning, to make use of formal teaching-learning situations, or to use learning resource materials on their own.

Chapter 3

Educational Objectives and Competence Descriptors – 'What exactly am I reasonably expected to become able to do?'

INTRODUCTION

In the previous two chapters, we mentioned the key parts played by *objectives* and *competence descriptors* in the design of teaching-learning processes and resources. In this chapter we will attempt to explain their importance and to illustrate the ways that they can be used. Behavioural objectives and competence descriptors have the common purpose of making it clear exactly what successful learners will be able to do at the end of specified stages in their learning programmes.

Historically, the development of the use of behavioural objectives in training and education was a milestone in clarifying, standardizing and specifying learning outcomes, and was a major part of teacher-training and trainer-training from the 1960s until the mid-1980s. The use of behavioural objectives was the cornerstone of the 'systems approach' to education and training. In the 1980s, 'competence' became the buzz-word in education and training in the UK, and major government moves encouraged vocational qualifications to be expressed in terms of the competences which successful learners should be able to demonstrate. In the early 1990s, National Vocational Qualifications are overseen by the National Council for Vocational Qualifications in the UK, and there is an ever-growing literature on topics such as specifying competences, assessing competences and so on. The competence-based approach is presently being extended into the school curriculum with the introduction of GNVQs (General National Vocational Qualifications) which run in parallel with GCSE (General Certificate of Secondary Education) and A-level curricula.

We see the 'competence revolution' as a logical, more flexible (and 'more humane') extension and development of the behavioural objectives era which preceded it, and in this chapter we will begin with a review of the formulation and use of behavioural objectives, and then offer some guidelines on how to extend and develop such specifications of learning outcomes into competence terms.

AN OBJECTIVES-BASED APPROACH TO LEARNING DESIGN

The identification and formulation of precise learning outcomes is generally considered to be the first crucial step in the processes of designing educational and training courses or learning resources, and remains at the heart of curriculum design. We showed 'objectives and competence descriptors' as one of the first steps in the model we presented in Figure 1.4. Various elements of this model are rearranged in Figure 3.1, concentrating for the moment on the formulation of objectives.

Within such a model, objectives serve three principal functions:

■ They define the general nature of the course or curriculum and give an idea of the material that should be covered.
■ They allow consideration of which teaching and learning methods should be employed.
■ They are of primary assistance in planning the content and processes to be used in assessment.

As shown in Figure 3.1, objectives (like all other parts of the model) should be adjusted in the light of experience of implementing courses or training programmes, and should be continuously refined in the light of emerging knowledge of the target population of learners and their existing skills, abilities and competences.

AIMS AND OBJECTIVES

Outside training and education circles, the terms 'aim' and 'objective' are almost synonymous, meaning 'targets' or 'that to which we decide to direct our energies'. However, in the jargon-ridden worlds of education and training, the words 'aim' and 'objective' have been endowed with a certain degree of special meaning, often quite unnecessarily.

Aims: these are broad statements of intent. They give a general picture of the intended learning outcomes. They illustrate the overall purpose of a course or learning resource.

Objectives: these are 'sharper'. They are more precise. One aim will usually lead to several objectives. They give more information. They describe in greater detail the intended learning outcomes of a course. They describe learning outcomes in terms of things that a successful learner will be able to do at the end of a specified part of a course. In open and flexible learning, objectives describe what

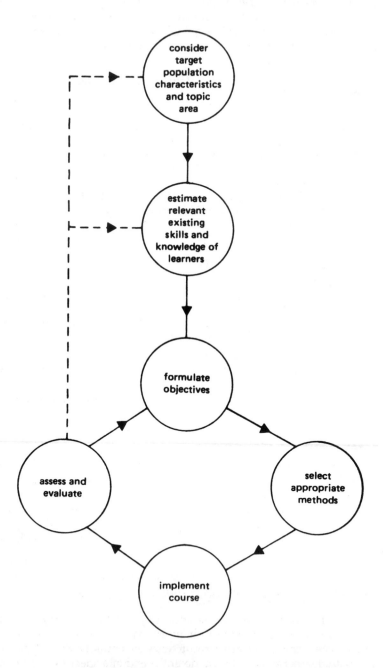

Figure 3.1 **A simplified systems approach to course design**

learners should be able to do after successfully completing their study of learning packages or resource materials. They are sometimes called *behavioural* objectives, since they are normally formulated to describe *terminal behaviour* of successful learners, in other words, what can be done by such learners at the end of a specified element of their studies.

To illustrate the difference between aims and objectives, let us look at a specific example, a typical basic chemistry course.

Aim: to develop students' understanding of the properties of chemical bonds and of the principles of bonding.

Objectives: at the end of the learning programme, students should be able to:

1. Define the term *orbital* in terms of the probability of finding an electron in a given region of space.
2. Explain the meaning of the terms: *s-, p-* and *d-electrons*.
3. Write the electronic configuration of an atom or ion, in terms of s-, p- and d-electrons, given the atomic number of the atom concerned.
4. Define the terms *ionic, covalent,* and *co-ordinate bond* and describe each of these bonds in terms of the electronic interactions involved.
5. Predict the likely types of bond formed between any two elements, when provided with the positions of these elements in the Periodic Table.
6. Define the terms *electronegativity* of an element and *polarity* of a bond.
7. List *five* of the important properties of bonds (strength, length, orientation in space, polarity and vibration) and, by giving suitable examples, describe each of these properties of bonds.
   and so on ...

Therefore, we see that *objectives* can be considered to be specific sets of well-defined activities which learners will be able to exhibit in order to demonstrate their achievement of more loosely-defined *aims*. (Equally, as we shall see later, the objectives are also statements of the *competences* which successful learners will become able to demonstrate after completing the appropriate element of their learning programme.)

FORMULATING AND WRITING OBJECTIVES

The most serious danger facing anyone trying to write objectives is that of formulating objectives which are too vague or too broad. In other words, the intended learning outcomes may be too imprecise. For objectives to serve both teachers and learners well, the objectives should:

- identify exactly what successful learners should be able to do;
- make sense to learners who have not yet achieved the objectives (in other words, not contain words or ideas that the learners can not understand);
- describe, where necessary, the conditions under which learners should become able to demonstrate their achievement of the objectives (specifying, for example, the data or information they will be provided with);
- describe, where necessary, the standards or levels to which learners should be able to demonstrate their achievement of the objectives (the basis on which learners' performance will be assessed in due course).

In the early days of behavioural objectives, they were usually prefaced by phrases such as:

At the end of the course, the student will...
After studying this package, the trainee will be able to...

and so on. Increasingly, objectives are being made more personal, giving learners and trainees a greater sense of *ownership* of the objectives and a greater incentive to achieve them. For example, a list of objectives can be prefaced by phrases like:

At the end of this course, you will be able to...
After working through this module, you will be able to...

Many designers of education and training courses and resources like to make the objectives less formal still, and use lead-in phrases such as:

At the end of this programme, you'll be able to...
When you've worked through this package, you should be able to...

For objectives to achieve their purpose (in other words, for learners – and teachers – to see exactly what is entailed in each objective), the first word or two of the objectives needs to be clear, precise, unambiguous and above all, *definite*. Looking back at the list of objectives we gave earlier, note the importance of the first word, (shown in bold this time, below).

1. **Define** the term *orbital* in terms of the probability of finding an electron in a given region of space;
2. **Explain** the meaning of the terms: *s-, p-* and *d-electrons*.
3. **Write** the electronic configuration of an atom or ion, in terms of s-, p- and d-electrons, given the atomic number of the atom concerned.
4. **Define** the terms *ionic, covalent,* and *co-ordinate bond* and describe each of these bonds in terms of the electronic interactions involved.

5. **Predict** the likely types of bond formed between any two elements, when provided with the positions of these elements in the Periodic Table.
6. **Define** the terms *electronegativity* of an element and *polarity* of a bond.
7. **List** *five* of the important properties of bonds (strength, length, orientation in space, polarity and vibration) and by giving suitable examples, **describe** each of these properties of bonds.

Certain words are unsuitable for use in objectives, because they are too vague or too broad. Such words include 'know', 'understand' and 'appreciate'. For example, the following statements would be far too vague to be useful objectives (and would perhaps only serve the purpose of broad aims):

by the end of the programme, you should know the plays of Shakespeare;
after working through this module, you should have developed an understanding of the Second Law of Thermodynamics and its applications;
when you have finished this course, you will appreciate the uses of Ohm's Law.

For objectives to be useful to learners (and teachers and trainers) more active, more explicit verbs are needed, such as 'state', 'explain', 'derive', 'define', 'discuss', 'describe', 'list', 'identify', 'predict', 'summarize', 'criticize', 'compare', 'contrast', 'name', 'give examples of' and so on.

With words such as those above included in objectives, the link to assessment is obvious and straightforward. If learners become able to achieve such objectives, they should expect to be able to handle corresponding assessments successfully. It should come as no surprise that when detailed objectives are not available to learners, they tend to look at past assessment questions for clues regarding exactly what they may in due course be expected to demonstrate.

Objectives: Mager's Approach

A leading proponent of the art of identifying and formulating tightly constructed behavioural objectives is the American psychologist Robert F Mager, whose published work is still used widely by educators and trainers. In his definitive work *Preparing Instructional Objectives*, first published in 1962, he paved the way for the widespread adoption of behavioural objectives as a key component in the design of educational and training materials and programmes. He proposed that objectives should be as clear and unambiguous as possible, so that learners could understand their meaning without further explanation or amplification. He argues that a well-formulated objective should include each of the following three dimensions:

1. a statement of exactly what the learner should be able to do at the end of a specified learning experience (ie, a statement of the desired *terminal behaviour*);

2. a description of any *conditions or constraints* under which this behaviour can be demonstrated (eg, 'under examination conditions' or 'in practical exercises' or 'in field work' and so on);

3. a clear indication of the minimum *standard of performance* which may be considered acceptable.

Some examples of objectives written in this fashion are given below, and in each case we have identified each of the three 'elements' that are required by Mager 'purists':

a. After working through this course you should be able to weigh an object (element 1) of less than 100 grams using an analytical balance (element 2) and obtain the correct answer to four decimal places at least nine times out of ten (element 3).

b. After this training session, you should be able to fire five shots from a standard-issue rifle (element 1) in 20 seconds at a standard circular target 50 metres away (element 2) scoring at least four bullseyes (element 3).

c. By the end of this course on writing computer-markable multiple-choice questions and responses, you should be able to compose a computer-marked test of ten 4-option questions (element 1) in less than three hours (element 2), where the responses are self-sufficient enough that 90 per cent of learners do not need to refer to the original questions to make sense of the print-out of responses they receive in reply to their test entries.

However, it can readily be seen that if all three elements were to be included in each and every behavioural objective, it would be quite impracticable to break down each element of curriculum into objectives in so detailed a manner. Therefore, it is sensible to exercise some judgement regarding whether the 'conditions' and 'standards' really need to be spelled out or whether they can reasonably be assumed to be understood by learners and teachers. However, there is no doubt that spelling out the desired learning outcomes helps both learners and teachers. As Mager himself put it: 'if you don't know where you're heading, you'll probably end up someplace else, and not even know it'. (One of your authors puts it rather more cynically: 'if you don't know where you're going, any train will do; if you do know where you're going, the train you wanted left Platform 7 three minutes ago'.)

SKILLS ANALYSIS

As far back as the 1950s and 1960s the 'skills analysis' or 'task analysis' approach of breaking down complex tasks into sequences of simpler tasks became popular. Now usually called 'training needs analysis', the technique has continued to be refined and developed. Such a breakdown can facilitate the specification of precise objectives relating to particular sub-skills, and also helps to identify the pre-knowledge or existing skills which may be necessary for learners starting out on a learning programme. Once the separate sub-skills related to an overall task have been identified, they can be described, in sequence, on a chart or diagram of the sort shown in Figure 3.2, which shows a skills analysis for the task of training people to use a mechanical micrometer, used for measuring the sizes of small objects with a high degree of precision.

Such skills analysis approaches have been particularly widely used in manipulative and industrial skills-training contexts. However, designers of training and educational programmes need to be aware that there are definite dangers to such an approach; for example, skills analysis may sometimes prove by no means the best – nor the easiest – way of determining course design objectives.

TYPES OF OBJECTIVES

With the general acceptance of the usefulness of behavioural objectives in designing educational and training programmes and processes, it became fashionable (for a while) to think in terms of three broad categories of objectives. A milestone in the thinking about behavioural objectives was provided by another American, Benjamin Bloom, who assigned behavioural objectives to three *domains*, namely the *'cognitive'*, *'affective'* and *'psychomotor'* domains. At the risk of oversimplification, these domains can be described as follows:

- cognitive domain: objectives relating to knowledge, theories, understanding;
- affective domain: objectives relating to feelings, attitudes, perspectives;
- psychomotor domain: objectives relating to skills, practical abilities, manipulation.

Bloom's Taxonomies of Educational Objectives

Bloom further subdivided each of the domains, as follows.

Cognitive Domain
1. *Knowledge*
   This Bloom considered the lowest level of cognitive objectives. Learning outcomes in this category include:
   - name parts of an object
   - identify a component
   - state a definition
   - list causes of an effect

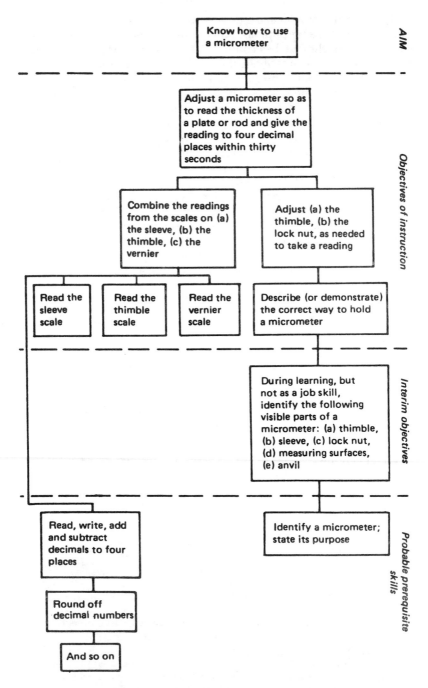

Figure 3.2 **Skills analysis for the operation of a micrometer**

2. *Comprehension*

This can be regarded as the simplest level of 'understanding'. Activities demonstrating learning outcomes in this category include:

- select an example which demonstrates a phenomenon
- give reasons explaining an observation
- classify objects into categories
- translate words into symbolic expressions

3. *Application*

This covers the links between theory and practice; examples include:

- perform a specified task
- calculate a mathematical result
- apply a given set of rules or procedures
- predict the result of a proposed course of action

4. *Analysis*

This involves the systematic breaking down of material into its constituent parts, and includes:

- compare and contrast alternatives
- justify the adoption of a particular model or explanation
- interpret the relationship between elements or variables

5. *Synthesis*

This involves the combination of elements or components to form new structured wholes. The higher-level skills included in the *synthesis* category include:

- compose an original essay
- propose ways to test hypotheses
- derive mathematical generalizations
- design systems to achieve stated aims

6. *Evaluation*

This is the highest level of Bloom's subdivisions of the cognitive domain. This includes:

- make judgements about the extent to which evidence satisfies criteria
- interpret evidence qualitatively and quantitatively
- indicate fallacies in arguments
- argue for and against a proposal
- compare a new model with established theories

It should be recognized that Bloom argued for a *continuum* spanning the cognitive domain, ranging from the simple and concrete to the complex and abstract. The six subdivisions mentioned above should not be regarded as 'watertight' or mutually-exclusive.

Affective Domain

This, as we have mentioned, is to do with attitudes and feelings. Bloom again attempted to divide the domain into subdivisions, as follows:

1. *Receiving*
   This could involve developing an awareness of the aesthetic factors of a subject, or 'tuning in' to the context of a discipline.
2. *Responding*
   This could be described as 'taking an interest' in a subject, or showing active attention, but at an uncomplicated level.
3. *Valuing*
   This could be described as acquiring a feeling for the 'worth' of a topic, culture, or pattern of behaviour, and acting accordingly.
4. *Organizing*
   This could include ordering the relationships between values, and sorting out one's feelings and attitudes towards situations or phenomena.
5. *Characterizing*
   An extension of organizing – for example, organizing values into a total and consistent philosophy.

Although at first sight these three domains, (and the subdivisions we have outlined for two of them) may seem to be usefully separate and distinct, in everyday life things are not so simple. Very often, all three domains are involved in any single objective, which has knowledge, feelings and practical dimensions.

Also, it is now increasingly recognized that some of the most important educational and training objectives should refer to much broader skills and abilities, including decision-making, problem-solving, interpersonal skills, creative thinking, time-management skills, teamwork skills and so on. Such skills and abilities defy being broken down simply into cognitive, affective and psychomotor ingredients. The 'Education for Capability' movement in the UK argues the need for attention to *process* rather than *content* in learning. Indeed, if the description of education as 'what is left after the facts have been forgotten' is accepted as having value, then the argument becomes very powerful for formulating objectives related to the 'broader skills' areas, and considering seriously the methods and processes most likely to foster the development of such skills.

A problem with Bloom's domain subdivisions is that it is by no means simple to decide into which category particular actions or objectives belong – indeed many can be justified as belonging to more than one category. Perhaps, some decades later, the principal benefits of Bloom's work are associated with a greater attention to the precision of the working out of objectives (and now competence indicators), as ways of clarifying the exact nature of intended learning outcomes. This in turn leads to useful information for those designing the processes, and the resources, which can usefully contribute to learners' achievement of such learning outcomes. Perhaps even more important is the fact that when learning outcomes have been clearly formulated, it becomes possible to design assessment instruments and processes which are directly relevant to such learning outcomes. In other words, we are slowly moving towards 'assessing the right things' after decades when learning and assessment sometimes seemed poles apart.

A Simpler Classification of Objectives

An alternative classification of objectives, which proves to be highly practicable and retains the main features of Bloom's classification but without as many overlaps, is as follows:

1. *Lower cognitive objectives*
   Comprising the first two levels (knowledge and comprehension) of Bloom's cognitive domain, and containing all objectives relating to acquiring knowledge and basic understanding.
2. *Higher cognitive objectives*
   Comprising the four higher levels (application, analysis, synthesis and evaluation) of Bloom's cognitive domain, and including all objectives related to decision-making, problem-solving, interpretation and planning.
3. *Affective objectives*
   Simply collecting together all objectives relating to the development of feelings, attitudes, and values.
4. *Psychomotor objectives*
   Comprising all objectives relating to hand-eye coordination, motor skills, practical abilities, manual dexterity and so on.
5. *Interpersonal objectives*
   Covering all the various 'life-skills' that were not catered for by Bloom's original tripartite classification, including interpersonal skills, communications skills (written and oral), listening skills, ability to work as a member of a team, leadership skills, entrepreneurial skills, higher teaching skills and so on.

ADVANTAGES AND DISADVANTAGES OF USING OBJECTIVES

Advantages

Detailed, well-formulated objectives allow teachers, trainers and learners to have a clear, *shared* picture of exactly what the learners will be expected to be able to demonstrate at the end of an episode of learning, whether a course or a learning module. Clear objectives also guard against over-reliance on particular teachers or trainers, and militate against idiosyncratic interpretations of syllabuses. However, even when clearly-worded objectives have been formulated, it is still, sadly, the case that some educators and trainers regard such objectives as 'private information', and fail to share the detail which these objectives provide with the learners who are intended to achieve them in due course. We feel that the objectives should *belong* to the learners themselves, as a means for them to decide what is important and what is not. We see no justification in the still-common practice of learners having to use old exam papers to work out exactly what their objectives really are.

When objectives are clearly-formulated and shared with learners, many benefits can be realized, including:

- learners and teachers know exactly what is intended as learning outcomes or targets;
- teachers and trainers can use objectives as planning tools in the organization of their teaching and training plans;
- objectives can be ranked in relative importance, helping learners to see what the priorities are in a programme of study or training;
- teachers and trainers can base their assessments on the intended learning outcomes specified by the objectives;
- learners can anticipate the standards required of them when preparing for assessment;
- learners can identify particular objectives that cause them difficulty, and seek help from teachers or trainers, or from fellow-learners or learning resources.

Disadvantages

There are several dangers which can be linked to 'slavish' following of objectives-based approaches to education and training. The following are only some of them:

- particular objectives may be given greater status than they deserve;
- teaching and learning may become far too prescribed;
- learners may become highly trained in narrow areas, but lack training in important broad areas;
- complicated learning outcomes are often difficult to express in terms of objectives, whereas it is usually easy to write objectives for straighforward learning outcomes; this can lead to the formulation of a set of objectives covering all the simple learning outcomes, but missing more important complex learning outcomes;
- a published set of course objectives can all too easily become a 'straitjacket' for an educational or training programme;
- objectives can be difficult and time-consuming to express and construct;
- there is always the danger that the published objectives 'belong' to the teacher or trainer, and that the objectives of learners remain unrecognized or undervalued.

A FRESH LOOK AT OBJECTIVES

Going back to the student-centred approach we advocated in Chapter 2, let us look again at the role of objectives, this time through the eyes of learners. When embarking on a programme of study or training, what do learners really want to know? We suggest it is as follows:

- **What** do I need to become able to do?
- **How** do I need to be able to demonstrate my ability?
- **By what means** will I be helped to develop such ability?
- **Why** is it important for me to develop these abilities?
- **When** will I be expected to demonstrate my ability?
- **Under what circumstances** will my ability be assessed?
- **How** will my ability be measured?
- **What evidence** will I need to furnish to demonstrate my ability?

The answers to these questions have a great significance in the model of learning with which we ended Chapter 1 – namely 'wanting', 'doing', 'feedback' and 'digesting'. The more learners can be informed about exactly what in due course they should be able to do, the easier it is for them to see the relevance of their achievement of stated learning outcomes, helping create motivation ('wanting'). Furthermore, explicitly stated learning outcomes give far more detail about what will be involved in the learning programme ('doing'). When assessment is based on published statements of learning outcomes, it becomes possible for learners to self-assess their own performance as they learn, and to gather information from trainers and tutors regarding how well they are progressing towards achieving the objectives ('feedback'). Clarification of the links between learning and assessment allows learners to make sense of their progress and plan and monitor their work ('digesting').

However, as we shall shortly see, there are many important and desirable learning outcomes where it is not at all simple to express the 'terminal behaviour' in terms of the sort of objectives we have been thinking about, or where it would be impossible to use traditional assessment methods to measure the learning outcomes (particularly relating to interpersonal objectives). This 'fresh look' at objectives led to the emergence of 'competence' as one of the key ingredients in the description of a wide range of educational and training programmes during the late 1980s and into the 1990s.

COMPETENCE: 'CAN DO' STATEMENTS

A phrase which was involved throughout the 'objectives' era was '*is able to* . . .' It may seem a small step to replace this phrase by '*can do* . . .'. Perhaps, it would be better to say '*does do* . . .'!

The 1990s (in the UK at least) seem destined to be the era of competence descriptors. In a book of this size, we can only skim the surface of the massive developments which are presently underway in terms of competence-based education and training. We have included in the bibliography references to some of the major publications that give far greater detail. Objectives, in their own way, were competence descriptors, but competence statements of the 1990s often go beyond the limits which could be achieved by objectives wording. In particular, the competence 'revolution' focuses on the *evidence* that successful learners will, in due course, be able to provide, to show that they have demonstrated identified competences (or, in past terminology, evidence that they have achieved specified objectives).

One example of the formulation of competence descriptors for a complex area of 'learning outcome' is as follows (adapted from BTEC Guidelines on 'Common Skills' in 1991):

Competence 7 *Can work effectively as a member of a team*

General Range Statement
This competence is about the achievement of goals and objectives in collaboration with colleagues. In the work place, this may be as a member of a small office or laboratory team, a maintenance team or a production or manufacturing team. At college, vocational situations could be devised where tasks are completed by team work.

Range Statement: The learner will have to be able to operate effectively as a team member and leader. Situations should be devised to enable the learner to identify where the use of team work would be of advantage and to manage the process accordingly.

Performance Criteria
(a)   Need and opportunities for team work are identified.
(b)   Team members' strengths and weaknesses are evaluated and shared responsibility for allocation of team tasks is agreed and undertaken.
(c)   Individual contributions to team tasks are delegated and accepted to meet organizational goals.
(d)   Other team members are listened to, helped and supported.
(e)   Potential problems are assessed and appropriate action is taken.
(f)   Self-evaluation of own contributions to team tasks is undertaken.

Looking at this specification of competence indicators puts the use of objectives into context. The assessment of the competence 'Can work effectively as a member of a team' would involve the compilation of a range of evidence relating to each of the *performance criteria* giving details of the nature of the desired manifestations of the competence. It is easy to see how impossible it would be to set a traditional written examination to 'measure' this sort of competence. Evidence would be made up of various components, including self-evaluation, peer-evaluation, observation by others (supervisors, tutors and so on). The collection of evidence upon which competence assessment is based is often called a *portfolio*, containing relevant evidence collected by learners from a range of sources.

It would not be easy to write objectives in the respective *cognitive, affective* and *psychomotor* domains to cover the statements of competence given in the example above. However, from the viewpoints of learners and teachers alike, expressions of competences can give a detailed picture of exactly what the intended learning outcome should be. In particular, competence descriptors give details of precisely what evidence learners should provide to demonstrate their achievement of the respective dimensions of the competences involved. Furthermore, employers can see from such competence descriptors the skills and qualities that successful learners should bring with them to their jobs. Employers can use such competence descriptors to select training courses and programmes (and learning packages and learning resources) appropriate to the different training needs of their various employees, thereby making their training as relevant as possible to the duties in which the competences will be required.

Formulating Competences or Objectives for a New Course or Training Programme

Choosing exactly which competences (or objectives) should be included in a new course or training programme could be viewed as essentially a series of subjective decisions, with the basis for such decisions having its roots in a wide variety of areas. Some of the most important factors to be taken into account when formulating a competence framework are as follows.

1. *Vocational needs.* These will reflect the specific skills and knowledge in the context of the learners' anticipated job profile, social role or profession.
2. *Training needs analysis.* This yields precise details of particular skills and knowledge needed to perform competently in identified jobs and duties.
3. *Cultural considerations.* This includes perceptions of what is needed in the area of 'the subject for its own sake' – skills, knowledge and abilities which are accepted to be important in the context of particular subjects.
4. *Social considerations.* These yield information about the knowledge, skills and attitudes which are rated as desirable by the society in which the learner or trainee will work.
5. *Learner-identified factors.* It is becoming increasingly common for

learners to have their own say in the content and processes to be involved in their education and training and for negotiated learning agreements to be constructed, including learning of topics chosen by learners themselves.

6. *Teacher factors.* Individual teachers and trainers, on the basis of their experience, can often identify preferences and interests which they feel should be built into courses and training programmes.

It should be remembered that the formulation of competences (and objectives) should remain a cyclical process. In other words, once the competence descriptors have been identified, formulated and written (however well-researched), they should not be taken as 'tablets of stone' or 'a millstone round the trainer's neck', but should be continuously kept under review. Probably the most profitable time to review competence descriptors is when the performance criteria are actually put to the test as instruments of assessment or appraisal. Only then may it be found that particular competence descriptors need revision, to make it easier for learners and assessors to match evidence to competence.

CONCLUSIONS

In this chapter we have been exploring ways of specifying learning outcomes by formulating behavioural objectives and competence descriptors. In other words, we have been looking at how best to define the *content* of educational and training programmes and also of learning resource materials. However, well-defined learning outcomes are also valuable to educators and trainers as a means of helping them to decide on the most suitable *processes* whereby learners will achieve the objectives or acquire the competences defined. Moreover, well-defined learning outcomes have a direct link to assessment, and help educators and trainers to choose the best forms of assessment, related to the skills and abilities which learners are intended to be able to demonstrate as a result of their learning. We will explore the issue of assessment in much greater detail in Chapter 7.

Chapter 4

Mass Instruction Techniques

INTRODUCTION

Let us suppose that a teacher, lecturer or trainer is involved in the development of a new course or curriculum and, as a first step, has produced a clear set of objectives or a competence framework. The next step is to choose the most appropriate methods for achieving these objectives or for developing these competencies, and just how he or she might go about this task will be the topic of the next three chapters of this book. The particular methods that are eventually chosen will depend on a large number of factors, including the detailed nature of the objectives or competencies in question, institutional constraints, student characteristics and his or her own preferences. They will, however, be of three broad types, namely, those associated with *mass instruction, individualized learning* and *group learning*, so we will look at these three types of instructional methods in turn.

In this chapter, we will examine some of the more common methods that are used in mass instruction, that is, the teaching or training of relatively large groups or classes, usually within the context of a teacher/institution-centred course of some sort. First, we will look at the methods themselves, identifying their main characteristics and discussing their respective strengths and weaknesses. Then, we will turn our attention to the various audiovisual media that can be used to support these different methods, dealing in turn with *non-projected visual aids, projected visual and audiovisual aids* and *audio aids.*

THE MAIN MASS INSTRUCTION METHODS

In this section, we will discuss four of the most common methods that are used in mass instructional situations, namely *lectures and talks, video presentations, educational broadcasts* and *practical activities.* Within each of these categories there are a wide variety of different approaches and tactics that may be adopted but, as we will see, a number of generalizations can be made, and it is on these tฺhat we will concentrate. It should be emphasized at this point that the techniques of 'mass instruction' may well be received by small numbers of students (or even by individual students) as well as by large audiences. Thus, the term 'mass' is used more in a qualitative than a strictly quantitative sense.

Lectures and Talks

Although the term 'lecture' is normally used in the context of tertiary education and training, we will take it to cover any situation in which a teacher or instructor talks to (or at!) a class of pupils, students or trainees. Despite a plethora of other teaching methods being available, the face-to-face talk or 'lecture' still holds a central position at many levels of education, and will undoubtedly continue to do so for some considerable time to come. It is therefore rather surprising that comparatively little is known about the educational effectiveness of the lecture. Also, what little information *has* been established as a result of controlled, empirical research is not particularly widely known, especially among practising teachers, lecturers and trainers. Thus, the strength with which opinions on the usefulness of lectures are held is frequently greater than the strength of the grounds upon which these opinions are based! In addition, the problem of defining what constitutes a 'good lecture' is exceedingly difficult, since several research studies have indicated that individual students appreciate not only different but sometimes conflicting things in a lecture.

Some advantages of the lecture method

Undoubtedly, one of the reasons why the lecture has retained its dominant place in the educational and training scene is that the method appears to be highly cost-effective, since it enables high student/staff ratios to be achieved; 100 students can, for example, be taught just as effectively as 10 in a lecture situation (see Figure 4.1). Indeed, with the expansion of higher education in the UK in the early 1990s, 400 students is a not-uncommon 'class-size'.

Another point in the lecture's favour is that it appears to be just as effective as other teaching methods at conveying information *when well done*. The majority of studies which have compared the lecture method with other methods designed for developing lower cognitive skills have not been able to detect any difference that is statistically significant, and those studies which have shown a measurable difference have been approximately equally distributed either way. (It is worth pointing out, however, that *most* teaching methods are not particularly efficient at imparting . information; a common figure quoted is approximately 40 per cent recall of information by students immediately after a lecture – and, unless reinforcement

Figure 4.1 **A typical lecture in progress**

takes place, even this ability to recall material falls off rapidly with time.)

Many teachers feel more comfortable using the lecture method than they do using other, perhaps more participative, methods. Also, the lecture method appears to be popular with students, although this may be largely due to familiarity, the opportunity to remain passive in comparative safety, and to a lack of appreciation of the possible advantages of alternative methods of teaching.

Some weaknesses of the lecture method

One aspect of the lecture method which causes some concern is that its effectiveness is inevitably very dependent on the skills of the individual lecturer. The ability to organize and explain a topic does not come naturally except to a fortunate few individuals, while fewer still are able to capitalize on their personal charisma in order to 'capture' their audiences. George Brown's book *Lecturing and Explaining* (1978) gives many useful guidelines on the art of structuring and presenting a lecture, and is heartily commended to all who lack these skills, as is the CICED booklet *Some Hints on How to be an Effective Lecturer* (Ellington, 1987).

In addition, the resultant effectiveness of a lecture relies heavily on the ability of the students to learn from it. Here, the study skills mentioned in Chapter 1 are extremely important, and it may well be necessary to make a conscious effort to inculcate good study techniques before the full educational potential of the lecture method is realized.

A number of research studies aimed at comparing the lecture with other teaching methods have been carried out. These studies have shown that the lecture is not particularly effective in developing high-level thought amongst students (Bloom's higher cognitive areas), or at teaching towards desirable attitudes (Bloom's affective domain) compared with methods of learning such as group discussions or participative simulations which involve more student activity. Thus, the lecture may not be quite as economical as it is generally believed to be in terms of achieving the entire range of course objectives, especially if a teacher does not appreciate the limitations of lectures and fails to combine their use with other, more active, methods.

Many of the disadvantages of the lecture method stem from the fact that students are normally completely passive in lectures, spending most of their time either listening or writing down notes. The method is usually non-interactive, although some teachers attempt to get round this deficiency by building in, for example, 'buzz' sessions (short problem-solving or discussion sessions) in which the students work on their own or in small groups and then feed back information based on the task set to the teacher and to the rest of the class. (See, for example 'Interactive Handouts: Open Learning Processes in the Lecture Room' in *The Open Learning Handbook* by Phil Race, also *500 Tips for Tutors* by Phil Race and Sally Brown.)

In a lecture, all students are forced to proceed at one pace, namely, that dictated by the teacher, with usually very little opportunity for feedback from the students. This inevitably produces a wide variation in understanding throughout a lecture class, making the method practically useless for achieving universal mastery of topics. Also, within a lecture structure, individual problems and difficulties cannot normally be dealt with in a satisfactory manner. A related difficulty is that the teacher's perception of a subject is not necessarily the same as that of the students in all cases.

Another problem caused by the passive nature of lectures is that student attention tends to fall off fairly rapidly with time. This fall-off takes the form of an increasing frequency of attention breaks (sometimes call *microsleeps*) in which the student 'switches off' concentration for a short time. The length of time for which a student can maintain full attention to the task of listening and writing is called the *attention span*. In a typical 50-minute 'straight' lecture, student attention span decreases steadily as the lecture progresses. Typically, it falls from about 12 to 15 minutes at the start of the lecture to around 3 to 5 minutes towards the end. Attention breaks usually last for about two minutes, although their pattern of occurrence is affected by a number of factors. It is found, for example, that, if the lecturer includes deliberate breaks in the lecture (practical demonstrations, 'buzz' sessions, visual stimuli and so on), the net effect is that the progressive decline in student attention is temporarily halted. Skilled timing of these variations can improve the attention span pattern considerably, and it is likely that any lecture time that is lost in providing these 'mental breathers' for students is more than recouped in terms of effective student learning.

Thus, if they are to used to optimum effect, the limitations of lectures *must* be recognized, both by course and curriculum planners and also by the teachers, lecturers and trainers who actually work at the 'chalk face'. The latter, in particular, should realize that lectures are much more effective if they are used in conjunction with a suitable combination of supportive and complementary teaching methods rather than entirely on their own.

Video Presentations

For many years, films were widely used in education (and, even more commonly, in training situations) as a mass-instructional teaching method in their own right. With the arrival of the videocas- sette recorder, which makes it even easier to show film-type pro- grammes in the classroom, this practice has become even more prevalent. Thus, an ever-increasing range of videocassette pro- grammes are now being made for all sectors of education and training. In addition to being a teaching method in their own right, short video clips can be incorporated into lecture-type presentations in order to provide illustrative visual stimulation and variety of approach, to provide enrichment material and so on.

Some advantages of video presentations

Video presentations can be used in education and training as an effective lecture-substitute. They are particularly useful if the content has a high visual impact, where a variety of techniques such as animation, time-lapse photography and close-up work can be used to good effect.

Video programmes can provide an impression of life outside the classroom which would otherwise be inconvenient or perhaps impossible to achieve. They can, for example, show lifestyles in other countries, scientific processes at the microscopic level, compli- cated industrial processes, theatrical productions, and so on.

A professionally-scripted and produced video programme may well be better structured that its lecture-type equivalent, and is almost certain to be more visually relevant and more stimulating than a lecture, even if the latter is supported by slides and other visual aids. Further advantages are that appropriate videos can help to add variety to lecture-dominated courses, and can be used to stimulate discussion and debate.

Some disadvantages of video presentations

The most common mis-use of videos occurs when the medium is used purely for convenience rather than for sound educational

Figure 4.2 **Use of video presentation as a lecture substitute**

reasons. The use of a video should not be thought of as an easy option, or 'something to keep a class quiet'. Indeed, it is important that a teacher or instructor should carry out a critical preview of the programme in order to check on its quality and to assess its relevance to the course. This will enable the teacher or instructor to introduce the programme properly, to explain its context and to prepare for class discussion after it has been shown.

Another possible educational disadvantage of using video presentations is that the teacher or trainer effectively relinquishes control over the class for the duration of the presentation, handing over control to the maker of the video. This makes it doubly important that such presentations should only be used where they offer some distinct advantage over other, more conventional, methods of teaching in achieving a particular set of objectives.

One practical disadvantage of the video is that it cannot be shown without the appropriate hardware. Also, there is often a financial implication associated with using a programme; indeed, in many cases, hiring or buying a video can be quite expensive, particularly if it is to be used in a commercial or industrial training context rather than in an educational situation.

An additional problem associated with the use of videocassette machines to record broadcast television programmes off-air is that there may well be copyright difficulties associated with showing the programmes in an educational or training situation. Although certain programmes are officially classified as 'educational' and can therefore be used with classes, the main television output (parts of which – documentaries, popular science programmes, etc – may in fact have a high degree of educational relevance) cannot legally be recorded on a videocassette recorder for subsequent use with a class unless the institution has paid for appropriate 'licensing' from the broadcasting authorities. Some of these programmes are, however, available for purchase or hire from the appropriate broadcasting authorities.

Educational Broadcasting

Broadcast radio and television have a long history of use in education and training, with programmes designed specifically for class use in schools and colleges being transmitted by a large number of broadcasting organizations in many parts of the world. In most cases, however, the role of such programmes has been limited to that of general interest, 'optional extra' or 'back-up' material, and it is only since the mid-1960s that such broadcasts have been used as front-line teaching tools. As we saw in Chapter 1, this development was pioneered in the UK by the Open University; since then, it has been used as a key part of similar distance learning schemes that have been set up in several other countries, including Israel, Canada and Norway.

Strictly speaking, the use of broadcast radio and television programmes in a distance learning as opposed to a classroom situation should be classed as an 'individualized learning' technique rather than a 'mass instruction' technique in the sense in which we are interpreting the latter term in this chapter. Such programmes are designed to be received by *individuals* and, in many cases, incorporate features (such as active participation on the part of the learner or viewer) that are more generally associated with individualized learning than with mass instruction. Thus, they are only 'mass instruction' techniques in the sense that they are capable of being received simultaneously by large numbers of people.

Some advantages of educational broadcasts

Educational radio and television broadcasts have the same basic educational advantages as video presentations in that they constitute high-quality material that can be used as an effective substitute for, or supplement to, a conventional taught lesson as and when appropriate, thus enabling a teacher, lecturer or trainer to introduce variety into a course. They have a further important advantage in that the material is made available free of charge.

Some disadvantages of educational broadcasts

They also share some of the disadvantages of video in that they are always liable to be used in the wrong way (eg for keeping classes quiet or filling slots in timetables) and again entail handing over control of one's class to someone else. A further disadvantage is that the timing of such broadcasts is fixed, so that they may be difficult (or even impossible) to fit into the timetable and cannot usually be previewed before showing to a class. Both of these problems can be overcome by recording the programmes.

Practical Activities

Within most teacher/institution-centred instructional systems, laboratory-type classes are a common way of demonstrating the practical elements of a subject and of 'using the theory'. On the face of it, the use of practical sessions in this context would appear to be capable of doing nothing but good; nevertheless, careful analysis of their use is often necessary if the fullest potential of such exercises is to be realized.

Some advantages of practical exercises
For subjects in which the development of manipulative (psychomotor) skills is important, a certain amount of practical experience is obviously necessary. Indeed, in many cases, there is simply no suitable alternative to 'hands-on' practice – as in the case of the pharmacy students shown in Figure 4.3, for example. However, it should be emphasized that such manipulative skills must be consciously taught for, and not just allowed to develop (it is to be hoped) of their own accord. In this context, specifying the competences to be gained as a result of practical work can be a particularly useful step.

Another strength of practical sessions is that students generally enjoy their participative nature, which may also provide a stark contrast to other, more lecture-oriented classes. Also, such sessions may give students an idea of some of the real-life applications of topics which have only been treated theoretically in lectures, thus helping to demonstrate the relevance of the course as a whole.

Some disadvantages of practical exercises
Practical and laboratory exercises tend to be very expensive in terms of time, manpower, equipment and materials. Hence, the reasons for using practical sessions should be well thought out, and they should not merely be used to fill allocated timetable slots, as is so often the case.

As mentioned in the previous chapter, it is highly desirable that the objectives of each practical session should be stated in advance, so that both staff and students know what should be gained from the work. The same benefits can be achieved by spelling out in advance the competences that learners are intended to develop during the course of their practical work. If this is not done, the results may

Figure 4.3 **A typical laboratory class in progress in the School of Pharmacy at The Robert Gordon University**

simply be 'recipe following', with little or no understanding of what is going on, or appreciation of the purpose of the exercise.

The design of practical or laboratory work is all too often completely unrelated to situations and problems which exist in real life. Thus, the perceived relevance of such sessions is often much lower than might be possible with a little more thought and ingenuity on the part of the designers.

Although we have stated that practical sessions have the advantage of illustrating practical applications of more theoretical work, it must be pointed out that student-based laboratory sessions may not be the most economical or efficient means of showing these. In some cases, a simple lecture/demonstration may be much more effective. Thus, while basic psychomotor skills may well be taught extremely effectively in the laboratory, question marks hang over the efficiency of the method in achieving other, higher level objectives that are commonly associated with 'practical work'.

AUDIOVISUAL MEDIA USED IN MASS INSTRUCTION

Within the context of the various teaching methods that can be employed as vehicles for mass instruction, it is possible to make use of a wide range of *audiovisual media*, both hardware and software.

In some cases, these are used to increase the effectiveness of the teaching method (for example, using visual aids to back up a lecture), while, in others, they constitute a vital part of the method itself (for example, video presentations or off-air broadcasts). As the name implies, an audiovisual medium can be thought of as a vehicle through which a message can be conveyed to learners; the medium, in other words, *mediates* between the teacher and the learner, as shown in Figure 4.4.

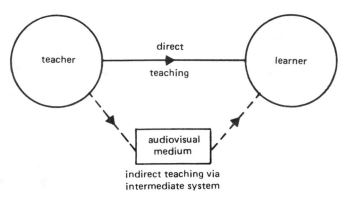

Figure 4.4 **The intermediary role of audiovisual media in teaching**

Thus, it is important that audiovisual media should be carefully chosen for use in particular teaching or training situations because of their suitability and not merely because they 'happen to be available'.

In the remainder of this chapter, we will look at the hardware and software that are associated with mass-instructional teaching methods under three broad headings, namely *non-projected visual aids*, *projected visual and audiovisual aids* and *audio aids*. In each case, we will discuss the medium in fairly general terms, outlining its main features and identifying its educational strengths and weaknesses rather than giving detailed instructions on its use. Readers requiring the latter type of information are referred to the many books that deal specifically with the use of audiovisual media – *Producing Teaching Materials* by Ellington and Race (1993) and Romiszowski's *The Selection and Use of Instructional Media* (1987), for example. (See the Bibliography for full details of these and other books on audiovisual media.)

Non-projected Visual Aids

As their name suggests, non-projected visual aids are those that do not involve the use of an optical or electronic projector. They include *chalkboards, markerboards, feltboards, hook-and-loop boards, magnetic boards, charts and wallcharts, posters, flipcharts, mobiles, models, realia* and *handouts*, all of which will now be examined.

Chalkboards

These are still often referred to as *blackboards*, although many are in fact now coloured – usually blue, brown or green. This is because coloured boards produce less glare and reflection, give less 'ghosting' (marks left when the chalk is rubbed out), and generally produce greater legibility than the traditional 'blackboard'.

Chalkboards are widely used in all sectors of education and training, and are most suitable for displaying impromptu notes and diagrams during a lesson and for working through calculations or similar exercises in front of a class.

A disadvantage of using chalkboards is that they tend to be difficult to write on and read from; practice in writing and drawing on them is thus often necessary. Chalkboards are also relatively messy to use, and even 'dustless' chalk tends to impregnate one's hair, fingernails and clothes. A further minor disadvantage is that the range of colours of chalk which can be used is often limited.

A major drawback of extensive use of the chalkboard in a classroom is that the teacher has, of necessity, to face away from the class for long periods. This not only means that the teacher is speaking 'into the board' for most of the time, but he also loses the advantage of eye-contact with the class – something that can help to convey meaning and provide useful feedback (by enabling the teacher to spot puzzled looks, loss of interest, etc).

Where group sizes are of the order of several hundred students, as in many higher education courses in the 1990s, it becomes very difficult to use blackboards well enough for them to be seen closely from the back of large lecture rooms.

Markerboards

These boards, which are often referred to as *whiteboards*, are used in much the same way as chalkboards, but have a number of advantages over the latter. For example, there is no mess from dust, the range and strength of colours which can be used is much greater, and, in an emergency, the markerboard can double as a projection screen. Against this, care is necessary to ensure that the correct, recommended markers and cleaning materials are used with a given board; use of the wrong markers may result in acute and even permanent 'ghosting' problems.

Feltboards

As its name implies, the *feltboard* is simply a board covered with felt or some similar material. Shapes cut out of felt will adhere to the board if pressed on to its surface, and paper or cardboard cut-outs may also be used by backing them with felt, thus allowing the user to write or draw on the shapes being displayed. To save time, felt-embossed wallpaper is a useful, relatively cheap substitute. Commercially-produced shapes and charts are available for some purposes, although those tend to have limited application.

Feltboards can be used for permanent or semi-permanent displays, but their main application is in situations requiring the movement or rearrangement of pieces, for example, demonstrating table settings, showing traffic movements, carrying out sports coaching, etc. They are also highly portable and comparatively inexpensive.

Hook-and-loop boards

The *hook-and-loop board*, which is also known as a *teazle board* or *teazlegraph*, works on the same basic principle as the feltboard. In this case, however, the display materials are backed with special fabric (such as Velcro) which incorporates large numbers of tiny hooks, while the display surface is covered with material incorporating tiny loops with which the hooks can engage. This creates a much stronger bond than that which is formed between two pieces of felt, thus allowing much heavier display materials to be attached to the surface of a hook-and-loop board. Such boards can be used for much the same purposes as feltboards, but only offer a real advantage over the latter in situations where the material being displayed is heavy – demonstrating the components of an actual piece of equipment, for example, or displaying items of realia such as rock samples.

Magnetic boards

Even more useful and versatile than feltboards and hook-and-loop boards are the various forms of *magnetic board*. These come in two main forms – *magnetic markerboards* and *magnetic chalkboards*. The former are sheets of ferromagnetic material with specially-painted light surfaces on which material can be written or drawn using suitable markers or pens, and the latter are sheets of ferromagnetic material covered with a thin layer of dark-coloured vitreous particles, producing a surface on which chalk can be used. Both types of board enable display items made of or backed with magnetic material to be stuck to and moved about on their surfaces, and both enable this moveable display to be supplemented by writing or drawing on the board. Thus, magnetic boards can be used to produce highly-sophisticated displays that enable movement and change in systems to be clearly demonstrated to a class. They are, for example, the ideal medium for demonstrating military tactics or carrying out sports coaching. For coaching a football or basketball team, for example, the field of play can be painted permanently on the board, with the individual players being identified by clearly-marked magnetic discs that can be rearranged and moved about as and when required, and the various movements, run patterns, etc being shown by adding suitable arrows or lines using chalk or marker pens (see Figure 4.5.)

Figure 4.5 **Use of a magnetic board in sports coaching**

Charts and wallcharts

The various forms of *chart* and *wallchart* have always been popular in all sectors of education and training because of their versatility and ease of use, and, even with the spread of more sophisticated visual aids such as slides and videos, are still capable of playing an important role in such work. Although the distinction between charts and wallcharts is sometimes a bit blurred, the former term is generally taken to refer to displays on large sheets of paper or cloth that are designed to be shown to a class in the course of a lesson. The latter term is used to describe similar displays that are pinned to a wall or bulletin board and are intended for casual study outwith the context of a formal lesson. Another distinction between the two is that material on charts is usually larger and easier to see or read than that on wallcharts, since the former has to be clearly distinguishable or legible at a distance whereas the latter can be studied at close quarters.

Large numbers of professionally-produced charts and wallcharts, covering a wide range of topics and often incorporating eye-catching features such as photographs, maps, diagrams, graphs and cartoons, are generally available to the educational and training community. In many cases, such charts and wallcharts are available free of charge from commercial organizations as 'goodwill' gestures, while others can be purchased at relatively low cost. Even if such 'ready-made' material is not available for a particular purpose, it is fairly easy to produce one's own, simply by using a little ingenuity and applying basic graphic and design skills.

In an educational or training situation, charts and wallcharts can play a variety of different roles. They can, for example, be used:

- to stimulate interest and provide motivation;
- to act as a source of ideas or topics for discussion;
- to be referred to at random in order to produce gradual familiarization with their content;
- to act as an information store and memory substitute.

The prominent display of a chart of the periodic table of the elements in virtually every chemistry classroom and laboratory illustrates most of the above uses.

Posters

These are similar in many ways to charts, but are usually smaller, simpler and bolder in content and style. Their main uses in the classroom are as a means of providing decoration, atmosphere and motivation, although they can also be used to make or remind learners of key points. As with charts and wallcharts, ready-made posters are available from a large number of sources – very often free of charge.

Flipcharts

These constitute a simple, and, when used in an appropriate context, highly effective method of displaying information to a class or small group. Such charts consist of a number of large sheets of paper, fixed to a support bar, easel or display board by clamping or pinning them along their top edges so that they can be flipped backwards or forwards as required. Such charts can be used in two basic ways. First, they can be used to display a succession of pre-prepared sheets, which can be shown in the required order either by flipping them into view from the back of the suspension system one by one or by revealing each successive sheet by flipping the previous one over the back of the suspension system out of the way. Second, they can be used to provide an instantly-renewable series of blank surfaces on which material can be jotted down on an impromptu basis in the course of a lesson, group discussion or other activity. They can, for example, be used to list replies from class members to questions or ideas generated by buzz groups.

'Electronic' flipcharts are now coming into use in educational and training institutions. These provide a reduced-size print-out of what has been written on the 'chart', which can be photocopied and distributed to the class.

Mobiles

A *mobile* is, in essence, a three-dimensional wallchart in which the individual components can move about. Instead of displaying a related system of pictures, words, etc on the flat surface of a wall, they are drawn on card, cut out and hung independently from the roof or a suitable beam using fine threads. The resulting display, which turns and changes shape as it is affected by random air currents, acquires a vitality which can never be produced in a flat display of the same material. Mobiles can be used in virtually any situation where pupils (particularly younger pupils) have to acquire and consolidate a set of related facts and where a wallchart would normally be used to reinforce this material.

Models

These are often used in cases where movement has to be illustrated (for example, the motion of the planets round the sun, wave motion etc) or when a three-dimensional representation is necessary (eg crystal structures, animal skeletons etc). However, it should always be remembered that, to a large audience in a lecture situation, even the best three-dimensional model invariably appears two-dimensional except to those who are very close. Thus, it is usually worthwhile getting the learners to gather round the model when its salient features are being demonstrated.

Realia

The supreme instructional 'model' is, in some cases, the article itself, since there are often considerable advantages to be gained from letting learners see or handle the 'real thing' as opposed to a mere representation thereof. In many cases, of course, this will not be practicable on grounds of availability, accessibility, safety, expense and so on, but there are many other cases where no such objections apply, and, in such cases, serious consideration should be given to the use of realia. When teaching geology, for example, there is simply no satisfactory substitute for getting the class to handle and examine real rock specimens, while the same is true in many aspects of the study of biology, physiology and similar subjects.

Handouts

Pre-prepared notes, diagrams and tables can be given to students in the form of *handouts*. This can save the student from tedious and perhaps inefficient note-taking, thus allowing him or her to concentrate better on what is being said. However, the use of very complete handout notes may encourage laziness or absenteeism and, for these reasons, some teachers prefer to use partial handouts which list the main points but allow the students to add their own notes in the spaces provided. Thus, the student has some involvement in the process, and interacts better with the handout. (See 'Interactive Handouts' in *The Open Learning Handbook*, Race, 1989.)

Projected Visual and Audiovisual Aids

These include all visual or audiovisual aids that involve the use of an optical or electronic projector, whether of the front-projection or back-projection variety. For our purpose, we will divide them into six broad groups, namely *filmstrips and filmstrip projectors, slides and slide projectors, overhead projectors, opaque projectors, films and film projectors* and *videocassette and videodisc machines*. Let us now look at these in turn. Though film has now been virtually eclipsed by video, we will include some discussions of film, for the benefit of teachers and trainers who continue to use it in some parts of the world.

Filmstrips and filmstrip projectors

Filmstrips come in two formats – *full frame* (as produced by a standard 35mm camera) and *half frame* (which gives smaller pictures, but twice as many of them on the same length of film). It is thus obviously necessary to have appropriate viewing equipment to accommodate the particular type of filmstrip being used. With large classes, a specially-designed filmstrip projector plus a standard projection screen will probably be necessary; most of these projectors can be adjusted to take both formats of filmstrip. With smaller classes or small groups, it may be possible to achieve satisfactory viewing conditions using a *filmstrip viewer* of the type that projects the image being viewed on to the back of a small translucent screen. Most viewers of this type can only be used with half-frame filmstrips, however. Filmstrips covering a wide range of topics are available from a large number of commercial and other organizations, many of these being accompanied by audiocassettes carrying a synchronized commentary. It is also possible to make one's own filmstrip using a 35mm camera.

The main advantage that filmstrips have over slides is that they are cheaper to mass produce, so that a commercially-available filmstrip tends to be considerably less expensive than a corresponding set of slides. They have, however, a number of disadvantages compared with slides, being less hardwearing and, because the sequence of frames cannot be altered, less flexible from a user's point of view. A further disadvantage is that a filmstrip can become out of date because of a single frame. For these reasons, filmstrips are sometimes cut up into their individual frames, which are then mounted as slides.

Slides and slide projectors

Ever since the days of the 'magic lantern', *slides* have been one of the simplest and most popular methods of introducing supportive visual material into a lecture or taught lesson. The original 'lantern slides' (which were roughly 3¼" square) are very rarely used nowadays, having been almost entirely superseded by 'compact' 2" x 2" (or 35mm) slides. These consist of single frames of 35mm or similar film mounted in cardboard, metal or plastic binders, often between twin sheets of glass for added protection, and are considerably easier to make, handle, use and store than their more cumbersome predecessors.

Slides are normally shown to a class with the aid of a suitable *slide projector*. Nowadays, these are usually fully automatic, having either linear (straight-through) or circular 'carousel'-type slide magazines. Such projectors can also be linked to a tape-recorder in order to enable synchronized tape-slide presentations to be shown.

If properly designed, slides can be of great assistance to a teacher or lecturer in providing visual reinforcement for what he or she is saying, and are particularly useful for showing photographs, diagrams, and other graphic material. However, they are also one of the most mis-used of all audiovisual media, largely because of the all-too-common practice of including far too much information on a slide. To be effective, a slide should be clear, simple, and capable of being seen and understood from all parts of the room in which it is being projected. If you are in any doubt about the clarity or legibility of a slide, go to the back of the room in which it is to be shown and see whether you have any difficulty in making it out; if you do, throw it away, for it is almost certainly worse than useless.

Overhead projectors

The *overhead projector* (or *OHP*) is probably the most versatile visual aid that can be used to support mass instruction methods, with the result that its use has become extremely widespread and popular over the last 20 years. Indeed, the OHP has now replaced the traditional chalkboard as the most commonly-used visual aid in many schools, colleges and training establishments, and many teachers and trainers have completely given up the use of slides, because of the greater ease of being 'in control' as they use overhead projectors.

The OHP has a number of definite advantages over other methods of presenting visual information. A teacher or trainer can, for example, use it in exactly the same way as a chalkboard or whiteboard (for writing up notes, showing diagrams, working through calculations, and so on) but with the great advantage of always facing the class. Another important advantage over the chalkboard or whiteboard is that the OHP can also be used to show pre-prepared material, thus enabling teachers and trainers to build up banks of notes, diagrams, etc that can be used over and over again. Such material can be prepared using a variety of production methods (free-hand writing or drawing, transfer lettering, thermographic or photographic copying, and so on) and can incorporate a wide range of presentation techniques (progressive 'build-up' using overlays, progressive disclosure, animation, movement and rearrangement of items, etc). Overhead transparencies are also extremely compact, and are therefore easy to store in suitable boxes, large envelopes, folders or files. Compared with other projected aids, the OHP also has the great advantage that it does not require the room to be blacked out, thus allowing students to take notes; indeed it can be used in all but the very brightest light (for example, direct sunlight). The OHP is also clean, quiet and 'user friendly', requiring no technical skill or knowledge on the part of the operator.

Disadvantages of the OHP include the fact that it requires a power supply, and needs a suitable flat (preferably white) surface on which to project its image. Also, unless this surface is inclined forward at the correct angle, the image will probably suffer from 'keystoning' (being wider at the top than the bottom due to the fact that the surface is not at right angles to the axis of projection). Unlike chalkboards, OHPs require a certain amount of routine maintenance, and are also liable to break down (generally at extremely inconvenient times), so it is always advisable to have a spare bulb close at hand; most modern machines do in fact have a built-in spare bulb that can be brought into use at the turn of a knob. A further disadvantage is that some users find the glare from the OHP troublesome, although this can generally be overcome by attaching a suitably-positioned shade to the machine.

Apart from these possible 'hardware' difficulties, the main problems associated with the overhead projector stem from the fact that many users do not give sufficient thought to the production of their display material. In many cases, writing is too small or too untidy to be read easily (both, in some cases), quite apart from the fact that it frequently extends beyond the visible area of the transparency (teachers often forget that the illuminated projection area in most overhead projectors is slightly smaller than the standard acetate sheet, and is usually cut away at the corners). As in the case of slides, there is also a tendency to include too much information on a single frame. Finally, teachers tend, if anything, to over-use the overhead projector just because it is so convenient, employing it in situations where other forms of visual aid might, on occasions, be more effective.

Opaque projectors (episcopes)

The *opaque projector*, or *episcope*, can be used to project an image of a small diagram or page of a book directly on to a screen. This has obvious advantages when, for example, the time or technical equipment needed to make an adequate slide is not available, or when the material is only to be used once. The main disadvantages are that complete blackout is usually required, making student note-taking difficult, and that the projection equipment is usually both bulky and noisy. Although modern opaque projectors have been greatly improved in these respects, few schools and colleges have invested in new machines recently. A further disadvantage of projecting pages of books directly is that the material is often difficult to read, and often contains superfluous information; this unnecessary detail may be both confusing and off-putting.

Films and film projectors

Films can be used to fill a number of instructional roles, ranging from front-line teaching to their use for illustrative or motivational purposes. They can, however, be expensive to hire or buy, and, for this reason, custom-built programmes developed 'in house' by schools, colleges or training organizations are now achieving much wider use – usually in video rather than film format.

Most of the standard films that are used for educational or training purposes are 16mm wide, and must be shown using a 16mm projector capable of reproducing the soundtrack, if there is one. Some films are only 8mm wide, however, and this produces further problems since 8mm films come in two formats – *standard 8* and *super 8*. Both formats have the same overall width, but the super 8 film has smaller sprocket holes, allowing a greater area of the film to be used for the pictures. Thus, a compatible projector is necessary for each type of 8mm film, although some 8mm projectors can in fact accommodate both types.

Short, single concept *loop films*, which can be 'slotted' into lectures or practical demonstrations in order to illustrate or demonstrate specific topics, are also produced on 8mm film, the resulting loop being mounted in a special cartridge. Such films can normally only be shown using a specially-designed loop film projector.

Videocassette and videodisc machines

The *videocassette recorder (VCR)* is essentially a television receiver minus a display tube, having facilities for recording television and other video inputs and playing back programmes recorded on videocassette. Nowadays, such machines are found in practically all schools and colleges, as well as in most homes. Most machines have the ability to 'freeze' the picture at a given frame, or to show frames in 'slow motion' – features that have obvious advantages in educational and training situations. However, as mentioned previously, there are copyright restrictions on the types of television programmes that can legally be recorded off-air for use with a class.

Although not as widely used as the videocassette recorder at the moment, the *videodisc player* seems likely to play an important part in future education and training. At the time of writing, videodisc players cannot be used to record programmes, but it is possible that the cost of pre-recorded videodisc programmes may, in the long run, become cheaper than the videocassette equivalent. Also, the range of features available on videodisc machines (eg fast search and slow motion reverse) far exceeds the capability of even the best videocassette machines. Such machines also play an important role in *interactive video* delivery systems, as we will see later (see Chapter 5).

Audio Aids

Apart from off-air radio broadcasts (which have already been discussed), the basic types of audio aid that are most widely used in mass instructional situations are the *tape recorder* and the *record player*. Let us therefore conclude this chapter by taking a brief look at each.

Tape recorders

These can be employed in a variety of roles, the most important being their use to play back pre-recorded audio lectures or talks to a class or to provide illustrative or supportive audio material in the context of a 'live' lecture or lesson. Audio programmes covering a wide range of subjects can be purchased from a variety of commercial and other organizations, and programmes can also be recorded off-air (having regard to copyright restrictions) and prepared 'in-house'. Audio-tapes can also be 'pulsed' to allow them to be used in tape-slide presentations.

There are two basic types of tape recorder, namely *reel-to-reel* and *cassette* machines. The former are generally used for making original recordings, and also for editing and mixing work. In most cases, monaural sound is all that is required, but, for certain special purposes (eg music appreciation) stereo obviously has advantages. Recordings made on open-reel machines are generally subsequently 'dubbed' on to compact cassettes, because these are much easier and more convenient to use in a classroom situation. This also has the advantage of keeping the master tape in reserve, so that a new 'using copy' can be run off in the event of damage or loss.

Record and compact disc players

Although they have now been largely superseded by cassette tape-recorders in many schools, colleges and training establishments, *record players* still provide a convenient method of playing audio material (particularly music and dramatic and literary performances) to a class. Their other main use is as a source of sound effects during the production of audio and video programmes.

The main disadvantage of the record player compared with the tape recorder is the fact that it can only be used to play back material that is commercially available on records. However, the high quality of sound that is available from compact disc players, and the robust nature of the discs themselves, make the compact disc player a highly useful – and portable – aid where sound extracts can enhance lectures or training sessions.

Also, in 1993, CD-interactive (compact disc interactive) players and software are sweeping the world of education and training, allowing high-quality video projection of motion-film, digitized graphics, stereo digital sound, in a highly interactive way. Such interaction is ideal for individualized learning situations (see Chapter 5), but is also very useful in mass instruction situations where the interaction is controlled by the lecturer or trainer.

Chapter 5

Individualized Learning Techniques

INTRODUCTION

In Chapter 1, we looked at the historical development of educational technology, and saw how the subject entered an 'individualized learning' phase during the mid-1950s. We showed how this had its roots in the behavioural psychology-based learning theories of B F Skinner, and how it led to the development of programmed learning, open learning and 'flexible' learning, and to an associated concern with the design of individualized learning materials.

In Chapter 2, we compared the radically different approaches to the instructional processes that are adopted in teacher/institution-based learning systems and in student-centred learning systems, showing how the latter are designed with the needs of the individual student in mind. In particular, we showed how they are made more flexible and open by reducing institutional constraints and giving the students greater control over how, when, where and at what pace they learn.

In this chapter, we will take a more detailed look at the range of approaches that can be used when developing individualized learning methods and discuss their respective characteristics. (The comparative advantages and disadvantages of the student-centred and teacher/institution-centred approaches have already been discussed in general terms in Chapter 2.) We will then take a brief look at the different types of hardware and software that can be used to support individualized learning methods.

THREE DIFFERENT APPROACHES TO INDIVIDUALIZED LEARNING

In Chapter 2, we identified three basic organizational systems in the context of which some form of individualized student-centred approach can take place, namely *institution-based systems, flexible-learning systems* and *distance-learning systems*. We will now examine these three systems more thoroughly and, in particular, will discuss the range of individualized methods that can be adopted within each. However, it should be emphasized at this point that the system of classification that we have adopted below is used purely for convenience. There can, in fact, be a considerable amount of overlap between the approaches and methods that come under the general umbrella of 'individualized learning', so these should be thought of as a continuous spectrum of flexible learning systems, in which the 'sections' that we have identified have no clearly-defined boundaries.

Institution-based Systems

In most schools, colleges, universities and training establishments, it is generally possible to accommodate some individualization of learning within the context of an overall teacher/institution-centred system. The amount of individualization in the system can vary considerably, from largely traditional courses which provide the option of a limited amount of individualized learning for remedial or back-up work, to highly-flexible personalized systems of instruction, which, although based in an institution, are nevertheless very strongly student-centred. In between, there is a continuous spectrum of emphases, both on the amount and on the type of individualization used.

The simplest, and possibly the most common, method is *unstructured reading* by the student, at home, in the classroom, or in the library. This type of reading may be actively encouraged by the teaching staff, or may be left entirely to the discretion and motivation of the individual student, but, in both cases, the method is self-paced and fairly flexible. Unstructured reading may prove very useful in reading 'around' a subject and in broadening a student's perspectives. However, unless the student has well-defined objectives in mind, the method may be inefficient in terms of time, effort and results.

In this respect, *directed reading* has a distinct advantage, in that the student's attention can be focused more sharply on those aspects of a subject which are deemed to be relevant and important. Directed reading may be used as a front-line teaching method in its own right, or as a back up to traditional expository methods, and may also serve as a foundation for future class discussion or practical work, or for a 'problem-solving' session of some sort.

More formalized attempts can be made to provide individualized learning material for *remedial* or *back-up* purposes, generally through the facilities offered in an institution's library or resources centre (see Chapter 9). For example, students who have been found to have problems in grasping subject matter taught by traditional methods in the classroom can be directed to a range of structured remedial learning packages; these may approach a given topic in a different way from the original teacher, and will probably also allow the student to progress through difficult areas at a more suitable pace. The format of the packages may be textual, audiovisual or even computer-based, but, in this particular context, they are almost always used to complement and support traditional teaching methods, and not to replace them. Other students, apart from those in real difficulties, are generally also free to use the packages on an optional basis. Indeed, research into student use of the remedial/back-up approach to individualized learning has tended to reveal that the middle-ability-to-better students make more use of the available materials than the weaker students for whom the materials were mainly devised. The learning packages used in such systems may either be purchased from a commercial organization or from another institution, or may be custom-made by teachers to support a particular course.

The main advantages of such a system are that students are given access to subject matter that is taught in alternative ways, and that weaker students have a 'safety-net' in the form of well-structured learning materials. In addition, students are introduced to individualized study packages as a legitimate learning method.

On the disadvantage side, it is very rare that there are enough suitable packages available to cover all aspects of a course, so the approach may well be piecemeal. A more serious problem is that those students who would probably benefit most from individualized learning material being available for back-up purposes are the ones who are least likely to use it in practice.

Another approach to individualized learning within an institution is to accommodate it within the four walls of a conventional classroom. Such *individualized classroom work* is most common in primary schools (see Figure 5.1), although a number of secondary school classrooms are now also operated in this mode. In such classrooms, the teacher is basically a manager of resources and learning opportunities for the students, who may be learning at different levels and also at different rates. The learning materials may be of a wide variety of types, but, as a general rule, the more content-based they are, the more highly they are structured. In such a system, the demands placed upon the teacher are much greater than when the teacher is in the traditional 'dispenser of knowledge' role, and it is perhaps only a minority of teachers who would feel comfortable in this alternative role. However, in the case of mixed-ability classes in particular, it is a flexible and appropriate method for allowing students to work and develop to the limit of their capabilities, without either being left behind by the 'high fliers' or held back by the less able. As the teacher is always present, this system also allows pupils to be given immediate personal assistance if they encounter a problem, a problem that may be specific to the individual rather than to the class as a whole.

Figure 5.1 **Individualized work taking place in a typical primary school classroom under the supervision of the class teacher**

One extremely common student-centred method, employed at all levels of education from the primary school to postgraduate university research, is the *project*. Projects are relatively lengthy activities (ranging in duration from an afternoon to three or four years) in which the students work either independently or within a small group. They involve the investigation generally being chosen by the students themselves, either on their own or, more usually, in consultation with a teacher or supervisor. Throughout the project, the role of the teaching staff is advisory rather than didactic, and it is the students who are largely responsible for making decisions which affect its progress.

Projects constitute an active learning method which allows students an opportunity to exercise initiative, to see practical applications of a subject, to cross subject area barriers, to probe deeply into a particular area of study, and to become responsible for organizing and structuring their activities. One drawback of this method is the difficulty of carrying out a fair and objective assessment of the student's work. This is often done by grading a tangible product of the project (a report, a thesis, a computer program, a model etc), but this may not accurately reflect the total amount of work that has been carried out. It may well be, for many students, that the actual 'planning and doing' aspects are more important educational outcomes than the end product itself.

As mentioned earlier, a number of courses use individualized learning materials mainly for remedial or back-up purposes, in support of more traditional 'front-line' teaching methods. A natural progression is for some courses or parts of courses to use materials as a front-line teaching method in their own right. *Individualized guided study* methods involve the student studying out of class (for example, in the library, in the institution's resources centre, or at home) using a range of carefully-prepared learning materials (textual, audiovisual, or computer-based) to achieve stated objectives. Students are normally provided with a structured *study guide* which can direct them towards appropriate learning materials and provide assignments and other exercises.

The use of individualized guided study for parts of some courses allows teaching staff to use their timetabled student-contact time in a different way. Instead of being almost entirely devoted to information-giving sessions, as is so often the case in traditional courses, class contact time can be used to rectify individuals' difficulties and to provide appropriate remedial work. The time can also be used to investigate the wider implications of the topic under study, and hence, through discussion, attempt to achieve objectives in Bloom's 'higher cognitive' areas, allowing the individualized study methods to cover the more content-related objectives in the 'lower cognitive' areas.

In some institution-based courses, self-instructional learning methods have almost completely replaced more traditional approaches. Learning schemes of this type have been termed *personalized systems of instruction (PSIs)*, the most popular paradigm of the approach being the *Keller Plan* that was discussed in some detail in Chapter 2. Although a number of variations are possible, personalized systems of instruction generally involve individualized learning materials, independent study, self-pacing and tutor support.

Flexible-learning Systems

Two important areas in which student-centred flexible course developments are currently taking place on an increasingly wider scale are *community adult education* and *further education and training*. In both these sectors, local systems of flexible or open learning are being used to accommodate the special needs and particular situations of potential students who reside in the catchment area of a given college. In many cases, such potential students cannot or will not attend formal, timetabled institution-based courses, for reasons such as distance, employers' attitudes and policies, age, and family commitments.

Awareness of the need to provide flexible educational, training and re-training opportunities for persons who are constrained in various ways was heightened in the United Kingdom by the Manpower Service Commission's (now part of the Employment Department) 'Open Tech' Programme of the mid-1980s. This had the following aims:

- to open up education and training opportunities for adults (most of them already in employment);
- to secure more and better provision for updating technicians and supervisors;
- to help employers and employees face up to the challenge of new technology;
- to help education and training make use of new technology to provide new skills where they are needed.

The three-year Programme, which ended in Spring of 1987, consisted of a series of sponsored projects, often involving an industrial firm and/or a college (or group of colleges) in developing open learning materials in one particular area. The projects were supervised by a central 'Open Tech Unit', which ensured that there was no unnecessary overlap between them, and that they were properly integrated and evaluated. The Programme was generally considered to have been a great success, and undoubtedly did a great deal to promote open learning in the UK.

Local systems of student-centred learning usually involve a host college or institution in providing (i) a source of learning materials, (ii) a tutorial system, (iii) an administrative system and (iv) a study support system (that is, counselling). The development of suitable learning materials can be one of the most exacting tasks, and is normally achieved via one of three paths: (i) adapting existing material, (ii) providing a study guide to 'conventional' resources, or (iii) developing custom-designed self-contained material. Mechanisms for practical work, student feedback and tutorials have to be carefully thought out; indeed, tutorials are often held over the telephone.

One well-known example of a local student-centred system is *Flexistudy*, which sets out to offer students all the resources of a conventional correspondence course plus local college support. It is targeted specifically at people whose lifestyle renders it impossible for them to conform to the rigid constraints inherent in conventional adult education and training courses. In Flexistudy courses, the student does not have to attend the host institution regularly, does not have to conform to conventional academic terms or years, is able to use a range of individualized learning materials, and has access to tutorial guidance as and when required. In such courses, a whole range of resources of the host institution are made available in order to complement the correspondence and tutor support. These normally include the library, any multi-media, self-instructional resources centre or language laboratory facilities that are available, counselling and career help, and the institution's administrative and examinations machinery. Although the majority of Flexistudy-type developments have, to date, been at the lower end of the adult and further education spectrum, this is not necessarily an intrinsic limiting feature of the system.

In effect, use of Flexistudy allows institutions to offer courses which students (and employers) want, when students want them, by means which suit their circumstances, and from which they can learn effectively. It is one extremely promising method of meeting the demands of recurrent and continuing education and training, and may even have implications for the long-term viability of some colleges. Against this, the development, organization and operation of a Flexistudy-type course is by no means an easy option, requiring tremendous efforts from both teaching and administrative staff, not to mention a considerable amount of self-motivation from the students.

Other examples of flexible local methods include *learning-by-appointment* and *open access* systems. In learning-by-appointment, potential students in the local community can 'sign up' for a given course and take appointments to attend the institution at mutually-suitable times. Normally, a range of individualized learning materials (textual, audiovisual and computer-based) is made available to the student in the institution's library or learning resources centre. In some cases, tutor help can also be 'booked'. Open access methods are less formalized in that the student can have access to the institution at any time. Both methods have proved particularly useful in the field of community education.

Distance-learning Systems

In *distance-learning* schemes, all (or nearly all) student learning takes place *away* from the host institution. In some cases, the 'distant student' may be on the other side of the globe from the host institution, and, as a consequence, the student is very dependent on the quality of learning materials available. However, even in such extreme cases, tutor support and feedback on assignments is an integral part of almost every distance-learning scheme.

The first distance learning developments came in the form of *correspondence courses*, which still have a place in the distance learning market today. In such courses, the material is almost totally textual, the student being provided with structured course units which direct learning activities and provide assignments. Students normally receive regular feedback on their performance, and may be required to reach a certain standard before being allowed to progress to the next course unit.

In recent years, distance-learning schemes have tended to make use of a much wider range of educational techniques, with *multimedia distance learning schemes* of the type pioneered by the Open University in Britain being developed in many parts of the world. Such schemes can combine a printed student study guide with broadcast material (radio and television), videocassettes, audiovisual learning materials, computer packages, practical 'do-it-yourself' kits, models, books and other textual materials. These materials, combined with tutor support (local and distant), student 'self-help' groups and occasional centrally-organized group learning sessions, allow the student to achieve a much wider range of educational objectives than is possible with purely 'correspondence' courses. As well as being educationally desirable, the use of a variety of methods also helps to reduce the strain and boredom of working in isolation.

MEDIA USED IN INDIVIDUALIZED LEARNING

In all three of the individualized approaches to learning described above, we have seen that self-instructional teaching materials play a 'front line' role in the learning process, with the actual teacher usually having a managerial and/or counselling role, as shown in Figure 5.2.

As with the exposition-based teaching methods that were discussed in the previous chapter, a wide range of hardware and software of varying technological complexity is now available to cater for individualized student learning methods.

We will consider the materials used in individualized learning under three broad headings: *textual materials, audiovisual materials,* and *computer-based materials*. Although this distinction has been made for convenience, it is often the case that a combination of media under all of these headings is used to achieve a particular range of objectives in an individualized learning situation. All the media to be described enable students to progress at their own speed and make provision for review and revision; many also provide the student with an on-going check on progress. Readers who require more detailed information about any of the media described are referred to

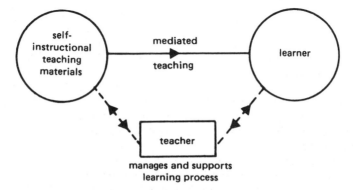

Figure 5.2 **The front-line role of teaching materials in individualized learning**

Producing Teaching Materials by Ellington and Race (1993); see the Bibliography.

Textual Materials

Directed study of materials in text books

Conventional *text books* can often be used in self-instructional situations, although, by themselves, they may not necessarily be suitable for enabling *mastery* of desired material to be achieved. This is because most text books are designed simply to *present* information, not to provide the users with a systematic learning programme. Also, it is very rare to find a single text book that covers all the material in a course or module in the manner that the person responsible for teaching that course or module requires. The effectiveness of text books as vehicles for self-instruction can, however, generally be greatly increased by the use of a suitable *study guide* which structures the learning process for the students by directing them to suitable chapters (or sections thereof) in appropriate books in a systematic and cumulative way, and provides supplementary notes and assignments, etc.

Some strengths of directed study of text book material

In the case of certain core subject areas, the course material may well be adequately covered in normal text books, and, if so, such books represent one of the cheapest and most convenient forms of self-instructional materials. Provided that suitable texts are available and the work is carefully structured, directed study of such text books can be a highly effective way of teaching basic facts, principles, applications, etc, ie, of achieving objectives mainly of the *lower cognitive* type.

Directed study of this type has a further great advantage of allowing learners to work at their natural paces. Research has shown that learners differ considerably in the rate at which they can assimilate new material effectively, so *any* method that allows self-pacing to take place is almost invariably more effective than a method (like the lecture) in which they all have to work at the pace directed by the instructor.

Another great advantage of the method is that it requires no specialized hardware or other facilities, and no specialized courseware other than standard text books. The latter can either be purchased by the students or made available through a suitable library.

A further advantage of the method is that study can be carried out at any time suitable to the learner, and (provided that the text books involved are not restricted to 'reference only' use within a library) at any convenient place.

Some weaknesses of the method

One possible disadvantage of the method is that it requires extremely careful planning and structuring on the part of the supervising teacher if it is to be fully effective; this, obviously, requires both skill and time.

Also, the method is totally dependent on suitable texts being available. In some cases, it may be possible to insist that all students purchase their own copies of the book or books involved, but, in many cases, this will not be a realistic option. In such cases, it will be necessary to ensure that the books are available in the library in sufficient numbers to enable *all* the students in the class to have suitable access. Ideally, this should be done by purchasing multiple copies and making them available for borrowing, but, if this is not possible, the books should be made available on a 'reference only' basis, for use in the actual library.

A further disadvantage is that the method is not really suitable for achieving many *higher cognitive* and *non-cognitive* objectives. Also, unless a deliberate attempt is made to build in participative student activities through the study guide, study of material in text books can be a very passive form of study, with little or no interaction taking place between the learner and the learning materials; this can lead to boredom and lack of motivation on the part of the students.

Study of open-learning packages

One of the drawbacks of using textbooks in self-instructional situations is that they may well be inappropriate either in their level or in the way they treat the subject matter, making it unlikely that they will match the intended learning outcomes required of the students. The use of carefully prepared, structured *handout notes* written and produced by teachers and trainers offer a way of increasing the relevance and suitability of text-based materials for individualized learning. However, since two key elements in learning are 'doing' and 'feedback' (as we explained at the end of Chapter 2), producing interactive open-learning materials provides learners with the opportunity to learn in a much more active way and also to receive immediate feedback on the efforts they make as they learn.

The design of open-learning materials is discussed in much greater detail elsewhere, for example *The Open Learning Handbook* (Race, 1989), *53 Interesting Ways to Write Open Learning Materials* (Race, 1992), *Exploring Open and Distance Learning* (Rowntree, 1992), and *Producing Teaching Materials* (Ellington and Race, 1993). However, perhaps the key ingredient in the best open-learning packages, relating directly to 'doing' and 'feedback is the *self-assessment question* and its accompanying *response*. Self-assessment questions (or 'activities' or 'exercises' or 'check-your-learning' quizzes) are interspersed throughout open-learning materials and allow learners the opportunity to perform a wide range of active-learning processes, including:

- selecting the correct option in multiple-choice questions
- picking the *best* option in multiple-choice questions;
- applying what they have learned to solve problems or do calculations;
- diagnosing faults or deliberate mistakes in diagrams, flowcharts, or text passages;
- arranging a series of steps into the most logical order (sequencing or prioritizing);
- recalling information they have learned and writing down answers to questions;
- extrapolating from information they have been given, to speculate or solve problems.

There are many more kinds of activity upon which self-assessment questions can be based. Most open-learning packages include space for learners to write in their answers to the self-assessment questions as they work their way through the package. This process of writing things into the package adds much to the feeling of *ownership* which learners can develop about their learning materials.

Perhaps the most crucial ingredients of good open-learning packages are the feedback *responses* which learners consult after they have tried each of the self-assessment questions. In the best open-learning packages, the feedback responses are far more than simply answers to the questions. Learners studying on their own need to find out the answers to two questions every time they consult a feedback response:

- Was I right? (did I answer the self-assessment question correctly?)
- If not, why not?

It is in connection with the second of these questions that the feedback responses are more than just 'answers'. A good response helps learners to see what went wrong if they did not answer the question correctly. For example, if they picked a 'wrong' option in a multiple-choice self-assessment question, the feedback response can explain what they may have been thinking to have done so.

Some strengths of open-learning packages

The principal strengths of open-learning packages are that they allow learners to learn in an interactive way, learning by doing, and drawing feedback from the responses built in to the materials. Learners use the materials at their own pace and normally (when provided with personal copies of the packages) at times and places of their own choosing. Learners can work again and again through difficult parts of an open-learning package, until they have mastered its contents. The best open-learning packages are written in 'user-friendly' language, helping to ensure that learners find them stimulating and interesting. The layout and design of open-learning packages can be made attractive and interesting, and the content can be adjusted to be directly relevant to the intended learning outcomes. Open-learning packages usually make it very clear to learners exactly what they are intended to be able to do after completing their studies of the packages, either by including a detailed list of objectives for the package, or by expressing the intended learning outcomes in terms of the competences that the learners will be expected to be able to demonstrate when they have studied the package.

Some disadvantages of open-learning packages

The task of producing high-quality interactive learning packages is very time-consuming, and requires a great deal of skill on the part of the writer. Another disadvantage is that the use of print-based packages for individualized study can become very tedious if it is the *only* medium being used in a programme of study or training. However, it is usual to include appropriate audiovisual components in learning packages (for example audiotapes or videocassettes) which can do much to break such monotony.

A short-cut to flexible learning

As noted above, the task of producing 'full-blown' open- or flexible-learning packages is very time-consuming. Furthermore, to produce high-quality open-learning materials ideally requires the 'subject-expert' to acquire additional expertise in the design of learning materials. However, when there is the opportunity for face-to-face contact with tutors or trainers from time to time, it is possible to separate the subject expertise from the materials-design expertise, and produce 'hybrid' learning materials which can work very effectively.

This kind of development has recently been introduced by Ellington and Lowis in a diploma programme for occupational health nurses run at The Robert Gordon University in Aberdeen (see the Bibliography). Self-study packs were produced for the distance-learning components of this course, with the subject matter for each pack being divided into up to six 'parts' (major subject areas), and each 'part' being further subdivided into 'sections' (specific topics within these subject areas). For each 'section', a 'course paper' was commissioned from an expert on the topic concerned and a self-study guide/workbook written round it by an instructional design specialist.

Each pack has the same 'preliminaries' – a statement of the philosophy of the pack, a full statement of the educational aims and objectives, a detailed list of the contents, and a list of associated further reading. The various 'parts' and 'sections' of which the pack is composed then follow in numerical order, each 'section' having an introductory page that describes its purpose and format and giving a detailed list of the intended 'learning outcomes'. This introductory page is then followed by a series of pages that give details of individual 'activities' which are intended to help the students achieve the learning outcomes, with each specific 'learning outcome' normally being associated with its own 'activity'. The 'course paper' round which the 'section' is built is reproduced at the end of the section, after the 'activity' pages.

In this way, the subject expertise and the learning-materials-design expertise are separated. It is relatively straightforward for an experienced materials designer who is not an expert in a particular topic to design activities around the content of a 'course paper' written by a subject expert, especially if the subject expert gives some suggestions regarding the learning outcomes to be achieved. The principal advantage of building up self-study materials in this way is that there is no longer any need to 'convert' subject-specialists into open-learning writers.

Audiovisual Self-instructional Materials

Audiovisual learning programmes

Although print-based, self-instructional material still has an important place in most individualized learning systems, many self-instructional learning packages now utilize a whole range of audio and visual media to increase their impact and effectiveness. Such packages may include audio and video tapes, filmstrips, loop films, slides, transparencies, models and practical kits as well as conventional printed material, the particular 'media mix' being carefully chosen with the objectives of the topic being covered in mind. For example, in a number of individualized learning packages that have been developed at Glasgow University to teach three-dimensional structures and relationships, printed material, audiotapes and slides have been used in conjunction with custom-built, three-dimensional models and construction kits; using the latter, students can build and examine their own models as directed by the programme (see Figure 5.3). The precise choice of media is therefore very dependent on the objectives that the package is designed to achieve or the competences which the learners are intended to develop.

A range of hardware of varying degrees of sophistication is available for use with the different types of software mentioned above. A wide variety of expensive automatic playback machines can be purchased for use in institutional libraries and resources centres. However, for students working on their own at home, suitable combinations of relatively inexpensive items of equipment (cassette players, simple slide viewers, etc) are generally just as effective from an educational point of view, and it can now be assumed that

Figure 5.3 **A student of chemistry studying organic chemistry using a self-instructional tape-model programme**

students will have access to video playback equipment, either at home or in learning resource centres.

Some strengths of audiovisual learning programmes

Because of the wide range of media available, audiovisual self-instructional materials can be used to achieve a wide variety of educational objectives, and although these again tend to fall mainly in the lower cognitive range, it is also possible to use them to achieve other types of objectives. By associating manipulative tasks with such materials, for example, they can be used to develop certain types of *psychomotor skills*, and they can also be highly effective in achieving certain types of affective objectives (eg, in producing desirable attitude changes). They also have the great advantage of allowing learners to work at their own pace.

In some cases (eg, language laboratories, or the tape-model systems developed at Glasgow University), they allow a high element of learner participation to be built into the learning process – another important educational 'plus'. Also, use of appropriate media enables things like sound, movement and realism to be introduced into a presentation, thus again increasing student interest and motivation.

Use of well-designed mediated presentations can save instructors from having to carry out a great deal of time-consuming, repetitive work – eg, in teaching all the members of a class individually how to use a particular type of machine, instrument or tool or how to carry out a particular process.

Some weaknesses of audiovisual learning programmes

The main weakness of the approach is that suitable ready-made courseware is seldom available, so instructors may have to produce their own. This is invariably time-consuming, often expensive, and (in many cases) requires specialist skills that the average teacher or lecturer simply does not possess. In some cases, it may be possible to learn the required skills by undergoing suitable staff development (eg, learning basic video production skills), but in other cases it may be necessary to rely on specialist support staff. Readers interested in developing such skills should find useful advice in *Producing Teaching Materials* by Ellington and Race (1993); see the Bibliography.

Although mediated self-instruction can be used to achieve a somewhat wider range of objectives than self-instruction based purely on the study of textual materials, there are still many higher-cognitive and non-cognitive objectives for which the technique is inappropriate.

By its very nature, mediated self-instruction relies totally on the availability of suitable hardware. In many cases, provision of sufficient hardware to enable extensive use of the method to take place may simply not be possible because of its cost, or due to lack of space for the provision of suitable study stations (*carrels*).

Language laboratories

These involve a specialist application of the tape recorder which allows students to interact individually with audio material. Although the original use of such equipment was for language teaching, language laboratories are now also used to present audio programmes in other subjects, and are therefore of more general interest. Basically, a language laboratory allows individual students to listen to a master tape and to record and listen to their own responses (see Figure 5.4, which shows students working in this way in a college of education language laboratory). The teacher can 'listen in' to any one student, and can communicate directly both with individual students and with groups of any size.

Language laboratories are an extremely expensive teaching resource, and, for this reason, are largely limited to individualized learning within groups in an institutional setting. The main advantage over the use of individual tape recorders is that, within a group, a teacher may 'listen in' unnoticed, and can therefore monitor each individual's progress and identify those who need help and feedback.

Broadcasting media

Through the media of radio and television, broadcast material is readily accessible to individuals in their own homes. The associated

Figure 5.4 **Trainee teachers working in a language laboratory**

hardware can be used to receive programmes transmitted either through an 'open' national or regional network or through a more local network such as a cable distribution or closed-circuit system. Also, by using the appropriate recording equipment, programmes that are broadcast at inconvenient times can be stored on tape and used at the convenience of the learner. Some years ago, such off-air recording by individuals was largely restricted to radio broadcasts, but, with the increasingly widespread domestic use of videocassette machines, recording educational television programmes is now just as common.

Computer-based Self-instructional Materials

Computer-assisted learning (CAL)

The computer can play a number of different roles in individualized learning schemes, including front-line teaching, assessment, managing resources and maintaining administrative records. The potential of the computer in each of these areas will be discussed in more detail in Chapter 10.

In an individualized CAL situation, a student may have access to a computer terminal linked to a large 'mainframe' computer, or to a small microcomputer with its own screen or video display unit (VDU). Whatever the hardware used, the computer acts in one of two basic roles in all CAL systems, namely, in a *tutorial* mode or in a *laboratory* mode (although it is sometimes used in a combination of both).

In the tutorial mode, the student interacts directly with the computer, which is programmed to understand and react to student responses. This is basically a sophisticated form of the branching programmed learning that was discussed in Chapter 1.

In the laboratory mode, the computer is essentially a learning resource rather than an instructional device. The computer can be used to simulate a laboratory situation, to model experiments, to provide data-bases, to set problem-solving exercises, and so on. For example, students can investigate mathematical models of physical systems, and see how specific factors vary under different conditions which they can control.

Some strengths of computer-assisted learning

Whether it is employed in the 'substitute-tutor' mode or in the 'simulated laboratory' mode, use of the computer as a delivery system for self-instructional materials enables an extremely wide range of educational objectives to be achieved, although (as with other types of self-instructional system) these tend to fall mainly in the lower cognitive area. It also enables learners to work at their own natural pace – a considerable educational advantage, as we have already seen.

Possibly the greatest strength of the computer as a delivery system is that it enables an extremely high degree of learner participation to be built into the instructional process, and also enables the system to adapt to the needs of the individual learner in a way that is simply not possible with other delivery systems, therefore providing opportunity for 'learning by doing', coupled with the benefits of immediate feedback to learners.

Use of the computer can also provide (through computer simulations) a wide range of otherwise inaccessible learning experiences. It can, for example, enable learners to carry out simulated experiments in fields like human genetics, macro-economics and sociology where actual experiments are impossible for ethical, economic or practical reasons.

A further advantage of using a computer as a delivery system for self-instructional materials is that it can allow on-going assessment and monitoring to take place automatically if this is thought appropriate. This can be extremely useful, especially if the learner is working in isolation (eg, on a distance-learning course).

Some weaknesses of computer-assisted learning

Computer-based learning has the same basic weaknesses as audio-visual learning in terms of general lack of availability of suitable ready-made courseware, total dependence on the availability of appropriate hardware and the fact that it is not suitable for use in achieving a wide range of higher-cognitive and non-cognitive objectives.

Figure 5.5 **The interactive video work station used as a delivery system for the BBC's 'Domesday Project'**

A further weakness specific to computer-based learning is that it requires computer literacy and (in some cases) a degree of programming skill on the part of the person designing the materials. With the development of user-friendly *authoring systems* of ever-increasing sophistication, however, it is now becoming very much easier for non-programmers to write CBL materials than was the case in the past, when ability to write programs in a language such as BASIC or FORTRAN was an absolute necessity for such work.

Other strengths and weaknesses of computer-assisted learning will be discussed in Chapters 10 and 11.

Interactive video

Interactive video systems are now to be found in most training centres and colleges. They utilize two relatively well-established teaching media – *videorecorders* and *computers* – in an integrated teaching resource. In marrying the two, the aim is to combine a flexible, interactive and accessible teaching programme (through the computer) with good visual and sound characteristics (through the videorecorder).

A large amount of development work has been carried out on interactive video systems, since their tremendous potential for providing high-quality learning materials to suit individual needs is obvious. The most important developments have been made by combining microcomputers with videodisc players rather than with videocassette machines. This is because it is very much easier to obtain access to specific sequences or frames of a programme using a videodisc system, since there is no need to wind a tape forward or backwards in order to do so.

The advent of the BBC's highly-ambitious *Domesday Project*, which uses videodisc-based interactive video as a delivery system for a comprehensive database on virtually all aspects of Britain (see Figure 5.5), provided a substantial stimulus. Now with the introduction of interactive compact disc software and hardware, the widespread use of interactive video principles and hardware is imminent, particularly as the compact disc hardware and software are being targeted at the domestic leisure market, rather than exclusively at education and training.

Chapter 6

Group Learning Techniques

INTRODUCTION

As we saw in Chapter 1, educational technology is currently very much concerned with the development of techniques that can be used to promote learning in group situations. Such methods normally involve very little use of technical hardware or sophisticated audiovisual software. Rather, they reflect a 'technology *of* educational and training' approach, their main concern being associated with directing the process of interactive group dynamics towards desirable educational or training goals. As a result, less tangible factors, such as room conditions, seating arrangements, group size and the role of the teacher, may play an important role in determining the success (or otherwise) of such methods. This chapter will begin with a discussion of group learning in fairly general terms, after which a number of specific group learning techniques will be considered.

GENERAL FEATURES OF GROUP LEARNING METHODS

The relevance of group learning techniques in an educational or training situation can often be assessed by carrying out a critical analysis of the aims and objectives of the course or programme in question. If the desired outcomes include the development of (for example) oral communication skills, interpersonal skills, problem-solving skills, decision-making skills, critical thinking skills, and certain attitudinal traits deemed to be appropriate, then group learning techniques may be more suitable for teaching towards such outcomes than the various mass instructional and individualized learning methods that have just been described. Indeed, one of the major strengths of a systematic approach to education and training is that when objectives are clearly specified, appropriate teaching methods can be matched with them. In particular, important competences which span all the objectives domains can often be developed and assessed in group situations, where it would not have been possible to address such competences either by mass instruction techniques or through individualized learning resources. The types of outcome which can be achieved through the use of group learning techniques will be discussed in detail later on in this chapter, after we have looked at some basic organizational considerations.

Organizational Considerations

Because of the fact that group learning techniques normally aim to stimulate effective interactive group discussions, it is obviously necessary to use a group of an appropriate size in each particular situation. The optimum group size depends on a variety of factors, including the purpose and nature of the exercise and any constraints that may be laid down by the logistics of the latter; many educational games and simulations, for example, specify the number of participants, particularly if they are highly structured. As a general rule, however, a group should be no larger than about 10 if it is to act as an effective vehicle for promoting group interaction and developing group skills, and, ideally, it should be somewhere between four and six.

In his book *Educational Technology in Curriculum Development* (1982), Derek Rowntree represents the 'group dynamics' that occur in two somewhat different small group situations in the way shown in Figure 6.1.

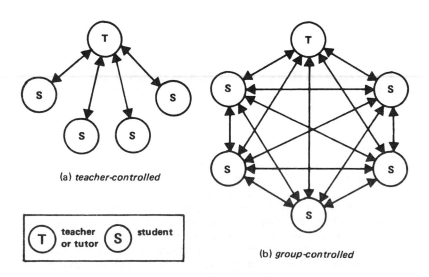

(a) *teacher-controlled*

(b) *group-controlled*

Figure 6.1 **Patterns of communication in two different group learning situations**

In situation (a), the teacher/tutor controls the discussion, the basic pattern being a succession of dialogues between the teacher and the various individual students. This is the somewhat limited pattern of communication that often takes place within a tutorial-type group environment. In situation (b), we see the multi-way communication pattern that takes place in a group-controlled discussion or seminar, in which the students can interact freely with one another, thus allowing ideas to be built upon from within the student group. Indeed, in such a group environment, it may not even be necessary for the teacher to become actively involved in the discussion provided that it is 'set off' in the right direction.

The role of the teacher or trainer in group learning situations is, however, very important, and calls for skills and adaptability which may, for some, be difficult to achieve. First, the teacher must exhibit good organizational skills in planning and structuring the learning experience. Thereafter, the role may be more adaptive and less authoritarian or autocratic than in exposition-based situations. Depending on the form, content and structure of the group technique adopted, and upon its particular educational aims and objectives, the teacher's role may include acting as *group leader* (giving strong direction to the discussion), *group facilitator* (generating self-expression and interaction within the group), *neutral chairman* (controlling the procedure, but not contributing substantially to the discussion), *consultant* (providing assistance and/or information as and when needed) or simply *observer*. In most group exercises, another important aspect of the role of the teacher is in *debriefing* the session. This involves going over with the participants the events that occurred during the group sessions and 'pulling out' any important points that arose, either in connection with the nature and content of the discussions or regarding the processes and interactions within the group itself. Obviously, the points that are highlighted in such a debriefing should be closely related to the main teaching objectives of the exercise. In *Workshops that Work* (1993), Tom Bourner, Viv Martin and Phil Race provide a wide selection of techniques and processes which can be used by facilitators of group work (see the Bibliography).

Group learning activities can range from being highly structured and pre-planned to being essentially free or open discussions. If a structured approach is to be used, the group may be organized in a pre-arranged way, and directed to discuss specific subject matter in a manner that is dictated by the teacher or predetermined by the format of the exercise. On the other hand, if a free or non-directed approach is to be adopted, the group processes are far more 'student-controlled' and flexible, and consequently the learning outcomes are much more difficult to predict. In between these two extremes is a whole range of techniques and approaches which involves the use of groups in a wide variety of different ways.

Some Strengths of Group Learning Techniques

In matching the desired outcomes, or objectives, of a course with the teaching methods likely to achieve them, it soon becomes obvious that no single method is suitable in all circumstances, and that an appropriate 'blend' of teaching methods (exposition-based, individualized and group) may be required. As mentioned above, there are a number of types of objectives for which group learning techniques are particularly useful as a means of teaching. Let us now examine these in turn.

Higher cognitive objectives

Within the general area of knowledge and understanding (Bloom's cognitive domain – see Chapter 3), we have already seen that mass-instruction techniques (for example, lectures) and individualized learning methods are well suited for teaching towards the lower cognitive areas of 'knowledge' and 'comprehension'. However, the understanding of factual material and its applications in a number of areas can often be much more effectively investigated in small group situations such as tutorial sessions. Indeed, in most colleges and universities, lectures and tutorials are generally closely linked and complementary.

Cognitive skills that lie further up Bloom's hierarchy (such as those involving the analysis or evaluation of given material) are often most effectively developed by using a group-discussion technique of some sort. Here, students can discuss problems and opinions with their peers in a relatively open environment.

Group methods have also proved to be useful in problem-solving sessions, with the students either working individually and interacting with the teacher, or working as a co-operative group in tackling a project of some sort. In such activities, the subject matter is often very specific to the students' course of study. However, exercises that foster the development of decision-making skills through the use of small-group methods need not necessarily be so content-related. Many management-training courses, for example, make use of exercises which enable the participants to improve their decision-making ability through activities in which the processes by which the decisions are reached are much more important than the actual content of the exercise.

Creative thinking skills and competences

In courses that contain objectives which involve the development of creative thinking skills (for example, the ability to perceive new relationships within a topic, or the ability to produce imaginative solutions to given problem situations), group methods have often been found to be extremely useful. In situations where wide-ranging and/or lateral thinking are required, for example, ideas can be 'bounced around' within the group for comment and criticism, with the result that individual group members benefit from the perceptions of others and from the subsequent interactions and discussions.

Communication skills and competences

A number of group learning techniques are ideal vehicles for the development of (or creation of an awareness of the importance of) the various skills that are associated with *oral communication, non-verbal communication,* and *written communication.*

Students are frequently criticized for their inability to express themselves coherently. Group techniques are particularly well suited to helping them to overcome these deficiencies, and, in recent years, a multitude of exercises have been designed specifically for this purpose. These provide situations in which students can develop oral communication skills (such as presenting and defending arguments and making a meaningful contribution to discussions) and through which they can generally build up their confidence. Ideally, a planned series of such exercises is desirable if significant and long-lasting improvements are to be achieved.

In the context of developing students' competences in the areas of written communication, it can be highly profitable to arrange group sessions in which written work such as essays, laboratory reports, assignments and project reports can be discussed. The purpose of such discussions can be twofold: first, to discuss the content of the written work for the mutual benefit of the group; second, to discuss the form of the written work in terms of, for instance, structure, sequence and clarity of expression. In many cases, open discussion of the latter may well encourage and catalyse improved future efforts.

Finally, group exercises may help the participants to develop an appreciation of the importance of non-verbal communication and to cultivate useful skills in this often-neglected area. This can be achieved through observation of the activities of the group by the teacher, by the actual group members, by independent observers, or via a videotape recording made for later analysis and discussion. Such techniques can be used for a variety of purposes: eg for demonstrating the nature of non-verbal communication to psychology students, or for helping trainee managers to recognize and develop the various non-verbal skills that play such an important part in interviews, meetings, etc.

Interpersonal skills and competences

The various skills that are required in order to operate effectively within a group or social situation are often best developed by group learning methods. In many instances, students leaving school or college enter jobs which require them to work in close co-operation with other people. For some, this may involve skills of leadership, administration and delegation, for some, the ability to work as part of a team, while for others it may involve social skills such as those needed in order to deal with the general public. Again, group methods are ideal for putting theory into practice, and a whole range of simulation and role-play activities can be used with small groups in order to help develop interpersonal skills of this type.

Desirable attitudinal traits

Research has shown that exposition-based and individualized methods are not particularly effective in the area of attitude (affective) development. It seems that active participation by students and exposure to views different from their own and to criticism by their peers are necessary if attitudes are to be changed, together with a less dominant teacher role than is found in most conventional learning situations. In other words, it appears that *student interaction* is the key to the achievement of such attitude changes.

The vital role that can be played by group methods in this area is self-evident. Such methods can provide an environment in which free discussion can break down prejudices and misconceptions and increase awareness of the range of factors that are involved in any given situation. An example might be the use of group methods to increase empathy towards a minority section of the community, or towards trade unions or representatives of management.

Group activities can also be an extremely powerful means of integrating an individual's cognitive and affective development within the context of a meaningful and relevant learning experience.

Some Disadvantages of Group Learning

Group learning also has a number of disadvantages, some of the more important of which will now be examined.

Organizational difficulties

Running group learning exercises can pose a number of organizational problems, not the least of which is the fact that it is often difficult to fit them into the normal teaching curriculum – particularly if the exercise is a long one or requires a large number of participants, extra teaching staff, special accommodation, etc. This is particularly true of many exercises of the game/simulation/case study type. Also, the fact that such exercises often require the participants to attend briefing or debriefing sessions or to carry out preliminary work can cause complications. Finally, it is often extremely difficult to assess student performance or evaluate the effectiveness of group learning exercises other than on a subjective basis.

Problems of attitude

One potential weakness of all group learning methods is that they require the active co-operation of the participants if they are to succeed. In some cases, however, this co-operation may not be forthcoming. Students may, for example, simply not turn up for the exercise because they feel that it will be a waste of time or are afraid of taking part. In other cases, they may be reluctant to make the very real personal commitment that many group learning exercises require, because they do not feel that they have the necessary skills and do not want to 'show themselves up' in front of their peers.

Nor are these attitude-related problems necessarily limited to students. As we saw earlier, running a group learning exercise can make heavy demands on the staff involved, often requiring them to take on a number of unfamiliar roles which may not fit in with their conception of what their job should entail. This is particularly true of many older, or more traditional, teachers, who, as a result, make little or no use of group learning techniques.

THE MAIN GROUP LEARNING TECHNIQUES

The type of group technique that is used in a particular teaching or training situation depends on a whole range of factors, including the objectives that it is wished to achieve, the relationship of the exercise with other teaching methods, the maturity of the students, the personality and experience of the teacher, and so on. The techniques described below by no means constitute an exhaustive list of those which can be used in small group situations; they do, however, illustrate a broad cross-section of approaches which vary in their degree of structure, teacher involvement and dependence on subject matter content. Some techniques can in fact be used within other group techniques, while others can be incorporated into exposition-based methods in order to generate student activity, discussion and feedback. More detailed descriptions of these and other group techniques can be found in Abercrombie's book *Aims and Techniques of Group Teaching* (1979) and in *Workshops that Work* by Bourner *et al* (1993).

In order to give this section of the book a workable structure, we will divide group learning techniques into six broad classes, namely, *buzz sessions and similar small-group exercises; class discussions, seminars, tutorials, etc; participative exercises of the game/simulation/case study type; mediated feedback/discussion sessions; group projects;* and *self-help groups.* Within each of these categories, it is, of course, possible to adopt a wide range of approaches and tactics, but, as we will see, it is also possible to make a number of generalizations, and it is on these that we will concentrate.

Buzz Sessions and Similar Small-group Exercises

Buzz sessions are short participative sessions that are deliberately built into a lecture or larger group exercise in order to stimulate discussion and provide student feedback. In such sessions, small sub-groups of two to four persons spend a short period (generally no more than five minutes) intensively discussing a topic or topics suggested by the teacher. Each sub-group then reports back on its deliberations to the group as a whole, or sometimes combines with another sub-group in order to share their findings and discuss the implications.

One variation of the buzz group approach is the *one-two-four snowball technique*. Here, the members of a class or large group are first asked to reflect individually on a question, then asked to form pairs in order to look for differences in these responses, then asked to form groups of four in order to arrive at a consensus response. As in the basic buzz group technique, each group of four is then asked to report on its findings to the class or group as a whole.

Some strengths of small-scale group sessions of this type

Buzz groups and similar small-group sessions constitute an excellent method of introducing variety into a lecture or formal presentation, thus helping to overcome the problems that can arise due to the limitations in the *attention span* of students (see the section on lectures in Chapter 4). Appropriate use of such sessions forces the students to undergo a radical change in their thought processes, thus helping to stop their attention from lapsing.

Such sessions can be used to achieve a wide range of objectives, both cognitive and non-cognitive. They can, for example, be used to develop oral-communication and interpersonal skills, as well as being ideal for helping students to develop their powers of decision-making, evaluation and divergent thinking.

Such sessions also serve as an ideal vehicle for getting students actively involved in a lesson, thus increasing the effectiveness of the learning that takes place. They also provide a teacher with a useful mechanism for obtaining feedback from a class.

Some weaknesses of small-scale group sessions

The main limitation of small-scale group sessions of this type is that they are not really suitable for use as a front-line teaching method in their own right, since they cannot, by themselves, be used to teach the basic facts and principles of a subject. Thus, they should only be used in a *supportive* role, in conjunction with other methods such as lectures.

Class Discussions, Seminars, Tutorials, etc

This class of techniques covers a wide range of activities designed to promote discussion between a teacher and a group of students, or within a group of learners.

Class discussions generally take the form of a *controlled discussion* in which the teacher is at all times firmly in control of the situation, either allowing the class to ask questions and controlling the way in which these are discussed, or else guiding the class through a structured discussion of some sort by asking carefully-chosen questions, providing appropriate prompts, and so on. Such discussions can be used in a variety of contexts, eg, as a follow-up to an expository session such as a lecture or the viewing of a film or video, as a class revision session, as a debriefing session for a game, simulation or participative case study, or as a teaching method in their own right.

Seminars can take a number of forms, and are generally run on somewhat less-restricted lines than class discussions, with the group members themselves having much more control over the course and content of the discussion. One common method of running a seminar is to base it on an essay, paper or prepared talk presented by one of the students in the group, with the group then discussing the presentation in depth. Figure 6.2 shows such a seminar in progress. Another method is to run the seminar as a *free group discussion* of a particular topic, the group either being given broad guidelines on how the discussion should proceed or being left to decide this for themselves. Another variation of the seminar approach is the *fishbowl technique*. Here, some of the members of the class involved sit in an inner circle and conduct a discussion while the remainder sit in an outer circle and act as non-participating observers; both sections of the group then combine for a general discussion of what occurred.

Yet another approach to the organization of a seminar is *brainstorming*. This involves group members in spontaneously noting

Figure 6.2 **A typical small-group seminar in progress in a business school**

down or suggesting a range of possible solutions to a problem or question posed by the teacher, eg, 'What items would be absolutely essential if you were marooned on a desert island?' Initially, the suggestions are compiled without comment, and the group as a whole then evaluates the various suggestions and modifies or rejects them in the light of the ensuing discussion. Brainstorming is very useful not only for stimulating discussion, but also for acting as an *icebreaker* at the start of a seminar by actively involving every participant right at the beginning. Once the 'ice' has been broken, the group's discussion will probably be a good deal more free and involve more students then might otherwise be the case.

Group *tutorials* can also take a variety of forms. One common form is the *working tutorial*, in which the class (or a section thereof) tackle course-related tasks set by the teacher or tutor, obtaining help or guidance if they experience difficulties. Another is the *problem-raising tutorial*, in which the members have the opportunity to ask their tutor about any matters relating to the course with which they are having problems.

Some strengths of class discussions, seminars and tutorials

Class discussions, seminars and tutorials can be used to achieve a wide range of educational objectives, both of the cognitive and of the non-cognitive variety. They can, for example, be used to build on *lower-cognitive* objectives (*knowledge* and *comprehension*) that have been developed in lectures or through individualized learning by providing a vehicle for achieving *higher-cognitive* objectives such as *application, analysis, synthesis* and *evaluation* in the areas in question. They can also be used to develop communication and interpersonal skills, and to achieve a wide range of affective objectives such as showing students that there are generally several ways of looking at an issue or making them more tolerant of the views of other people.

They enable relevant topics to be examined in great depth or discussed at considerable length.

Like buzz sessions and similar exercises, they have the great advantage of *getting the learners actively involved in the learning process*, since they are, by definition, participative rather than passive.

Some weaknesses of such methods

With all group learning methods of this type, there is always the danger that some of the members of the class or group will not take an active part in the exercise, leaving all the thinking or speaking to others. Thus, if such an exercise is to be fully effective, it is necessary to take steps to ensure that *everyone* takes part – either by careful structuring or control and/or by limiting the size of the group.

Building group learning sessions such as group tutorials or seminars into a curriculum can cause timetabling and logistical difficulties because of the fact that they generally involve the class being split up, thus making extra demands on staff support and accommodation.

One major drawback of subject-based tutorials and seminars is that there is often a tendency for the teacher to become over-dominant, and, in some cases, to use the session as a 'mini-lecture'. If this happens, the opportunity to achieve the full range of higher-cognitive and other objectives of which such sessions are capable will almost certainly be lost.

Participative Exercises of the Game/Simulation/ Case Study Type

During the last decade, the use of *games, simulations* and interactive *case studies* as a group learning technique has increased dramatically. Such exercises were originally largely confined to the military and business management training sectors, but they have now spread to virtually all sectors of education, where they are used in a wide range of subject areas to teach towards a wide variety of educational objectives.

The scope and range of applications of the techniques are much too wide to allow them to be discussed in any great depth here, and interested readers are referred to the various books that have been written on the subject. (Ellington, Addinall and Percival, for example,

Figure 6.3 **Chemistry pupils playing a typical educational game –
'Formulon' (a card game designed to reinforce understanding of how
elements and ions combine to form chemical compounds)**

have written a number of books on the design and educational uses of games and simulations, and other useful books have been written by Tansey and Unwin, Boocock and Schild, and Taylor and Walford, to name but a few – see the Bibliography for details.)

The different types of exercise

In an educational or training context, *games* are exercises which involve competition and have set rules. The term covers an extremely wide range of exercises – everything from simple card and board games to large-scale. management games and sophisticated competitions. When playing a game in a group learning situation, the participants, acting either individually or in co-operation with others, use their skills and knowledge to compete with one another in order to 'win'.

Simulations, on the other hand, are exercises that involve an on-going representation of some aspect(s) of a real situation of some sort. In many cases, they involve the members of a group in taking part in *role-play*, during which each member acts out the part of another person such as a lawyer, local councillor, trade union representative or conservationist.

Finally, *case studies* are exercises in which the members of a group have to carry out an in-depth study of a process, situation, event, document, etc in order to examine its special characteristics, characteristics that either may be limited to the particular case under examination or may be general features of the broad set or class to which it belongs. Obvious examples are the group discussions of specific cases that are carried out in the context of medical or legal training, but the case study technique can also be used in a wide range of other areas.

There are also various types of 'hybrid' exercises in the game/ simulation/case study field, exercises which have characteristics that are drawn from two or even all three of the basic areas that have just been described.

Simulation games, for example, have a competitive element and also involve a simulation situation, a well-known example being MONO-POLY. Other variations might involve using the actual process of playing a game as a case study in itself (in the study of probability theory, for example) or basing a case study on a simulated rather than a real situation (as in the simulated patient technique developed at McMaster University in Canada for use in the training of medical staff). Such hybrid exercises are described in detail by Ellington, Addinall and Percival in *A Handbook of Game Design* (1982).

Some advantages of games, simulations and case studies

Let us now examine some of the reasons why games, simulations and interactive case studies are useful in a group learning situation.

The techniques constitute a highly versatile and flexible medium whereby a wide variety of educational aims and objectives can be achieved. In a group situation, they can be used to achieve objectives in all parts of Bloom's cognitive and affective domains. Although the methods are no more effective than any other method when used to teach the basic facts of a subject, they have been found to be particularly valuable in teaching towards high-level cognitive objectives relating to such things as analysis, synthesis and evaluation, and also for achieving a variety of affective (attitudinal) objectives. Thus their use is often as a complement to, and a support for, more traditional teaching methods, and they can also be used for reinforcement purposes (see Figure 6.3) or to demonstrate applications or relevance.

The use of a simulated as opposed to a real situation as the basis of a group exercise allows the situation and learning experiences to be tailored to meet the needs of the group, rather than requiring the exercise to be designed within the constraints imposed by the situation. Only very rarely does a real-life situation have all the features that the designer of a case study-type exercise wishes to bring out, whereas a simulated situation can have all such features built in. Also, real-life situations are often much too complicated to be used as the basis of an educational or training group exercise as they stand; the simplification that the use of simulations allows can often overcome this difficulty by reducing the complexity to manageable proportions.

Work by Paul Twelker (see the Bibliography) has indicated that well-designed games, simulations and interactive case studies can achieve *positive transfer of learning*, that is, they can produce in participants the ability to apply skills acquired during the exercise in other situations. It would, in fact, be difficult to justify the use of many exercises of this type if no such transfer of learning occurred.

In many cases, exercises in the game/simulation/case study field constitute a vehicle whereby students can use and develop their initiative and powers of creative thought. This feature may prove increasingly important in the future if the educational system continues to place progressively greater emphasis on the cultivation of divergent thought processes.

Apart from their specifically content-related outcomes, many exercises of the type under discussion help to foster a wide range of useful skills (such as decision-making, communication and interpersonal skills) and desirable attitudinal traits (such as willingness to listen to other people's points of view, or to appreciate that most problems can be viewed in a number of different ways). Indeed, many people believe that it is in these areas that games, simulations and case studies can make their most valuable contribution to education. Exercises which have been designed to involve a high degree of interaction in the group are found to be particularly effective in this regard.

In cases where a competitive element is involved (not necessarily at the expense of co-operation), this can provide strong motivation for the participants to commit themselves wholeheartedly to the work of the exercise. This competitive element may be overt (when sub-groups or individuals are in open competition with one another) or it may be latent (as, for example, when sub-groups or individuals have to perform parallel activities and report their findings to the group as a whole).

Many exercises in this field have a basis in more than one academic discipline, a feature that can help the participants to integrate concepts from otherwise widely-related areas into a cohesive and balanced 'world picture'. Exercises which require the students to formulate value judgements (for example, weighing economic benefits against social costs) or examine problems from a number of different perspectives are particularly valuable in this respect.

Multi-disciplinary exercises have an additional advantage in that they can provide a situation in which participants with expertise in different subject areas have to work together effectively in order to achieve a common end. Interpersonal skills of this type are very important in a student's later life, and constitute an area of education and training in which the multi-disciplinary simulation and simulation game may be the only means of providing practical experience in a school or college environment.

Finally, one universally-observed advantage of game/simulation/ case study techniques is that student involvement and motivation are normally very high – features that are particularly beneficial when using these techniques with the less able. In addition, most participants find the approach extremely enjoyable.

To sum up, participation in games and simulations can address the development of a wide range of competences, in ways which are close to the natural ways in which people learn, with abundant 'learning by doing' and feedback to participants.

Some disadvantages of games and simulations

Apart from the various organizational and attitude-related disadvantages which they share with other group learning techniques (see p 108), there are two main disadvantages that are specifically associated with games and simulations.

First, there is always a danger of using such exercises for the wrong reasons, for example using them as 'diversions' or 'time fillers' rather than for some specific educational purpose. Also, with some 'educational games', it is possible for students to play them purely as games, without deriving any worthwhile educational benefit, because the 'educational' and 'gaming' elements are not fully integrated. (A number of commercially-available card games tend to have this weakness to some extent, as do many board games.)

Second, if a game or simulation is to be of any real use in a given educational situation, it must not only be capable of achieving the desired educational outcomes but must also be properly matched to the target population with which it is to be used; in other words it must be pitched at a suitable level. It is, however, very unusual to find an exercise that is ideally suited to the purpose which the teacher/tutor has in mind, so it may be necessary to carry out a certain amount of adaption or modification, or even to 'start from scratch' and design a completely new exercise. Obviously, this requires a certain amount of expertise and (preferably) some previous experience.

The role of the teacher

In most exercises of the game/simulation/case study-type, the role of the teacher is mainly organizational, with the actual activities that take place within the exercise being largely under the control of the students. The extent to which an exercise is pre-structured (and hence the extent of student freedom) can, however, vary considerably.

One of the most important roles of the teacher is in *debriefing* the participants after the completion of the exercise, such debriefing being absolutely vital if the full educational value is to be derived from their experience. The form of the debriefing will depend on the nature and function of the exercise concerned, but should generally include the following four elements:

1. review of the actual work of the exercise, and discussion of any important points raised by the students;
2. discussion of the relationship between the exercise and the subject matter on which it is based (for example, discussion of the degree of realism in the case of a simulation);
3. discussion of the group processes which occurred during the exercise;
4. discussion of any broad issues raised.

The debriefing session is particularly important in the case of exercises that involve role play, or which place the intrinsic subject matter in a social, political, economic or environmental context; indeed in such cases, it is often the most important part of the whole experience.

Mediated Feedback/Discussion Sessions

Another important class of group learning techniques includes all those that involve mediated feedback on and discussion of an activity of some sort. One well-known example is *microteaching*, which is widely used in the training of teachers. In microteaching, attention is focused on specific teaching skills, which the trainee teacher practices for short periods (from 5 to 20 minutes) with a small group of pupils (usually 4 to 7). The session is recorded, usually on videotape, and is then played back to the trainee teacher, normally in the presence of other trainees, in order to obtain immediate feedback and catalyse discussion of the performance. The resulting group feedback (together with the supervisor's comments and any observations made by the actual pupils) helps student teachers to analyse their performances and thus enables them to restructure the lesson in order to teach it to a second group of pupils. Again, this is followed by immediate video replay, so that further analysis and evaluation can take place in order to identify any areas where further improvement could be made. By employing this 'teach-reteach' cycle, it is possible to give student teachers the opportunity to put into immediate practice what they have learned from the video replay and from the peer group and other feedback on the previous attempt.

There are many variations of microteaching, and indeed, such video-replay methods for analysing performance are now used in many areas of skills training other than teaching practice. Examples include the recording of simulated interviews or other interactive situations for subsequent analysis, criticism and discussion by a class.

Some strengths of mediated feedback/discussion sessions

Use of mediated feedback followed by class or group discussion provides an ideal vehicle for in-depth examination of a whole range of situations and processes (individual presentations, simulated interviews, group-dynamics situations, and so on).

Such techniques can be used to develop a wide range of useful skills, including the skills associated with the situation or process being examined and the various skills that are developed by the subsequent critical discussion (communication skills, evaluative skills, and so on).

Again, such techniques have an extremely high 'learner involvement' factor – a great educational advantage, as we have seen earlier.

Some weaknesses of such techniques

One of the main drawbacks of such techniques is that some students may well find them rather off-putting at first; thus, getting the most out of such techniques may require considerable skill and empathy on the part of the organizing teacher.

Another obvious disadvantage is that the technique requires suitable hardware to be available, and may also require back-up by technical staff. Use of techniques of this type may also cause time-tabling problems, particularly if a class has to be split up for the work.

Readers who want to learn more about microteaching and similar techniques are referred to the books that have been written on the subject by Brown and by Hargie and Maidment (see the Bibliography).

Group Projects

One group learning technique that has become increasingly popular in recent years is the *group project*. Here, students carry out project work in small co-operative groups (generally containing between 3 and 6 people) rather than as individuals. Such group projects can be carried out as teaching exercises in their own right (eg, for providing part of the practical or case-study work of a course, as in Figure 6.4) or can be built into other, larger exercises (eg, in the form of *syndicate* work).

Some strengths of group projects

Group projects can be used to achieve the same basic range of objectives as conventional practical and project work (see Chapter 4), and, in addition, help the participants to develop the various interpersonal skills that are so essential for success in later life. Furthermore, the constructive exchange of ideas and division of labour that are generally associated with group projects can make such exercises far more useful learning experiences than individual projects, with the group being able to produce work of a quality that would probably be completely beyond even the best students if they had to work on their own.

Figure 6.4 **Students at The Robert Gordon University carrying out a mathematical modelling exercise as a group project**

Group projects are also ideal vehicles for cross-disciplinary work, an aspect of education that is assuming more and more importance as traditional subject barriers become less rigid than was the case in the past.

Some weaknesses of group projects

One obvious weakness of such exercises is the problem of making sure that all the members of the group play their full part in the work; in such projects, it is often all too easy for a lazy or incompetent member to 'opt out', leaving colleagues to do all the hard work. It is therefore important to try to build into such projects measures which help ensure that everyone pulls his weight.

An associated problem is that of *assessing* a group project. While it is obviously fairly easy to assess the work of the group *as a whole*, it is generally much more difficult to assess the work of the individual members unless the group is constantly monitored by supervisory staff (something that can be counter-productive). One solution is to build an element of *peer assessment* into the assessment process, eg, by asking every member of the group to award every other member a mark reflecting his evaluation of their respective contributions of the work.

Self-help Groups

These arise when students meet on their own (that is, with no teacher or tutor present) in order to discuss common problems, share ideas and generally help one another by a process of *peer teaching*.

In many cases, such groups form spontaneously; in others, some encouragement from the teacher or institution may provide the necessary catalyst. Students obviously need to be motivated to participate in such groups, but the peer teaching aspect can be extremely valuable in helping them to cope with difficulties. In many distance learning courses, such as those offered by the Open University, the formation of self-help groups is actively encouraged, and, in such circumstances, can often do a great deal to help offset the isolation of independent study.

Chapter 7

Assessment

INTRODUCTION

In the previous editions of this book, this chapter provided a thorough review of various approaches to assessment, giving examples and suggesting advantages and disadvantages of different methods. Many of these assessment methods are used to assess the achievement of learning objectives by students and trainees. All of these methods are still practised widely now, and we decided to retain all of the original discussion. However, in the previous edition, only a few paragraphs were devoted to self- and peer-assessment. These kinds of assessment are particularly relevant in the assessment of the evidence which demonstrates the achievement of competences. Furthermore, there is now growing concern at the artificiality of some traditional forms of assessment, not least the formal written examination. We have therefore decided to add a substantial new section at the end of this chapter, under the general title 'Learning and Assessment: a Critical Overview', looking critically at the main limitations of examinations as assessment devices and leading into a detailed discussion of the relative benefits of self- and peer-assessment and linking assessment in general to the 'Fresh Look at Learning' we presented at the end of Chapter 1.

EDUCATIONAL TECHNOLOGY AND ASSESSMENT

In Chapter 1 we discussed the main features of a systematic approach to the design of educational and training programmes, and in Chapter 3 we argued the case for clearly formulated statements of intended learning outcomes, both in terms of behavioural objectives and in terms of competence descriptors. A logical argument for taking structured steps in expressing learning outcomes is that it is much easier to design assessment criteria when details of the competences learners are intended to gain are well defined and expressed. It is equally useful for learners themselves to be able to see such details of their anticipated performance (and even more useful when learners have the opportunity to *apply* assessment criteria to their own performances or each others performances).

We believe that it is in the formulation of valid and reliable assessment processes and instruments that the technology *of* education and training has its most important part to play. In addition, aspects of technology *in* education and training play their part in assessment, for example in the use of computerized assessment systems to provide feedback to learners and keep records of their progress.

The results of assessment are very useful in the context of evaluating the effectiveness and quality of educational and training courses and resources. It is important at this stage to draw a clear distinction between the terms 'assessment' and 'evaluation', which can have radically different meanings in education and training contexts from the everyday meanings of the words.

By *assessment*, we mean the processes and instruments that are designed to measure learners' achievements, normally after learners have engaged in an instructional programme of one sort or another, or after they have worked through open- or flexible-learning resources on their own. *Evaluation* (in the context of education and training) normally refers to a series of activities that are designed to measure the effectiveness of the instructional system as a whole, or the effectiveness of educational and training resources used within such a system. The data from learners' assessments clearly contribute one form of evidence which can be used in evaluation of an instructional system, but there are many others which need to be included to make a 'whole' evaluation. A much fuller discussion of the relationship between assessment and evaluation can be found in *Assessing Students: How shall we know them?* by Derek Rowntree (1987).

In this chapter we will first review the general principles that underlie effective assessment procedures and will then describe a range of approaches to test construction and assessment design. We continue the chapter by providing a broad review of the range of assessment methods in use in education and training, commenting on their functions and their respective strengths and weaknesses. As we mentioned in the Introduction above, we then conclude this chapter by taking a highly critical look at the most common form of traditional assessment – the written exam – and by introducing an extended discussion of self- and peer-assessment, which we believe to be a much more important part of the 'technology *of* education and training' than has hitherto generally been accepted.

DESIRABLE CHARACTERISTICS OF ASSESSMENT PROCEDURES

We will now turn our attention to the basic features that should characterize a 'good' assessment procedure. Such a procedure should, ideally, be *valid, reliable, practicable,* and *fair and useful to students.* Let us now discuss these in turn.

Validity

A *valid* assessment procedure is one which actually tests what it sets out to test, ie one which accurately measures the behaviour described by the objective(s) under scrutiny. Obviously, no one would *deliberately* construct an assessment item to test trivia or irrelevant material, but it is surprising just how often non-valid test items are in fact used – eg questions that are intended to test recall of factual material but which actually test the candidate's powers of reasoning, or questions which assume a level of pre-knowledge that the candidates do not possess.

As we will see later in the review of assessment methods, validity-related problems are a common weakness of many of the more widely-used methods. For example, a simple science question given to 14-year-old schoolchildren ('Name the products of the combustion of carbon in an adequate supply of oxygen') produced a much higher number of correct answers when the word 'combustion' was replaced by 'burning'. This showed that the original question had problems of validity in that it was, to some extent, testing language and vocabulary skills rather than the basic science involved.

Reliability

The *reliability* of an assessment procedure is a measure of the consistency with which the question, test or examination produces the same results under different but comparable conditions. A reliable assessment item gives reproducible scores with similar populations of students, and is therefore as independent of the characteristics and vagaries of individual markers as possible; this is often difficult to achieve in practice.

It is obviously important to have reasonably reliable assessment procedures when a large number of individual markers assess the same question (eg in national school examinations). A student answer which receives a score of 75 per cent from one marker and 35 per cent from another, for example, reveals a patently unreliable assessment procedure.

To help produce reliability, the questions which comprise an assessment should (ideally) test only one thing at a time and give the candidates no choice. The assessment should also adequately reflect the objectives of the teaching unit. Note that the reliability and validity factors in an assessment are in no way directly linked – a test or examination, for example, may be totally reliable and yet have very low validity, and vice versa.

Practicability

For most purposes, assessment procedures should be realistically *practical* in terms of their cost, time taken, and ease of application. For example, with a large class of technicians being trained in electrical circuitry, it may be convenient to use only a paper-and-pencil test rather than set up numerous practical testing situations. It should be noted, however, that such compromises can, in some cases, greatly reduce the validity of the assessment.

Fairness and Usefulness

To be fair to all students, an assessment must accurately reflect the range of expected behaviours as described by the course objectives. It is also highly desirable that students should know exactly *how* they are to be assessed. Indeed, it could be argued that students have a *right* to information such as the nature of the materials on which they are to be examined (ie content and objectives), the form and structure of the examination, the length of the examination, and the value (in terms of marks) of each component of the course.

Also, students should (ideally!) find assessments useful. Feedback from assessment can give students a much better indication of their current strengths and weaknesses than they might otherwise have. In this respect, the non-return of assessment work to students greatly reduces its utility. We emphasize the importance of feedback to students more fully in the 'Critical Overview' later in this chapter.

CRITERION-REFERENCED AND NORM-REFERENCED ASSESSMENT

Two contrasting general approaches to student assessment are *criterion-referenced* and *norm-referenced assessment.*

Criterion-referenced assessment involves testing students in order to measure their performance in tasks described by a particular objective or set of objectives (the criterion). In any systems approach to education or training (which is invariably geared towards the achievement of clearly-specified objectives), it is normal to use some kind of criterion-referenced test for student assessment. In such a test, the *relative* performances of the various individuals in the class are of little consequence – indeed, in the unlikely event of the whole class demonstrating complete mastery of the objectives, this would simply indicate that a highly-successful teaching/learning system had been developed.

A good example of a criterion-referenced test is the standard driving test, in which learner drivers have to demonstrate a certain level of competence before being allowed to 'pass'. Their performance relative to other learner drivers should (in principle) be of no consequence.

This approach contrasts sharply with *norm-referenced assessment*, which is altogether more competitive. Norm-referenced assessment involves tests of ability or attainment which are intended to probe differences between individual students, and hence to determine the extent to which each individual's performance differs from the performance of others of similar age and background.

In cases where there is a choice of questions in a norm-referenced test, a need is highlighted for *standardization* of scores for comparison purposes. A typical norm-referenced test may have a fixed pass rate (say 55 per cent) which is strictly adhered to, no matter how high or how low is the general level of attainment. This is, on the face of it, a much less fair approach to assessment than criterion-referenced assessment, since only *relative* attainment, not *absolute* attainment, is recognized. However, the approach is widely used – in many national school examinations and professional examinations, for example.

Basically, criterion-referenced assessment and norm-referenced assessment differ in the *purpose* for which the assessment is carried out, the *style* in which the component tests are constructed, and, finally, in the *use* to which the information derived from the results of the assessment is put.

In the remainder of this chapter, we will attempt to demonstrate the role of assessment techniques in a general systems approach to course design. Thus, our main concern will be with criterion-referenced assessment related to the attainment of pre-specified objectives and identifiable behaviours.

TEST CONSTRUCTION

As mentioned earlier in this chapter, a student assessment should be directly geared towards the stated course objectives (while remembering that not all objectives are formally assessable, yet may nevertheless be very important). The attainment of assessable objectives may be measured in a relatively sporadic programme of *set examinations*, or, more consistently (and possibly less stressfully for students), by some form of *continuous-assessment* procedure. However it is done, it is likely that a *combination* of assessment techniques will be necessary in order to assess the range of objectives under investigation validly and comprehensively.

In order to ensure that particular sets of skills are being assessed, some individuals and organizations have drawn up 'tables of specifications' for tests to ensure that due weight is given to all skills and content areas. For example, Figure 7.1 is a typical specification of the cognitive skills to be assessed in the UK Ordinary National Certificate (ONC) in chemistry. The course syllabus is written in the form of behavioural objectives, and the specification is given in terms of Bloom's classification of educational objectives (which was men-

Subject and topic	Ability				
	Recall	Comprehension	Non-routine application	Analysis/ evaluation	Totals
Inorganic chemistry					
Revision and extension	7	6	4	6	23
Chemical reactions	8	10	2	0	20
Group I and II elements	5	10	2	2	19
Group VII elements	5	10	2	2	19
Group V elements	5	10	2	2	19
Totals	**30**	**46**	**12**	**12**	**100**
Organic chemistry					
Nomenclature	3	2	0	0	5
Stereochemistry	1	6	2	0	9
Hydrocarbons	5	7	4	2	18
Halogen derivatives	1	6	3	0	10
Hydroxyl compounds	2	8	3	2	15
Carbonyl compounds	3	10	3	3	19
Acids and derivatives	3	6	2	1	12
Bases	2	6	2	2	12
Totals	**20**	**51**	**19**	**10**	**100**
Physical chemistry					
Gases	4	5	3	1	13
Solutions	8	9	6	3	26
Thermodynamics	3	4	2	1	10
Chemical equilibrium	3	3	2	2	10
Electrochemistry	6	7	4	2	19
Ionic equilibria	6	7	6	3	22
Totals	**30**	**35**	**23**	**12**	**100**

Figure 7.1 **Typical tables of specifications for the UK Ordinary National Certificate (ONC) examinations in chemistry**

tioned in Chapter 3) and the various areas of course content. Tables of this sort, while perhaps a little rigid, do enable exam setters to design assessments to cover the full range of skills (in this case, cognitive skills) that are under scrutiny, and to promote good syllabus coverage. They also ensure that certain skills (eg factual recall) are not over-emphasized, and that due attention is paid to higher cognitive skills.

The type and range of techniques used within a given assessment strategy will depend upon a number of factors – the most important (at least from an educational point of view) being the student behaviours that are specified in the objectives being tested. The basic characteristics of the range of commonly-used assessment methods will now be discussed, together with their respective advantages and limitations.

A REVIEW OF ASSESSMENT METHODS

Assessment methods can have a wide variety of forms. The most common general approach is via some form of written response, ie the 'paper-and-pencil' approach. This approach encompasses a whole range of 'traditional' assessment methods such as *essay-type questions, short notes questions* and *problem-solving questions*, all of which require an extended written response of some sort.

Another form of 'paper-and-pencil' approach involves the use of *objective tests*, although such tests seldom involve the student in writing very much; in most cases, a mark made beside one of a range of possible options, or a single-word answer, is all that is required. Also, the word 'objective', when used in the 'objective test' context, can be somewhat confusing, since it neither means that the questions are necessarily related to the course objectives, nor implies that the questions are objectively chosen. The term simply indicates that the answers to such questions can be marked *totally reliably* by anybody, including non-subject specialists, and, in some cases, even by a computer. The most common type of objective question is the *multiple-choice question* (or, more correctly, *multiple-choice item*), together with its range of variations. Other types of objective questions include *completion items, unique-answer questions,* and *structural communication tests.*

Practical tests are often used to assess psychomotor objectives, and include such techniques as *project assessment, assessment of laboratory work,* and other *skill-tests* designed to assess specific manipulative skills. Also in this category are *situational assessment* techniques, which involve students using non-cognitive skills (such as decision-making skills) in a real, or (more likely) in a simulated environment.

There is a range of *unobtrusive assessment* techniques which can take place without the student necessarily being aware that he is in fact being assessed. Finally, variations of self- and peer-assessment are currently being researched and used; we go into these in some depth later in this chapter.

Let us now look at each of these techniques in turn, starting with traditional paper-and-pencil tests that involve extended writing of some sort.

Traditional 'Extended Writing' Tests

As we have seen, the most common test techniques that fall into this category are *essay-type questions, short-notes questions* and *problem-solving questions*. Let us therefore examine these in turn.

Essay-type questions

Essay-type questions are often considered to be one of the 'bluntest' instruments of assessment, having very low reliability and, in many cases, low validity. Often, in a single question, the setter attempts to test *knowledge, reasoning, written communication skills* (including English language skills, and, perhaps, graphical skills and mathematical skills), *creative thinking abilities,* and *interpretation* (not only of the question itself, but often of the implied objectives of the setter). All these factors and skills are interwoven in an extremely complicated matrix, and much is left to the judgement (or caprice!) of the marker. Even with the best of intentions, it is almost impossible to tease these skills out and mark them independently. Even when an *assessment grid* is used, thus enabling the various components of the essay to be marked independently, research has shown that inter-marker reliability is still very poor, with markers varying widely in their scoring of this kind of question. Despite this, essays do have a number of points in their favour.

(a) They give students an opportunity to organize their ideas and express them in their own words. Also, scope is provided for the demonstration of written communication skills and for the expression of unconventional and creative thinking. (These opportunities are, however, often lost when 'essays' consist simply of regurgitated class notes).

(b) They allow students to display a detailed knowledge of related aspects of the course being assessed, as well as a knowledge of relevant topics outwith the course proper.

(c) The questions are relatively easy to set.

(d) Many teachers and users of the results of assessments (eg employers) hold the opinion that student tests and examinations should contain at least an element of essay writing (except, perhaps, in mathematical subjects).

Balanced against these advantages, however, are many disadvantages, some of the main ones being listed below.

(a) Essay questions are exceedingly difficult to mark reliably, and, with only one marker, the subjective element can be considerable. The correlation between the scores of two markers for the same set of answers on different occasions is seldom sufficiently high to justify confidence. Essays are also very time-consuming to mark, especially if the marker adds comments and criticisms in order to provide feedback for the student.

(b) Only a small number of long essays can be answered in a given time, thus effectively restricting the assessment to a few (often student-selected) areas of the course content. Other equally-important areas may be completely neglected, and the total mark may therefore be an unreliable index of the student's grasp of the course as a whole. Also, in an examination which consists of a limited number of essays, luck in 'spotting' questions beforehand is often a significant factor.

(c)   Where there is a choice of questions, this enables different students to answer, in effect, different papers, so the same total mark may not represent comparable performances. This will almost certainly be the case when the questions vary in difficulty, in content, in the types of skills involved, and are scored by different markers. For example, a '5 from 8' paper contains a total of no less than 56 different combinations in which the 5 questions can be selected!

(d)   Occasionally, students may not appreciate the true intent of an essay question because of inadequate directions (eg 'Write an essay on proteins'). Markers then have the choice of ignoring the answer, accepting the student's interpretation as an answer to a question which was not intended, or adopting an uneasy compromise. Clearly, this adds neither to the reliability nor to the validity of the assessment.

(e)   Irrelevant factors often intrude into the assessment, eg speed of handwriting (especially with restricted time), style and clarity of handwriting, and grammatical errors.

Short-notes questions

In cases where 'short notes' on a subject or topic are required, rather than an extended essay, many of the problems associated with long-essay questions are reduced, although not necessarily eradicated. 'Short-notes' questions should (in principle) be more valid and reliable than essay questions, because the marker is able to concentrate more sharply on particular aspects of the answer. In addition, they allow wider coverage of course content, and are generally more specific.

However, although reliability is increased, some deviation in scores may still occur between markers. Also, course coverage may still not be adequate, and students' individual written and presentational skills may again cloud the validity of the questions.

Problem-solving questions

Problem-solving questions are an excellent method of testing some of the middle-to-higher cognitive skills (such as comprehension, application and analysis), and for demonstrating extended reasoning skills. Mathematical, scientific and engineering subjects, in particular, lend themselves readily to assessments of this sort.

With such questions, validity may well be high, but problems of reliability may arise in respect of the marking of partially-solved problems, or answers in which an error is made.

Objective Tests

Objective tests are assessment procedures which can be marked totally reliably. Although such items are often criticized on account of assessing only at low intellectual levels, this is not necessarily the case. It is possible (although more difficult) to design items to test skills in the higher cognitive areas, and even to test logical thinking and skills related to structuring arguments.

Before looking at the characteristics of specific techniques of objective testing in more detail, we will summarize the main advantages and disadvantages of using objective tests in general.

Some of the main points in favour of objective tests are listed below.

(a)   The tests can be marked with complete inter-marker reliability.
(b)   Large numbers of questions can be answered, thus ensuring a thorough sampling of course objectives and content.
(c)   Objective items can be designed to test specific abilities in a controlled way.
(d)   The difficulty of the items is often known from trial-testing. Hence, by selection of appropriate items, the difficulty level of the test can be adjusted to meet particular requirements.
(e)   Items can be 'banked' and re-used.
(f)   There is no need to provide a choice of questions for the students, and, indeed, this is not desirable, since it tends to reduce validity.
(g)   Tests lend themselves to inexpensive and easy marking, and also to thorough statistical analysis. This allows investigation of individual difficulties, and also permits the general problem areas of the student population as a whole to be identified.

Against these advantages, objective items have the following disadvantages:

(a)   They are very difficult and initially expensive to construct, and considerable preparation time is necessary. Their *apparent* ease of construction often leads to amateurish attempts, resulting in very poor, invalid terms. (This, in turn, has been responsible for some of the criticisms levelled at objective tests.) Expert advice is often required in designing items, and all items should be pre-tested in order to measure their level of difficulty and the extent to which they discriminate between the better and poorer students in a given population.
(b)   The teacher or marker cannot see the reasoning behind the choice of a wrong answer.
(c)   It is difficult or impossible to construct tests to assess certain

high-level abilities such as extended reasoning and written communication ability. Thus objective tests are probably best suited for testing lower cognitive skills, and items at these levels are certainly the easiest to write.

Let us now look at the different types of objective test items that can be used.

Multiple-choice items

Multiple-choice items are probably the most widely used component of objective tests. Several variations on the multiple-choiced theme are possible, such as when several items arise out of one situation, graph or set of figures. A number of references to sources of further information on the construction of multiple-choice items are given in the Bibliography.

The advantages and disadvantages of objective items in general (as listed above) apply in full to multiple-choice items.

An example of a multiple-choice item that is designed to test knowledge is given below:

Which city is the capital of Australia?
  (a)   Melbourne
  (b)   Brisbane
  (c)   Sydney
  (d)   Canberra

Multiple-choice objective testing has its own associated jargon, the most common terms being as follows:

Stem: the introductory part of the question out of which the alternative answers arise. Ideally this should be a self-contained question containing all the basic information which the student needs in order to respond to the item, so that he or she does not need to read through the options to discover what is being asked. The stem should be concise, should use unambiguous language appropriate to the student's ability, and should avoid negatives if at all possible.

Options: the range of possible answers. The options should be parallel in content and structure, ie they should all have the same kind of relationship to the stem, and should all follow grammatically from it. Obviously, the item should not contain clues in the structure of the options (eg mixtures of plurals and singulars).

Key: the correct answer. This must be unarguably correct; hence the option 'all of these' should never be used.

Distractors: the wrong answers. These must be unarguably incorrect answers, yet should appear plausible to weaker students.

Non-functioning distractors: those distractors which attract less than 5 per cent of the responses. When an item is re-written, an attempt should be made to replace such distractors with more plausible ones.

Facility value (FV): the fraction (normally expressed as a decimal) of the candidates choosing the key in any given item. Thus, if half the students answer correctly, the facility value for that item is 0.50. In tests of achievement designed to rank students in order of merit, the facility value should lie between 0.35 and 0.85, since very difficult or very easy items do not normally contribute to the role of such a test.

Discrimination index: a figure which represents the degree to which the item separates the better students from the poorer students, since a 'good' item (particularly in an achievement test) is one which the better students should get right and the poorer students should get wrong. There are several ways in which the discrimination index can be calculated, but one of the simplest is to calculate the difference between the facility values for the top third of the population (on the test as a whole) and for the bottom third for each item under consideration.

The discrimination index can obviously never be greater than + 1.0, and should always be greater than +0.2 for a 'good' item. A negative discrimination index is a sign of a very poor item that should be either discarded or revised.

When there is a choice of pre-tested items of known quality, the facility values and discrimination indices chosen will depend on whether the test is meant to be of a simple 'pass/fail' type, is meant to produce a meaningful class ranking, is meant to serve as a diagnostic instrument providing feedback on progress for students, or is designed to help evaluate the efficiency of a teaching/learning system.

Completion items and unique-answer questions

In both these types of assessment question, the student must *supply* the answer rather than select from a set of choices provided. Examples are given below:

Completion item: 'The United States equivalent to the British House of Commons is known as the ....'
Unique-answer question: 'What is the equivalent temperature in degrees Centigrade to 185° Fahrenheit?..........................'

In both these cases the answer is unique, and so the test can be marked reliably; it has, however, to be marked manually. In such items, skills can be examined one at a time, eg mastery skills (recall, using formulae, simple calculations, etc), organizing skills (categorizing, etc) and interpretation skills (of graphs, tables, etc). Such items can, in fact, be set at surprisingly high cognitive levels. Again, relatively full and representative coverage of course objectives and content is possible, since only very short written answers are required.

Structural communication testing

This is a fairly recent development in objective testing in which an attempt is made to carry out a reliable test of a student's ability to select relevant information from irrelevant information and to present structured arguments logically.

Basically, students are presented with a grid containing statements pertaining to a particular topic, all of which are factually correct. The grid can contain any number of statements, but 16 or 20 are typical. Students are then asked questions on the topic, to which only *some* of the statements are pertinent. The student has to select from the grid the *relevant* pieces of information to answer the question(s), and then has to *arrange them in a logical order*, in order to present the argument. Allowance in the scoring can be made if several logical sequences are permissible. In some cases, structural communication testing can be computer-marked.

Practical Tests

Practical tests are highly appropriate in cases when the development of psychomotor or manipulative skills is an important part of a course. Their main drawbacks are that they may be logistically difficult to arrange and administer, and may have low reliability. However, the face validity of actually performing a set task would seem to be high compared (for example) with giving a simple written description of how the task *should* be performed.

Let us now examine some of the most important types of practical test.

Project assessment

In such assessment, a student may be assessed in terms of his or her cumulative work over a period of time, or perhaps on only the end result of the project (such as a working model), the results of a set of experiments, or a computer program. Such assessment can also be carried out on *groups* of students who have collaborated on a group project of some sort. However, this can give rise to problems in assessing the contributions made by the different members of the group unless some form of *peer assessment* is used.

Assessment of laboratory work

In cases where the development of manipulative laboratory skills are important (eg in science courses), assessment of actual laboratory work may be carried out. This usually takes the form of continuous assessment over a period of time or a one-off practical examination at the end of a course or section thereof. The latter has the disadvantage that it may be unfair to students who have an 'off-day', and also to students who react badly to exam pressure but have otherwise performed well during the course. From the marker's point of view, it can also be exceedingly difficult to monitor the progress of even a small number of students effectively during such an examination.

Skill tests

Tests of the ability to carry out specific manipulative tasks may be important in some courses, eg dismantling and reassembling a car engine, cutting hair in a particular way, or repairing a piece of technical equipment. For each of these, a suitable practical test can generally be devised, depending on the circumstances. Such tests are more common in 'training' courses than in general educational courses, however.

Situational assessment

Procedures of this type stem originally from management education, and involve the appraisal of complex decision-making skills. They may involve the student in performing such activities as dictating letters, dealing with personnel problems, formulating agendas, and dealing with budgets or financial problems. The situations that are used in such assessment are normally simulated, and a whole range of activities and crises can be 'built in' to arise in the same way as they might in the real world. Such an approach is often called an *'in-tray'* exercise.

Again, the validity of such a technique would appear to be high, but care must be taken in marking the performance in order to ensure reasonable reliability. To this end, a checklist containing the objectives under assessment provides a useful guide for the marker.

Unobtrusive Assessment

Unobtrusive techniques involve the students being observed and assessed without their prior knowledge. Such techniques can be important in assessing a student's *commitment* and *attitudes* to work, rather than simply his ability to perform tasks under the controlled conditions of more formal assessment. They can, therefore, be more valid than (for example) written examinations, which invariably contain a large element of artificiality. On some occasions, video techniques are used for recording student performance, and for subsequent analysis and assessment of personal skills and traits. However, there are often considerable logistical problems in operating such an approach, not to mention the obvious doubts over the ethics of unobtrusive assessment.

LEARNING AND ASSESSMENT: A CRITICAL OVERVIEW

The various kinds of assessment discussed so far in this chapter have one thing in common: they all, in one way or another, involve assessment being 'done to' the learner. They all depend on the skills and objectivity of assessors and the designers of assessment devices and instruments. We have tried to indicate ways that assessment can be made reliable, valid, practical, and fair and useful.

In Chapter 1, we included a model of learning based on 'wanting', 'doing', 'feedback' and 'digesting'. In this critical overview, we would like to reflect on the dangers of many traditional assessment methods. We then wish to present some ideas showing how self-assessment and peer-assessment can not only provide ways of escaping from these dangers, but can also provide deep, valuable learning experiences for learners.

Let us look first at the conflicts between the most commonly used form of assessment, (the timed, written examination), and the natural processes by which people learn that we introduced at the end of Chapter 1.

■ **Wanting to learn (motivation).**
Not many people like exams! The fact that there is an exam coming along at the end of the road is not the strongest motivator for most people. The inevitability of traditional forms of assessment is a key factor in preventing many people from participating in learning. Assessment processes are at cross purposes with learning processes.

■ **Learning by *doing* (practice, learning from mistakes and so on).**
Learning by doing can indeed happen during assessments, including written exams. Mistakes are indeed made during assessment – plenty of them! But learning by doing *while being assessed* is hardly the best way of using experiential learning. Besides, it is usually presumed that the learning should have taken place *before* the assessment event. Again, assessment processes are at cross purposes with learning processes.

■ **Learning through *feedback* (to develop positive *feelings* about the learning).**
All assessment results in some sort of feedback. However, it is often the absolute minimum of feedback – for example a mere score – and even then weeks or months after the event. There is usually little or no real feedback, and chances to learn from the feedback are minimal. Once more, assessment processes are at cross purposes with learning processes.

■ *Digesting* **(taking stock, making sense of the experience and of the feedback).**
Exams are better known for producing *indigestion* than for allowing

people the chance to consolidate their learning. As we have already suggested, the feedback is usually very limited in scope (and often delayed in time) and is not a useful means towards 'digesting'. Such feedback as there is tends to be one-way. There is little or no chance to discuss the details or negotiate what best to do next. Yet again, assessment processes are at cross purposes with learning processes.

Perhaps traditional forms of assessment have only one real contribution towards learning – people are frightened (shamed) into doing some learning so that they may minimize their chances of being shown to be 'lacking'. Much intensive learning is done just before exams, but most of it is of a superficial nature and soon forgotten again. We would next like to present a series of concerns about traditional assessment processes, and to give some suggestions about how these concerns may be addressed, particularly pointing towards the use of self-assessment and peer-assessment, which we consider in detail later in this chapter.

1. *Assessment is often done in a rush, to meet exam board deadlines. It is rarely carried out under the best of conditions!*

    This is because assessment tends to be done *to* learners, not *by* them. Assessment tends to be done at the end of learning something, rather than as a means to help the learning processes. In public exams, examiners often face piles of some hundreds of scripts, which all need to be finished within only a week or two.

    Two ways to improve the situation are as follows:

    - allow much more time for assessment, so that it can be done well.
    - allow learners to use self- and peer-assessment, so they can learn by assessing.

2. *Assessment is often done by bored people, tired of reading the same answers to the same questions (and seeing the same mistakes).*

    Examiners get thoroughly fed-up as they wade through hundreds of scripts. They get discouraged when they see things they hoped their learners would have mastered, only to find that messages have not got across. Any tedious or repetitive task causes people to change their mood. If assessors' moods plunge, the objectivity of assessment is likely to be affected accordingly.

    Two ways to improve the situation are as follows:

    - decrease the emphasis on traditional written exams altogether.
    - allow *learners* to learn by reading their own mistakes and those of their peers.

3. *Assessment tends to be governed by 'what is easy to assess'. Therefore, traditional written exams (relatively straightforward to assess) are used. These measure learners' skills at tackling traditional written exams.*

There is still not enough attention being paid to what should constitute the *evidence* upon which to base awards. Many important competences are simply not assessable by traditional methods. While it is perfectly possible to use traditional methods to measure recall of facts and information, it is not at all easy to use such methods to measure innovation, judgement, or personality. Figure 7.2 shows an overhead transparency which works well in alerting students to the various agendas that may be served by traditional exams.

Two ways to improve the situation are as follows:

- look carefully at exactly what is being measured by each form of assessment.
- refrain from measuring the same things all the time, especially recall. People who can *find* and *apply* information are usually more valuable than people who simply happen to remember a lot of it.

How much you know?
How much you don't know?
How fast you can write?
How good your memory is?
How much work you did the night before?
How well you keep your cool?
How competent you are?
How well you can read the questions?
How good you are at answering exam questions?
How practised you are at answering exam questions?
How you perform under pressure?
How good you are at time management?
How well you can keep addressing the question?
How often you've practised on similar questions?
How well you read your own answers?

Figure 7.2 **What do exams really measure?**

4. *Learners rarely know the intimate details of the assessment criteria and how examiners interpret them.*

    There really is no excuse for this. The *reason* may be sinister – that those who design the assessment criteria are not sufficiently confident about them to show them to the learners. Assessors often fear that learners may demand to know 'why did I get 65 per cent for this, when my friend got 75 per cent?' Surely, they have every right to ask this sort of question – and to learn from the feedback they should be given by way of a response. An even more sinister fear could be that learners knowing the criteria may score 100 per cent. In many subject areas, examiners are extremely reluctant to award full marks, often giving only 80 per cent for a really excellent performance. However, such behaviour is in direct contradiction to the principles of formulating objectives and competence descriptors. Surely, learners who achieve all the objectives *deserve* 100 per cent? Or is it that there remains a 'hidden agenda' of unrevealed objectives?

    Two ways to improve the situation are as follows:

    - help learners to feel that they know all the 'rules of the game', and to believe that they can indeed *completely* achieve stated objectives, or demonstrate stated competences
    - give learners the opportunity not only to see the intimate details of assessment criteria, but also to *use* the criteria.

5. *How should we develop learners' unassessable qualities? Should we refrain from developing them because we can't measure them?*

    'Don't bother to learn anything, when you can't see how they can ask you about it at the end of the day': this is a perfectly rational view taken by learners, deciding what to learn and what not to learn.

    Two ways to improve the situation are as follows:

    - bring the unassessable qualities firmly onto the agenda. Formulate clear descriptors of the competences which learners need to be able to demonstrate, even when it is not possible to measure these particular competences systematically
    - explain to learners why they are important, and work out with learners what kinds of *evidence* can be linked to these qualities and how the demonstration of that evidence can be built in to assessment procedures.

6. *Almost all assessment processes in common use foster learner competition rather than collaboration. No wonder our educated people are so bad at working in teams.*

    Learners preparing for exams are often quite secretive about the work they do. No one likes to be thought of as 'a swot'!

However, it is more sinister than this: we actually *compound* the competition by using norm-referenced assessment far too much. In other words, only a certain proportion of learners are allowed to receive 'A' grades, or first class honours degree classifications. Therefore, learners *are* in competition.

Two ways to improve the situation are as follows:

- use criterion-referenced assessment only – abolish the use of norm-referencing
- help learners to feel that they can help each other prepare to demonstrate their competence without disadvantaging one another.

7. *What competences are measured by assessment anyway? Are they 'can do' competences? Or are they simply 'did do, once' ghosts?*

Exams tend to measure 'did once' competences. At their worst, they still tend to measure 'knew once' competences rather than 'did once' competences.

Two ways to improve the situation are as follows:

- increase the proportion of assessment schedules allocated to continuous assessment – which measures 'is doing' competences rather than 'did once' ones
- involve the learners in self-assessment and peer-assessment, both of which allow them time to reflect on their own performance.

8. *If we were to introduce a set of guidelines defining 'Quality of Assessment' what should the criteria look like? What evidence of competence should assessors demonstrate?*

At present, it is automatically assumed that anyone appointed to a post involving teaching, lecturing or training is blessed with all the skills needed to design assessment schemes and implement fair assessment. People are usually appointed to teaching (and assessing) posts not on the basis of how well they can do either task, but often on the record of their own academic performance.

Two ways to improve the situation are as follows:

- assess the assessors. Have a system of 'licences' to assess, and police the system thoroughly
- increase the uses of self-assessment and peer-assessment, which depend far less on subjectivity of assessors and allow far greater amounts of feedback to contribute towards successful learning experiences.

9. *'If you can't measure it, it doesn't exist. If you can measure it, it isn't it'. What should we be trying to measure?*

It has been said that one of the main faults of our education and training systems is that we tend to teach people things that are already understood, instead of equipping them to understand new things. Assessment reflects this. Moves towards expressing competences in terms of performance indicators are a positive step on the path towards ensuring that important things are placed on the assessment agenda in an appropriate way, even when they can not be directly measured by traditional assessment devices.

Two ways to improve the situation are as follows:

- use self- and peer-assessment as an inherent part of *learning* processes, with the emphasis on learning rather than assessment outcomes
- help learners themselves to formulate the assessment criteria, giving them a sense of ownership of the assessment agenda.

10. *Whose fault is it that assessment is so artificial? Heads of department in universities and schools? Employers? Assessors themselves? Validators? External moderators? The government? Yours? Ours?*

If one implies that there is something suspect about people's abilities to assess, it is badly received. Assessment is something that is usually done privately rather than publicly, and people go to great lengths to ensure that they retain privacy. Is not such privacy really needed mainly because of the prevalence of the 'put down the number you first thought of' syndrome?

Two ways to improve the situation are as follows:

- be brave! Experiment with assessment design
- talk to colleagues about the limitations of traditional assessment methods and ask them to help you monitor the objectivity of assessment methods you use (and volunteer to help them do the same).

SELF- AND PEER-ASSESSMENT – LEARNING BY ASSESSING

Close Encounters with Assessment Criteria

This is the crucial difference between formal assessment and self- and peer-assessment. Learners find out a lot about any subject simply by applying assessment criteria to examples of work in that subject (whether the examples are self-generated, made by other learners, or issued by a teacher). Previously, assessment criteria have seemed to learners to be the property of examiners. There has been a tendency for teachers to regard assessment criteria as quite private. Even where model answers and marking schemes have been required to be sent to external examiners or moderators, the vital information in such schemes has seldom been shared with learners, and until recently hardly ever *applied* by learners themselves. Yet when learners get the chance to get their hands on assessment criteria, they seem to develop a thirst for the information they can derive from them, leading to much deeper learning.

Self-assessment and peer-assessment are not just self-testing. These forms of assessment when well-developed involve two processes:

- involving learners in identifying standards or criteria to apply to their work
- allowing learners to make judgements about the extent to which they have met these standards and criteria.

Assessment Criteria: Black and White or Shades of Grey?

In subjects like maths, science and engineering, things are often either right or wrong and it is relatively easy to devise assessment criteria for tests and exercises. However, even in subjects such as law or social studies, there are identifiable *hallmarks* of a good or an unsatisfactory answer to a question. Such hallmarks can be turned into checklists of a flexible kind, which enable the characteristics of good and less-good answers to be compared and contrasted. Students can benefit by learning in the act of applying assessment criteria to their own work and each other's work.

There are significant benefits to learners in becoming closely involved in using assessment criteria. Learners can quickly find out about incorrect assumptions they have been making. They are able to find out the answer to the question: 'What am I expected to become able to do?' There are, of course, many more benefits, depending on *how* we involve learners in using assessment criteria – including helping learners themselves to formulate the criteria (when this is possible or appropriate) – leading to the most obvious form of ownership of assessment.

Some Examples of Self- and Peer-assessment Mechanisms

Self-assessment is not confined to the variety that is widely used in open and distance learning (though of course that is one powerful form of it). Self-assessment processes can include any of the following:

- providing learners with assessment criteria and a marking scheme and allowing them to mark their own work
- as above, but then allowing learners the chance to compare *their* mark with that of a 'professional' marker

- as above, but *also* giving learners feedback about the *quality* of their self-assessment
- enabling individual learners to generate assessment criteria and use them to assess their own work
- enabling a group of learners to generate assessment criteria and so on
- allowing learners to use *core* criteria generated by a group, plus *additional* criteria specific to their own pieces of work, with an agreed weighting
- groups of learners can be issued with criteria to apply to each other's work
- groups of learners could *produce* criteria and apply them to each other's work.

There are further combinations of these. There is also the additional matter of whether the grades or scores contribute in a formal way to the performance records of learners.

Eliciting Assessment Criteria from a Group

The following approach gives useful results with groups of 10–20 people:

- ask each learner to *privately* list, for example, six things you would expect of a good 'x' (where 'x' could be essay or presentation or handout and so on)
- ask learners to go to groups of three or four and discuss criteria
- ask the *groups* to make a list of criteria and to *prioritize* them
- put on a flipchart the most important criteria from each group, then the next most important, etc
- ask the whole group whether anything important is missing from the flipchart list
- tidy up the flipcharted items if necessary, for example, and number them, 1–8
- ask each learner to privately distribute (say, 20) 'marks' among the criteria
- write each learner's 'mark' alongside each criterion on the flipchart. Then either average them out, or allow each learner to apply his or her own weightings in the peer assessments to follow
- allow learners to prepare the task (individuals or groups)
- produce for them a grid with *their* criteria and weightings, ready for peer assessment (see Figure 7.3 for a typical grid structure).

Learners' Ownership of Assessment Criteria

The sort of peer-assessment described above is suitable for tasks such as presentations, where many people can assess the same piece of evidence and where scores can then be compared and discussed by

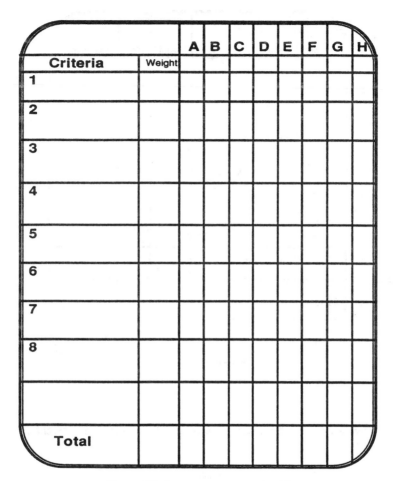

Figure 7.3 **A peer-assessment grid**

the group. For individual tasks such as essays, reports, projects, dissertations and so on, it is likely that each piece of work will reflect slightly different criteria (or even *very* different criteria) and then it is often best to allow for some 'agreed' criteria and some 'idiosyncratic' criteria so that each learner can exercise more ownership of the assessment criteria. An example of a grid that can be adapted for such purposes is shown in Figure 7.4.

The most important outcome of involving learners in the formation of self-assessment or peer-assessment criteria is that learners address the task with criteria in their minds, and the quality of their work seems to be much higher than it may otherwise have been.

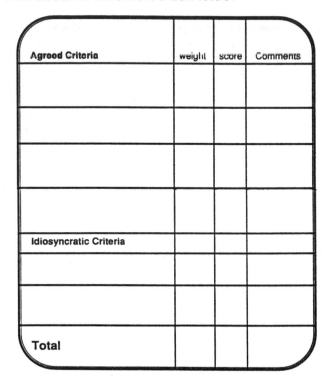

Agreed Criteria	weight	score	Comments
Idiosyncratic Criteria			
Total			

Figure 7.4 **A self-assessment grid, using agreed and idiosyncratic criteria**

How Well can Students Assess Themselves and Each Other?

In general, students are quite accurate in their assessing. It has been found that when students are asked to 'guess' their own performance scores just after completing an exam, around 90 per cent of students 'guess' within 5 per cent of their actual scores. It is useful to identify the 10 per cent who had an inaccurate perception of how they had done – they usually benefit from a discussion to probe the causes. Those 10 per cent may be over-anxious and underestimating their achievements, or over-confident and over-estimating their achievements. When discrepancies in self-assessment occur, they are usually due to one of the following causes:

■ there is some tendency for learners to over-rate themselves in areas to which they are new; this tends to happen with the weaker members of a group
■ there is a tendency for some learners to under-rate themselves in areas in which they are experienced; this tends to happen with the more skilled members of the group.

Peer-assessment and self-assessment can be usefully combined. Peer-assessment can be conducted 'blind' so that 'arranged' scoring is avoided. If the peer-assessment mark or grade is equal to the corresponding self-assessment mark (eg within 5 per cent) then the self-assessment marks go forward into the assessment system, possibly with a staff 'scan' to ensure that fair play is in operation. (It is far quicker to *scan* a piece of work to check whether the assessment is fair, than it is to *mark* the work from scratch.) When self- and peer-scores differ, negotiation or staff intervention may be necessary, but this happens surprisingly rarely in practice.

Self- and Peer-Assessment and the Processes of Learning

Earlier in this chapter, we looked critically at the mismatches between traditional formal assessment (exams) and the processes by which people learn. Let us end this analysis of the benefits of self- and peer-assessment by repeating the same approach.

- **Wanting to learn (motivation).**
Motivation can be improved by early success. Self-assessment in particular can be used with the comfort of privacy, and learners can gain confidence by finding that they are 'doing alright' long before they need to prove so publicly or formally.

- **Learning by *doing* (practice, learning from mistakes and so on).**
There is no better way to find out about one's successes and failures than by finding them out for oneself, or having a peer help one do this, rather than an 'authority figure' like a tutor or examiner. The very act of assessing is intrinsically 'learning by doing' – it involves the application of criteria, decision-making, judgement and reflection.

- **Learning through *feedback* (to develop positive *feelings* about the learning).**
The worst factor of formal assessment has to be the dreadfully limited feedback that is the norm. Peer-assessment can allow for a great deal of feedback – far more than could ever be given by a tutor or assessor. In addition, the feedback gained in peer-assessment is usually far less threatening than that from 'professional' assessors. Indeed, peers will often argue and debate issues, further deepening the usefulness of the feedback exchanges they receive.

- *Digesting* **(taking stock, making sense of the experience and of the feedback).**
Both self-assessment and peer-assessment can help learners to make sense of their learning experiences and of the feedback they gain. Furthermore, the time lag between the learning and the feedback can be much less than with traditional methods of assessment. Therefore,

the feedback is much more actively received and the learning thereby enhanced.

Conclusions on Self- and Peer-assessment

It can be argued that people who need a 'tester' are inadequately prepared to be sent out into the world outside. Self- and peer-assessment can both be an important part of the learning process. The learning experience resulting from such forms of assessment is more important than the result of the assessment. Self- or peer-assessment do not necessarily have to lead to any 'formal' (recorded) assessment. The aim can be to serve purely as a learning experience, with the 'marks' simply part of the process through which that experience is facilitated.

Self-assessment and peer-assessment are skills, and become more reliable with practice. Receiving feedback on the quality of these forms of assessment is vital if learners are to derive the maximum benefit from engaging in them. 'Ownership' is the most crucial aspect of successful learning, and both self- and peer-assessment are closely connected to the development of ownership of learning.

Self-assessment and peer-assessment should be introduced early, for example during the first term rather than being left until the final year. Late in a course, students may see little point in embracing new ways of learning. Not all students warm to the 'exposure' of self- or peer-assessment. They may begin their studies with expectations that they will be assessed by professionals. 'What's in it for me?', they naturally may ask. They need to be convinced that self- and peer-assessment have direct benefits for themselves, and do not represent an abdication from duties on the part of tutors. Some tutors, however, feel it is dangerous to 'lose control' of assessment. If such tutors try to employ self- or peer-assessment, but constantly safeguard their right to step in 'should things go wrong', the whole concept of such forms of assessment is undermined.

CONCLUSIONS

In the final analysis, the quality of education and training depends upon the quality of the assessment devices and processes which are in due course used to accredit learners and trainees for their achievement of the planned objectives or demonstrations of the intended competences. In this chapter, we have reviewed a range of assessment devices and processes, each lending itself to particular sorts of competences or objectives. We have emphasized the value of assessment not only being valid and reliable, but also providing learners themselves with useful learning experiences and valuable feedback on their efforts. Since each type of assessment device has its own limitations and practicalities, we conclude that the most sensible strategy is to employ a *battery* of several different forms of assessment, both to give learners the opportunity to experience different ways of demonstrating the competences they develop and to avoid learners who happen to be poor at one particular form of assessment (we are thinking here of formal examinations in particular) from being penalized unduly.

Chapter 8

Evaluation

INTRODUCTION

In the previous chapter, we distinguished between assessment and evaluation by describing the former as those activities that are designed to measure *student learning* achieved as a result of a teaching/learning situation, and the latter as a series of activities that are designed to measure the *effectiveness of a teaching/learning system* as a whole.

Mary Thorpe (1988) gives the following definition of evaluation:

> Evaluation is the collection, analysis and interpretation of information about any aspect of a programme of education or training, as part of a recognized process of judging its effectiveness, its efficiency and any other outcomes it may have.

Commenting on the above definition, Derek Rowntree (1992) offers the following:

1. Evaluation is NOT just another word for assessment. The quality of our learners' learning may well be one of the outcomes we need to evaluate. But many other factors may be equally worth looking at.
2. Mary Thorpe's phrase 'any other outcomes' reminds us that evaluation is concerned with what happens rather than merely with what was meant to happen. It should be capable of picking up the unexpected – eg unwanted side effects or interesting new possibilities.
3. By 'a recognised process' she means that evaluation needs to be planned, systematic and openly discussed. Evaluation is not just keeping records or writing a final report. It is a public commitment to purposeful enquiry.

Whatever forms evaluation may take, the results of student assessment may well form part of the wider evaluation process.

Within the systematic approach to instructional design which was described in Chapter 1 and which is argued for throughout this book, the role of on-going monitoring and evaluation of the system is of vital importance to its development and evolution. Because of the cyclical and interactive nature of the systems approach, each cycle can benefit from the experiences and feedback obtained from previous cycles. Evaluative feedback can be gained from a wide range of sources and via a wide range of methods, and, in many cases, a whole battery of evaluation techniques are used in order to gain an overall view of the effectiveness of the instructional system in question. Whether this is a complete course, part of a course, a particular teaching session, a self-contained programme, or a teaching aid such as a film or video, the designer (or team of designers) should never be happy with their first attempt, or even with revised versions. If one takes the view that 'the system can always be improved', on-going evaluation should always be an integral part of the design process.

The scope and depth of the evaluation that is carried out in any particular case will vary according to the nature of the situation, as, indeed, will the evaluation methods used. Whatever the circumstances, however, the importance of using evaluation procedures to monitor the instructional system should shed light on the appropriateness of the *teaching methods* used, the *structure* adopted, the *implementation strategy*, the *assessment methods* and even the *aims and objectives* themselves. With each successive cycle of the system, the teaching/learning situation should become progressively more finely 'tuned', and should consequently become *more efficient* and *more effective* through a continuous process of evolution and improvement.

In this chapter, we will first describe more fully the philosophy that underlies the role of evaluation in the evolution of instructional processes. In order to do this, we will adopt the basic 'error elimination' approach advocated by the philosopher Karl Popper and adapt it for use in the on-going development of instructional systems. We will then describe two contrasting paradigms (or models) of evaluation – one of which concentrates mainly on the *outcomes* of an instructional system (the *agricultural/botanical* or *scientific approach*), and one which pays more attention to what happens during the educational process itself (the *social/anthropological* or *illuminative approach*). Finally, we will review the range of diagnostic techniques which are commonly used as part of an evaluation strategy, and discuss the evaluation of cost-effectiveness.

INSTRUCTIONAL DEVELOPMENT BY ERROR ELIMINATION – A 'POPPERIAN' APPROACH

The philosopher Karl Popper originally used the concept of 'error elimination' to explain how progress is made in developing scientific theories. The same concept can be applied to the logical development and improvement of instructional systems of all kinds. (See the Bibliography for details of Karl Popper's work.)

Underlying Rationale

The 'error elimination' approach to the development of instructional systems is based on two assumptions: first, that the instructional system is not an independent entity, justifying its existence *a priori,* but is part of a total system – fulfilling a specific function by helping to get from Situation A to Situation B as in the diagram below:

Situation A		Situation B
Students thought capable of achieving certain objectives, but lacking some or all of the necessary knowledge, skills and attitudes	➤ Instructional system designed to supply all or part of the necessary education and/or training ➤	Qualified people who have achieved the specified objectives, and can proceed to the next stage of education or training (or take their place in society)

The second assumption is that the development and improvement of the instructional system can most effectively be tackled by adopting the general methodological approach proposed by Karl Popper, an approach that can be summarized by the following schema:

P_1	TS	EE	P_2
initial problem situation	*trial solution*	*error elimination*	*new problem situation*
(identification of need for the instructional system)	(development and operation of the instructional system)	(looking for ways in which the instructional system is failing to achieve its objectives)	(identification of areas in which the instructional system could be improved)

Stages in the Development of an Instructional System

We can see that there are four general stages in the above approach.

Stage 1: the identification of the initial 'problem situation' (P_1)

This itself can be seen as having three sequential stages:

(a) Identification of the desired objectives (knowledge, skills and attitudes) – let us call those X.

(b) Identification of the relevant knowledge, skills and attitudes already possessed by the prospective students – let us call these Y.

(c) Identification of the objectives represented by X-Y, the gap to be bridged by the instructional system.

Stage 2: development and operation of the instructional system (TS)

This falls into two sub-stages:

(a) Designing an instructional system capable of achieving the objectives represented by X-Y (or at least part of the difference). This involves developing the overall structure, selecting and sequencing the content, choosing appropriate teaching methods, and so on.

(b) Making appropriate administrative arrangements to put the instructional system into operation (ie implementation of the system).

Stage 3: the 'error elimination' process (EE)

This stage involves carrying out a *critical analysis* of stages 1 and 2. It is the key stage in Popper's methodology, according to which a new instructional system can be regarded in the same way as a new scientific theory which has been developed in an attempt to resolve a specific problem situation, but which has not yet been subjected to rigorous experimental testing. According to Popper, such a theory should be tested not by trying to prove it *right* (an impossible task from a logical point of view) but by trying to prove it *wrong*, ie by looking for specific ways in which the theory can be shown to be incompatible with experimental evidence. In the case of a new instructional system, the testing should be carried out not by trying to prove that it is succeeding in achieving its objectives (a very difficult task to do with any degree of rigour) but by looking for ways in which it is manifestly *not* succeeding (a much easier task). Needless to say, such an approach requires a healthy attitude towards criticism that is sometimes lacking in those who develop and operate educational and training courses; all too often, these try to defend their course against criticism by contrived arguments and rationalization rather than accepting valid criticism and attempting to rectify the situation through improvements to the instructional system.

Stage 4: identification of the new 'problem situation' (P₂)

If carried out correctly, stage 3 should reveal areas in which the instructional system needs to be improved, and (hopefully) point to how these improvements might be carried out. It therefore leads to a new problem situation, P_2, that can form the starting point of a further development cycle.

$$P_2 \longrightarrow TS \longrightarrow EE \longrightarrow P_3$$

Thus, Popper's methodology is seen to be both open-ended and on-going, forming a basis for the continuous development of instructional systems of all types.

How the Error Elimination Process may be Carried Out

There are two basic questions that should be asked of an instructional system:

1. Are there any ways in which the instructional system is manifestly failing to achieve its design objectives?
2. Are there any ways in which the organization and logistics of the instructional system are unsatisfactory?

Finding answers to question 1 is essentially a long-term process and can be done:

(a) by surveying students who have undergone the instructional system (ie former students); and
(b) by surveying people who are not directly involved in the instructional system under scrutiny, but who nevertheless may have relevant comments and observations, eg employers who subsequently take on the students, or the teachers and organizers of any subsequent courses or training situations to which the students proceed.

Finding answers to question 2 is usually easier, and can be done:

(a) by surveying the staff who are involved in implementing the instructional system; and
(b) by surveying the students who are involved in the system.

Techniques through which the above information can be obtained are reviewed later in this chapter.

TWO CONTRASTING PARADIGMS OF EVALUATION

A major area of debate in educational evaluation is concerned with the relative merits of two distinctly contrasting approaches. On the one hand, there is the so-called *agricultural/botanical approach*, which reflects a 'scientific' approach to evaluation; on the other, there is the *social/anthropological approach*, which is more concerned with the hidden *processes* which occur during an educational experience. The latter approach has become known as *illuminative evaluation*.

The *agricultural/botanical approach* has its origins in scientific experiments set up to assess the effects of specific variables (the nature of the soil, fertilizers, etc) on the growth of crops. Such experiments have tight controls, and the resulting outcomes can be measured relatively easily. When applied to education, this approach has led to the use of systematic, objectives-oriented evaluation procedures. This 'traditional' strategy sets out to measure the extent to which a given instructional system has achieved certain specific goals (its objectives) in relation to the students' pre-knowledge or existing skills. To this extent, the agricultural/botanical evaluation approach measures *output* against *input*, and often treats the differences statistically. Other factors in the system, such as the learning environment, teaching personnel, course content and structure, and teaching methods, normally receive only incidental examination, if they are considered at all. This general approach has been used when measuring the relative efficiency of different methods in teaching towards a common end, and also to measure the effectiveness of self-instructional programmes in achieving stated objectives.

By comparison, the *social/anthropological approach* is more concerned with studying the on-going process of education, and, in general, the techniques used are far more subjective and often involve personal value judgements of the results. The arguments in favour of this type of approach are that the variables in educational developments cannot be readily identified or controlled, and that 'inputs' and 'outputs' can be varied, complex, difficult to specify with certainty, and often virtually impossible to measure. In such cases, the evaluator explores the perceptions, opinions and attitudes of staff and students, using a variety of methods, in an attempt to reveal what was otherwise hidden in the educational process. The evaluation process is generally not rigidly structured or constrained, and usually gives the evaluator scope to follow up specific areas of interest as and when they become apparent. Illuminative evaluation of this kind has been referred to as 'attempting to open up the black box of the educational process'. Malcolm Parlett and David Hamilton, amongst others, have been influential in presenting the case for a greater emphasis on illuminative evaluation. (See the Bibliography.)

These two basic paradigms of evaluation differ significantly both in their methodologies and in their treatment of results. They also differ in their focus. The agricultural/botanical approach is basically designed to find out if *specified goals* have been achieved. The social/anthropological approach, on the other hand, is more flexible, and is designed to find out *what* has been achieved and *why*.

Clearly, there must be some middle ground between what, on the one hand, purports to be a purely objective approach, and the largely subjective approach that is embodied in illuminative evaluation. Where the correct balance lies, however, depends to a large extent on what is being evaluated, and for what purpose. A useful review of how appropriate evaluation strategies can be matched with different types of educational development has been given by Tony Becher (1981) – see the Bibliography for details.

A REVIEW OF EVALUATION TECHNIQUES

There is no *single* correct way to conduct an evaluation exercise. One may, for example, be looking for outcomes (whether intended or not) in cognitive, affective and skills areas, and also for an insight into possible problems concerning the implementation and operation of an instructional system. Much depends also on whether one is adopting an 'illuminative' strategy or a more rigid 'objectives-based' approach.

Because of the variety of information that one may be seeking during an evaluation, it is normally advisable to use an appropriate *battery* of evaluation techniques. Some of the possible information sources are listed below:

(a)   Results from student assessment.
(b)   Student questionnaires and interviews.
(c)   Observations of the instructional system in progress.
(d)   Feedback from teaching staff directly involved with the instructional system.
(e)   Feedback from people having an indirect link with the instructional system.

Each of these approaches generally has an important part to play, regardless of whether the evaluation is of a course or unit of teaching that is still in the process of development (*formative evaluation*) or of a fully-developed instructional system that is ready for use (*summative evaluation*).

Let us look at each of these sources in more detail.

Results from Student Assessment

When an instructional system has sharply-defined objectives, a critical study of the results obtained from student assessment (as described in the previous chapter) can be of great assistance in the error elimination process described above. Two basic techniques can be used.

Analysis of student assessments that form a part of the instructional system

When student assessments are an integral part of a course or other instructional system, the results of and trends indicated by these assessments can usually shed considerable light on the operation of the system as a whole. The evaluator should, as a result, be able to judge which objectives are being well achieved, and, more importantly, which objectives are *not*. When students do not perform as well as expected, there is a traditional tendency to conclude that it is basically the fault of the students. This may occasionally be the case, but, more often than not, there are other factors involved. A systematic approach to instructional design allows *all* aspects of the system to be analysed, and may reveal that there are in fact a number of reasons for unsatisfactory student achievement, for example:

(a) the teaching methods were not well matched to the course objectives;
(b) there were problems in the operation of the instructional system;
(c) the assessment methods used were not suitable;
(d) the objectives themselves were not realistic.

Critical analysis of this sort allows the instructional system to be continuously monitored and progressively 'tuned'.

Analysis of student assessments carried out solely for evaluation purposes

When an instructional package of some sort is being trial tested, or when the relative effectiveness of two methods is being measured, specially designed student assessment techniques can be used to evaluate the effectiveness of the *methods* involved, rather than to assess the *students* themselves. Such approaches are normally essentially 'agricultural/botanical' in nature, and often involve the use of pre- and post-tests, 'control' groups, and statistical analysis of differences. They are one of the standard methods of evaluating new systems, techniques, packages, etc.

Student Questionnaires and Interviews

Obtaining feedback from students regarding their experiences and their opinions of an instructional system is one of the most common approaches to evaluation. The information can be sought through *questionnaires* and/or *interviews*, and can be treated either objectively or in a more illuminative manner. Student feedback can be obtained through a variety of so-called 'self-reporting' techniques. Several of these have been adopted from the field of attitude measurement. Let us now examine some of the more important of these techniques.

Likert scales

Essentially, a Likert rating scale is an attitude measurement instrument consisting of a list of statements, the person responding having to make a judgement on each statement, often selecting one response from a number of degrees of agreement and disagreement. A typical example is shown below.

The number of points on the scale depends on the specific requirements of the setter, although the use of an even number of

	Strongly agree	Agree	Disagree	Strongly disagree
1. I find the course easy				
2. The course contains too many lectures				
etc				

options has the advantage of making it impossible for students to 'duck the issues' by repeatedly taking refuge in a completely neutral category.

In practice, it is harder to produce 'good' statements than it first appears, and some trial testing of the statements may well be necessary. Indeed, there is a fair amount of skill associated with preparing statements which are *valid* and which, at the same time, provide good discrimination.

Likert scales can be used to monitor students' general opinions of an instructional system. It is also possible to use such statements for comparative purposes, eg by pre- and post-testing the students, or by comparing an 'experimental' group with a matched 'control' group.

Semantic differential scales

This is another type of attitude scale, and it can be used to measure connotations of any given concept for an individual. Here, word pairs of antonyms such as 'valuable/worthless' are joined by a 3, 4, 5, 6 or 7 point scale. The method is based upon the premise that the word pairs are opposites, although this may not always be valid in practice, because particular words sometimes have different meanings for different students. Part of a typical semantic differential scale of the type used in course evaluation is shown below.

I consider the course to be: (mark appropriate box on each row of scale)

easy							difficult
inflexible							flexible
too theoretical							too applied
poorly structured							well structured

Objectives rating scales

Student ratings of the degree of achievement of learning objectives is sometimes used in student feedback questionnaires. Here, the objectives of an instructional system are listed, and the student is asked to indicate whether each objective has been 'well achieved' through to 'not achieved at all'. The rating is generally carried out using a five-point scale, but variations are possible. This type of scale is particularly useful in cases where no other suitable technique exists for measuring the achievement of certain objectives, or as a cross-check on other evaluation techniques.

Free student comments

If students are allowed to respond freely on topics raised in a questionnaire, unexpected outcomes and attitudes may often emerge. Although it may be difficult to categorize free responses, these should normally be sought as a matter of principle, since they can often add a completely new dimension to an evaluation.

Some ways of using questionnaires

There are several ways in which questionnaires can be used, each with its advantages and drawbacks. Some of the techniques for using questionnaires include:

- privately by individual teachers or trainers, who design their own questionnaires and interpret the findings privately. This can be useful for 'intimate' feedback about lecturing, tutorials and so on
- 'short and often, rather than long and once': any feedback form should be short enough not to bore or alienate learners. A good guide may be that it should be possible for a group to complete the form in a few minutes or so. This means separate forms for lectures, tutorials, learning modules, laboratory work and so on
- formative as well as summative: we recommend seeking feedback during a programme, so that something can still be done about matters emerging. Feedback after completion of a programme is still useful, but is not seen by learners as so valuable as when they have the chance to suggest changes they themselves will benefit from directly.

Some advantages and limitations of questionnaire feedback

Questionnaires can be very useful to gather feedback on a wide range of issues, from the quality of teaching and learning situations, to the effectiveness of learning resource materials. Some of the advantages of using questionnaires are as follows:

- they can be used anonymously, allowing learners the chance at least of giving negative feedback without the embarrassment of giving it publicly

- they can be quick to administer, enabling feedback on many things to be gathered in a few minutes
- they are amenable to statistical analysis. However, there is always the possibility to taking the statistics too far. For example, if 84 per cent of the learners are 'highly satisfied' with a series of lectures, it is quite possible that the other 16 per cent have a serious concern that is well worth looking into
- they can be used on a 'deeper' level. It is possible, for example, to get learners to go through a questionnaire twice. The first time they respond as they feel, the second time they respond as they would *like* to feel. This can help to get over the problem of different learners preferring different things. The 'gap' between 'how it is' and 'how you'd like it to be' is often more important – and more revealing – than learners' reactions to 'how it is'

Some limitations of the use of questionnaires are generated by the somewhat casual way that learners may address them, particularly if confronted by too many questionnaires, too often. The limitations include:

- the 'Ticky-box' syndrome: people become conditioned to make instant responses to questions. Getting through the questionnaire quickly becomes a virtue. Responses are made on a surface level of thinking rather than as a result of reflection and critical thinking. (This is all right where 'instant' reaction is what is wanted, but the feedback is not usually analysed on that basis)
- the 'Performing Dogs' syndrome: many people filling in questionnaires tend to want to please. They can usually tell which responses will please the people giving them the questionnaire and the people whose work is involved in the issues covered by the questionnaire. If they like the people, they are likely to comment favourably on things
- lost learning opportunities: questionnaires are often used after the event rather than during it. This tends to minimize any real learning outcomes of the process of completing questionnaires. The sense of ownership is reduced
- the 'wysiwyg' syndrome: (what you see is what you get): questionnaires produce feedback on the particular issues covered but often *not* on other important issues. There is a tendency to design questionnaires which will give positive feedback
- 'Blue, Rosy and Purple' questionnaire: a major limitation of most questionnaires is that responses are coloured by how people *feel* at the moment of filling them in. If the same questionnaire were used a few days later, some responses may be completely different. Yet the results are often statistically analysed as though they reflected 'permanent' reactions to questions and issues, rather than fleeting, transient reactions.

Feedback from groups of learners

This can be more useful than feedback from individuals, for the following reasons:

- the feedback reflects the benefit of group discussion and debate, rather than instant reactions of individuals
- the group can present negative feedback with less embarrassment than an individual
- where a questionnaire is used as an agenda for group feedback, the group is more likely to be willing to go beyond the agenda.

Interviews with students

Student interviews are basically a verbal form of student questionnaire. A well-run interview can, however, probe more deeply and sensitively into specific areas of interest than can normally be done in a written questionnaire. One drawback is that individual interviewing is a time-consuming procedure. Thus, the most effective role of sampled interviews may well be to check the validity of a more widely-used formal questionnaire.

Observation of Instructional Systems in Progress

An understanding of the hidden educational processes occurring within an instructional system may be developed by means of careful and sensitive observation of these processes. The observation can be direct and immediate, or may be recorded in some way (eg on videotape) for later analysis. Such techniques are particularly useful when one is evaluating exercises designed to develop communication and interpersonal skills. The ethical problems associated with 'unobtrusive assessment' that were mentioned in the last chapter are not really a problem in this case, as it is the *instructional system* which is under scrutiny, not the students.

It should be remembered that effective observation is a high-level skill and that seeing is not observing. Similarly, making a video recording does not in itself amount to structured observation, though structured observation of the video recording is possible later. For observation to be effective and in due course useful to the teachers or trainers being observed, it is important to map out in advance the skills and qualities which are to be analysed in the observation. It is equally important to secure the cooperation and trust of the people being observed, ensuring that they appreciate the purposes of the forthcoming observation and that they are aware of the agenda being used for the observation. In fact, when it is possible to allow the people who are going to be observed to contribute substantially to the observation agenda, they are much more likely to benefit from the results of the observation, due to their feeling of ownership of the criteria to be employed.

In preparing the agenda for the observation, it is useful to design a checklist or matrix, so that important data can be entered easily by the observer. One of the best ways to formulate such an agenda is to discuss with the teachers or trainers to be observed what they consider are 'critical incidents' in the particular sorts of instruction to be observed. Experienced teachers can usually give a much sharper picture of the things that really matter in the way they go about their teaching, than would be given by an observer with only a general understanding of teaching and learning processes. In addition, teachers themselves can provide much help in deciding the order in which the 'critical incidents' should be expected to be observed in a typical session, helping to make the checklist or matrix much more straightforward to use in practice.

Observers should give careful thought to whether to make notes during the observation, or immediately after it. There is no doubt that the sight of someone making notes on one's performance affects most performers. Furthermore, the act of making notes interrupts the observation itself, and important things may be missed even in a few seconds. Probably the most sensible compromise is to limit direct observations to less than 15 minutes or so, and to then make notes immediately afterwards while incidents are still fresh in the observer's memory. Alternatively, where it is possible to make a video recording showing not only the teacher or trainer in action, but a view of the learners as well (ie, a minimum two cameras in most circumstances), longer periods of work can be recorded. Then both the observer and the teacher can sit down together with the checklist or matrix, filling them in together, and rewinding the tape from time to time so that important incidents are not missed while making notes.

It should be remembered that however much we try to formulate an agenda for any kind of structured observation, the act of observing is always quite subjective. Think of the problems in criminal courts with eye-witness reports. There is no known method of teaching structured observation – it is done by practice and feedback. Useful practice at observing interpersonal behaviour can, however, be done in safety, for example by making notes of the processes of television interviews and debates and then discussing the findings with other observers who have done the same.

Feedback from Teaching Staff Directly Involved in the Instructional System

Through questionnaires, interviews and solicited comments, the opinions of staff directly involved in the implementation and operation of an instructional system can be of great value in course evaluation. Their comments may be influential in evaluating all aspects of the system, including the validity of the objectives, the course structure, the teaching sequence, the assessment methods, and the day-to-day organization and management.

Feedback from People Having an Indirect Link with the Instructional System

People who do not have a direct link with the actual teaching/ learning system under investigation may still be able to make an important contribution to its evaluation. Again, questionnaires, interviews and solicited comments are appropriate means of gathering information.

The advice of *employers*, for example, may be sought if a vocational course is being evaluated. This may be done at the *formative evaluation* stage, before a course has been fully developed (in order to assess the skills and qualities which employers are looking for from students). It may also be done as part of a *summative evaluation* process (to gather information on the relevance of the course to the actual work situation and on the general strengths and weaknesses of former students).

Similarly, the opinions of *former students* can be important, as they can comment on the relevance of the course or other instructional system in retrospect, and perhaps suggest improvements with the benefit of hindsight and experience.

If a course has *external examiners*, their comments are invariably extremely influential in course development. This feedback may prove even more valuable if the external examiners are given some guidance as to what particular aspects should be commented upon.

Finally, the opinions of *teachers* who subsequently take on a particular group of students for a related course are often highly relevant. Their comments on the students' strengths and weaknesses can be important when revising a particular instructional system, or part thereof.

EVALUATION OF COST-EFFECTIVENESS

The perceived balance between the cost of an educational programme or innovation and its educational effectiveness depends upon a multitude of factors. Deciding whether or not the initial costs and on-going running costs justify the end results is a value judgement, involving a wide range of educational, financial, social, and political considerations. Improvements in the effectiveness of teaching/learning can also be measured in several 'dimensions', as discussed in Chapter 1.

It is not our intention in this book to deal in any depth with the complexities of cost-effectiveness. It is, however, important to bear in mind the overall financial implications and on-going financial commitment associated with *any* educational development, and to weigh these against the expected educational benefit using whatever criteria are deemed important.

The financial costing of an educational development is a complex process in itself. Fielden and Pearson, in their book *Costing Educational Practice* (1978), describe a practical approach which they believe could be generally adopted, and give an insight into some of the associated problems, using a number of case studies for illustration. Other interesting case studies of educational costing are provided by Birch and Cuthbert (on open learning methods) and by Fielden and Pearson (on computer-assisted learning). (See the Bibliography for further details.)

SUMMARY

Systematic evaluation is an essential component of the process by which the on-going development of instructional systems and learning resources takes place. Evaluation (like the demonstration of competence) is best achieved by the collection and analysis of as wide a range as possible of different kinds of evidence relating to the quality of the educational or training system being evaluated. No single evaluation tool is sufficient. As in the case of assessment, it is generally more profitable to use a *battery* of appropriate techniques. With the spread of systems of 'total quality management' into education and training provision, the various expressions of quality often lend themselves to the design of specific evaluation tools and parameters, so that evidence can be collected as a continuous process and used to feed back into the delivery of high-quality learning.

Chapter 9

Resources Centres

INTRODUCTION

In Chapter 5, we looked at a range of individualized learning approaches and techniques. These all give the student greater control over such factors as *how*, *when*, *where* and *at what pace* the actual learning takes place than is the case in most traditional institution-centred courses, thus making them more flexible from the student's point of view. One of the key components of many individualized learning approaches is a *resources centre* of some sort, in which much of the learning material and many of the aids that are provided to support self-learning may be housed. In this chapter, we will first take a more detailed look at the role of resources centres in education and training, and will then examine some of the practical considerations that relate to their operation.

We will begin by distinguishing between *resources, resources centres* and *resource-based learning*, and indicating how these three concepts are linked. Then we will describe how resources centres are used in different educational systems and at different levels of education. Finally, we will discuss some of the factors that are involved in the planning, organization and operation of a learning resources centre.

RESOURCES, RESOURCES CENTRES AND RESOURCE-BASED LEARNING

In essence, resources, resources centres, and resource-based learning may be thought of as progressively more highly structured systems through which flexible, *student-centred learning* can be achieved. Let us illustrate this thesis by examining each in turn.

Resources

Basically, a *'resource'* in education or training is a system, set of materials or situation that is deliberately created or set up in order to enable an individual student to learn. To qualify as a true learning 'resource', the resource must satisfy all of the following three conditions:

(a)   it must be *readily available;*
(b)   it must allow student *self-pacing;* and
(c)   it must be *individualized,* ie it must cater for the needs of students working on their own.

It therefore follows that a 'resource' must, by definition, be *student-centred.* Thus, in a traditional teacher/institution-centred system involving teaching methods such as lectures or talks, timetabled laboratory classes, and text books, it is only the text books which normally satisfy the criteria for being 'resources', in the sense we have described here. However, in such a course, lectures *could* be made more like true 'resources' by having them 'packaged' in some way, eg by recording them on videocassettes or making them available in some other self-study format such as duplicated notes backed up by audiotape commentaries. Similarly, a laboratory situation could be made into a 'resource' by allowing more flexible student access to the laboratory facilities than may normally be the case.

Resources can come in many forms. *People* can be 'resources' as, for example, when teaching staff make themselves available on a flexible basis in order to deal with individual student difficulties as and when they arise. Similarly, *places* can be 'resources', as in the case of an open-access laboratory of the type mentioned above. Finally, a whole range of *instructional media* can be 'resources'; examples include books, structured notes, videocassettes, tape-slide programmes, computers, etc. Self-instructional materials in all their various formats are probably the most common type of learning resource, and these are often housed centrally in a *resources centre.*

Resources Centres

A *resources centre* is a place (anything from part of a room, as in Figure 9.1, to an entire complex of buildings) that is set up specifically for the purpose of housing and using a collection of *resources,* usually in the form of self-instructional materials.

Resources centres (which are sometimes given equivalent names such as *learning aids laboratories* or *self-study centres*) may serve the needs of an individual department within a school or college, an entire institution, or even a collection of institutions, as, for example, when several schools are served by a single central resources centre. In many cases, such centres are housed in libraries, which often double up as resources centres by providing for the storage and use of both book and non-book learning materials.

Student use of resources centres may, at one extreme, be very loosely structured, and, in some institutions, may not be an integral

Figure 9.1 **A resources centre in a typical primary school classroom**

component of courses. On the other hand, in strongly student-centred courses, students may spend a large proportion of their time using the facilities offered by such centres.

The different uses that are made of resources centres, and the various factors that are involved in their planning, organization and operation, will be discussed later in this chapter.

Resource-based learning

Courses that involve *resource-based learning* generally provide for individual study by including some measure of self-teaching and self-pacing. Such courses invariably make wide use of learning 'resources' in the sense described above, and *may* make use of the facilities of a resources centre. However, true resource-based learning goes far beyond the mere use of a resources centre, involving a highly structured system of individualized, student-centred learning experiences that make full use of both human and non-human resources. The class of resource-based learning systems encompasses all the individualized learning approaches that were discussed in Chapter 5; for example, Keller Plan, Flexistudy and distance learning courses, including all correspondence courses.

Within the broad spectrum of resource-based learning, resources centres *can* be used as a basis for implementing and supporting developments of this type. Such centres are not, however, essential prerequisites for *all* resource-based learning schemes, since it is perfectly possible to operate a resource-based learning system without such a centre.

Several texts which further explain the concepts of 'resources', resources centres and resource-based learning are listed in the Bibliography.

THE ROLE OF RESOURCES CENTRES IN DIFFERENT EDUCATIONAL SYSTEMS

Resources centres are exploited in fundamentally different ways in different types of educational institutions, and the way in which they are used also depends to a considerable extent on the nature of the strategic approach to instruction that is adopted.

Within flexible *student-centred* approaches to learning of the type discussed in Chapters 2 and 5, a resources centre may have a key role to play in providing students with a whole range of learning resources, together with any associated hardware that may be required for the use of these resources. Within such flexible learning systems, students are often given free access to a resources centre within a host institution, and are permitted to attend at times which suit *them* rather than the institution. Advice is normally given (via a 'study guide') regarding the range of resources which may be suitable to assist in the achievement of a given set of objectives within a given course unit. Teaching staff may be present in order to assist with any problems or difficulties that may arise, and, as such, constitute another 'resource' within the centre.

In the case of courses which are based on the more conventional, more constrained *teacher/institution-centred approach* (see Chapter 2), the role of resources centres is generally completely different. Here, their role is not so much to serve as a means of providing a front-line teaching facility, but rather to provide remedial or back-up material to support other teaching methods.

In primary and secondary schools, a centralized resources centre may store and supply both book and non-book materials which individual teachers are able to borrow for use with their classes. Similar centralized collections of teaching materials are found in teacher training colleges and teachers' resources centres (see Figure 9.2). In such cases, the resources are most often used as aids within a traditional expository approach rather than for individualized instruction.

Individual use of resources centres by students undertaking traditional teacher/institution-centred courses is often completely voluntary (that is, it is an 'optional extra'), although students may sometimes be directed or recommended to use certain resources by particular teachers or lecturers. All resources are again normally available at most times, but the choice of what particular resource(s) to use is often left to the student. Indeed, students may elect to use the

Figure 9.2 **Part of the teaching resources centre in the library of a large teacher training college**

facilities of a resources centre in order to study subjects that are not directly related to the content of their course, for example learning foreign languages for holiday purposes, or studying computer programming out of general interest. However, the main uses of resources centres by such students include remedial study, immediate follow-up of class work, revision before exams, and extra study carried out in order to benefit from an alternative approach to specific subject matter.

Some institution-based resources centres also lay on a programme of displays and exhibitions for general motivation and background interest purposes. This practice is most common in resources centres that are based within a particular department, or which deal only with resources in specific areas (eg the biological sciences or health education).

THE PLANNING, ORGANIZATION AND OPERATION OF A RESOURCES CENTRE

As we have seen, a resources centre can be used in different ways at different levels and in different systems of education. Clearly, the method of use will have a marked effect on how the resources centre is organized and developed. Thus, there are many factors that have to be considered before embarking on the planning and operation of a resources centre, and, in the remainder of this chapter, we will take a detailed look at some of the more important of these.

Constraints

The development of a resources centre is often constrained by a number of factors, including *finance, space, staffing, attitudes* and *general educational policy*. Let us now look at these in turn.

Finance

Money is obviously required both to set up and to operate a resources centre. An initial outlay is required to buy furniture (for example, study carrels, desks, chairs and storage shelves), to purchase any necessary hardware (for example, microcomputers, interactive video work-stations, on-line printers, tape-slide players, cassette players and videocassette recorders) and to purchase appropriate commercially-available resources (in both print and non-print format). In addition to this 'pump-priming' money (which may be considerable), an annual operating budget is required in order to maintain and enhance the equipment and resources housed within the centre.

Space

Suitable space clearly has to be found in order to site the development. In some cases, it may be possible and desirable to place the resources centre within an existing library; in others, it may be better to use separate accommodation – particularly if the resources centre is to be departmentally rather than centrally based. The amount of space required will obviously be directly related to the amount of use that students are expected to make of the centre. Experience shows that there are liable to be peak times of use (lunch times, free periods, etc), and the size of the development should (ideally) be sufficient to cater for such 'peaks', although in many situations, this is simply not practical.

In addition to providing adequate student spaces, an appropriate amount of storage space is required, both for equipment and for resources; if possible, this should be flexible enough to cater for any planned future expansion of the resources centre.

Staffing

Several staffing problems will almost certainly have to be faced. The cataloguing and administration within the centre should (ideally) be handled by a specialist librarian, but such a person may not be available, so it will often be necessary to find a suitable 'volunteer' to do the job. It may be desirable to use teaching staff within the resources centre as 'human learning resources' to which students can have access, but this may lead to timetabling problems, and also to problems related to staff willingness (or unwillingness!). Finally, some technician back-up is generally necessary in order to check and maintain any audiovisual equipment housed in the resources centre.

Attitudes

Positive attitudes to the resources centre from both staff and students are absolutely vital to the success of the venture. Unless a resources centre is generally considered to be capable of playing an effective and valuable part within the teaching system in which it is to be used, the development is almost certainly doomed to failure. All too often, teaching staff in particular (especially the older members) are highly sceptical regarding the value of a new development such as a resources centre. If this is the case, it may be necessary to take positive steps to convince them that all the expense and effort are worthwhile, and that a more flexible student-centred approach is capable of producing a significant increase in the overall effectiveness of the learning process.

Politics and policy

Factors ranging from intra- and inter-departmental politics, through general institutional policy to local and central government policy, can all affect the development (and effectiveness) of a learning resources centre. For example, if a college of further education is attempting to implement a policy of flexible course provision that includes community education, this will probably stimulate the development of a resources centre in the college; conversely, in the absence of any policy of this type, any attempts to establish such a centre may well be stifled. Similarly, important central government initiatives such as the setting up of the 'Open Tech' programme in the UK (designed to foster the training and re-training of adults at technician level by open learning methods) may give an impetus to the development of resources centres in a wide range of educational institutions and training centres.

Organization and Management

Thought must also be given to a number of other factors, including the centre's *management structure*, the *resources* themselves, the *equipment*, and the *general administration* of the centre. Let us again consider these in turn.

Management structure

Problems related to the *organization, management* and *operation* of a resources centre must be faced on a regular basis, and firm decisions must be made as a result. In some resources centres, these decisions are made by a single person or a small team, whereas in others, a committee of some sort is responsible for deciding policy. Such a committee might involve teaching staff, administrative staff, library staff, educational technologists, students and technicians.

Resources

Basically, the instructional media which comprise the actual learning resources in a resources centre can come from two sources: those that are 'bought in' from commercial organizations or from other educational institutions, and those that are 'internally produced' in order to cater for the requirements of a given set of students within a specific subject area.

'Bought-in' resources have the obvious advantage of allowing a usable collection of resources to be assembled relatively quickly. However, some resources, particularly those with an audiovisual component, can be expensive, and, in most cases, their content is not entirely compatible with the objectives of the course in which they are to be used.

Resources which have been 'internally produced' by a teacher, on the other hand, may be much more relevant to the specific needs of a course, but, at the same time, can be extremely time-consuming to plan, produce and evaluate. In addition, devising effective student-centred learning resources may call for a wide range of new skills on the part of the teaching staff, skills which often have to be nurtured and developed over an extended period.

The various media which might be used in the production of resources have been discussed in detail in Chapter 5, where it was argued that the media should (ideally) be chosen to match the objectives being taught towards. However, the precise choice of media may be influenced by other factors, one of the most important being the range of equipment available in the resources centre. If, for example, basic slide viewing facilities are the only visual equipment available, staff will clearly have to use slides rather than filmstrips or videotapes. Also, when buying in audiovisual resources, care must be taken to ensure compatibility with any standardized equipment already installed; for example, any pre-recorded videocassettes that are purchased should be of the appropriate format to be played on the videocassette players that are available in the centre.

Finally, the effective production of resources within an institution depends on having adequate production facilities available, including reprographic, photographic, graphics, audiorecording, and possibly also television services, together with adequate secretarial support. In some cases, it may also be necessary to provide facilities for reproducing certain types of resources within the centre itself. For example, a student-centred course involving extensive use of a resources centre may have a relatively large number of students progressing through the course at roughly the same pace. If reproduction facilities within the centre allow rapid duplication of resources, such as textual notes and audiotapes, this may reduce the need to store multiple copies of particular resources in order to cope with peak demand, and may well result in greater overall efficiency. Where such immediate duplication facilities are not readily available, consideration should be given to the optimum number of copies which are to be held. With 'bought in' materials, copyright restrictions may preclude direct copying, and, in such cases, any additional copies required would obviously have to be purchased.

Equipment

The range and type of equipment that needs to be installed in a resources centre depends on a number of factors, including the nature of the media to be deployed and the amount of money available. For example, if tape-slide instructional programmes are to form a significant proportion of the resources in the centre, specialist machines, through which the audio commentary is automatically linked to the slides by means of electronic 'pulses' recorded on the tape, can be provided in order to enable students to study these programmes. If finances do not permit the purchase of this type of (relatively expensive) hardware, however, simple manually-operated slide viewers and basic cassette players can be combined to provide a reasonably inexpensive alternative.

The number of sets of equipment to be installed in the centre has also to be determined, and should (ideally) be sufficient to cope with the expected peak demand. If this proves to be impossible, some form of 'timetabling' or booking of student use of the resources centre may well be necessary, albeit somewhat undesirable.

The actual location of the equipment within the centre may also cause problems. If the equipment is permanently set out in the resources centre ready for use, as in Figure 9.3, there may be problems relating to its security. If the equipment is stored centrally, on the other hand, and has to be collected by students every time they want to use it, this inevitably reduces the 'openness' of the resources centre by erecting a (perhaps unnecessary) administrative barrier, and may well deter some students from making full use of the facilities.

As mentioned previously, regular technical maintenance of all audiovisual equipment is extremely important. If minor faults are not immediately rectified, student interest and motivation may again be lost; it is, after all, extremely frustrating for a student to go to a resources centre, get hold of the material he or she wants, and then find that the hardware needed to study it is not working properly.

General administration

A whole series of factors have to be considered regarding the running and administration of a resources centre. One of the most important of these is the question of whether the students are to be allowed free access (open access) to the resources, or whether access is to be via staff (closed access). In an *open access* system, the resources are usually housed in the main body of the resources centre, so that

Figure 9.3 **Some of the equipment in a typical audiovisual resources centre**

the students can select and use resources 'off the shelf'. In a *closed access* system, on the other hand, the resources are usually held in a central store, and students must request resources more formally. This factor is linked both to the staffing levels that are available to run the resources centre, and to the degree of student supervision that is thought necessary for educational, operational and security reasons.

Regardless of whether open or closed access is used, the resources of the centre must be systematically catalogued in some way in order to facilitate efficient retrieval. Where resources are stored on a closed-access basis, or are intrinsically 'non-browsable' (eg videocassettes), it may help to annotate the catalogue entry with a fairly detailed description of the contents of the resource. The importance of a good cataloguing system becomes progressively more crucial as the number of resources in the centre increases. Indeed, in the case of a resources centre where a large collection of materials is being built up, there is a strong case for placing the cataloguing of the resources in the hands of a specialist audiovisual librarian.

Other administrative duties which may be important in a resources centre include arranging the booking and borrowing of resources (since it may be desirable for students to be able to use the resources outside the premises of the resources centre itself). Also, someone must be responsible for obtaining for preview and eventually purchasing resources produced elsewhere, on the basis of staff recommendations or other appropriate criteria. A further duty may be the keeping of records of usage of resources, possibly for the purpose of student 'credit' assessment, or, alternatively, for more administrative reasons such as assessing relative demand for different resources or establishing the level of use made of the resources centre.

Finally, the possibility of using 'human resources' in the centre has already been raised. Normally, these will be full-time teachers or lecturers who have a certain amount of 'resources centre duty' built into their timetables, but they can also be part-time members of staff or retired staff who are brought in specially for the purpose. It is also possible to make use of senior students in such a role.

In large learning resources centres such as those found in most universities, it is normal to employ 'subject librarians' who are well-qualified in the principal subject areas or fields. Such staff provide an invaluable service to students looking for specific educational resources relevant to their studies, and often provide much-appreciated informal tutorial support. Subject librarians can also run short introductory courses on making the best use of the learning resources centre and of the particular subject-specific resources contained therein.

With increasing emphasis on individualized learning as a component of further and higher education, it is becoming more common for specially designed learning resources centres to remain open for extended hours (particularly when most of the learners are residential on the campus or in the immediate vicinity). Bournemouth University, for example, provides a purpose-designed suite of rooms containing a range of computer terminals and printers and accompanying educational software, which remains open 24 hours per day. This helps reduce the problems of queueing for particular learning resources, and learners can be found working in the centre even in the early hours of the morning (especially when deadlines for finishing project work approach). Round-the-clock availability necessarily requires careful planning regarding security and safety, and a central station with a battery of TV monitors is continuously staffed so that any security or safety problems can be identified and dealt with. Where a learning resources centre can be designed with a single exit (apart from 'alarmed' fire-exits), and this main exit can electronically detect any stock being removed without authority, it is possible to staff such a centre in the late evening and at weekends with security staff only. For example, the learning resources centre at the University of Glamorgan remains open till midnight and at weekends, but without the presence of library staff after 9.00 pm. In the initial trial period of extended opening, it was made clear to students that the continuation of this provision was dependent on the lack of any disturbance or misconduct. It was found that the student community was highly appreciative of the availability of quiet study facilities, and there were very few problems.

Educational Considerations

Once the idea of setting up a resources centre has been firmly established in a school or college, a number of additional factors regarding the educational (as opposed to the administrative) aspects of its operation and function have to be taken into account. These include *integration with the teaching/learning system, the role of the teacher, student characteristics, group work, photocopying facilities* and *feedback and evaluation,* all of which will again be examined in turn.

Integration with the teaching/learning system

We have already pointed out that there are many possible ways in which resources centres can be used in educational and training systems. One key decision that has to be made is whether the resources centre is to operate in a 'front line' role or in an optional 'back-up' role.

Within the context of an open, student-centred learning facility such as a resources centre, the amount of guidance given to students in the selection and use of resources must strike an appropriate balance between constructive direction and freedom of choice on the part of the learner. This depends upon just how 'open' and 'flexible' the learning situations can be while still remaining relevant to the course objectives.

When a resources centre is used within a strongly student-centred, self-paced course, there is also the very real problem of coping (on the one hand) with students who complete work quickly, and (on the other hand) with those who fall far behind. Some resources centres do in fact provide 'mind-broadening' or 'enrichment' materials for the 'high-fliers'. Another approach is to use the better students to help their weaker colleagues through a process of *peer teaching.*

In many schools and colleges, there is an increasing awareness of the need to integrate the actual teaching and learning process with the entire range of available support services. This has led some institutions to combine library, computer and media resources under one 'umbrella' service in order to co-ordinate their activities, and thus (it is hoped) to best serve the needs of the institution's courses and students.

The role of the teacher

In a resources centre, the role of the teacher effectively changes from being the sole supplier of information to being a provider of counselling and assistance for those who need it. Within a student-centred resource-based learning course, the teacher is much more a 'manager of resources' based learning course, than a 'provider of information'. As we saw in Chapter 5, this role is not easy for some

teachers to adopt, especially if skills related to the in-house production of resources have also to be learned. These factors indicate a very
real need for appropriate staff development programmes on such
things as the production of resources, the organization of resources
centres, and the use of resource-based learning.

Student characteristics
It is a well-established fact that different students learn in different
ways. To cater for individual differences in learning style, it may well
be desirable to present similar information in alternative resource
formats. In some instances, there may even be a case for introducing
small-group teaching methods for the benefit of those who find
studying on their own particularly difficult (eg self-help groups).

When the main role of a resources centre is that of being an
'optional extra', there is often the additional problem of attracting
those students who have seldom or never used the facilities on offer.
It is a disturbing fact that many institutions which provide resource
material of a remedial or 'back-up' nature find that it is the *better*
students who use it voluntarily, rather than the weaker students who
would, perhaps, have most to gain.

Group work in learning resources centres
Most people associate libraries and resource centres with 'virtual
silence'. However, in Chapter 6 we discussed the importance of
group work and the fact that learners engaging in peer-group
discussions and group project work learn much more actively than
if working alone, and benefit from a great deal more immediate
feedback from their peers. In many large learning resources centres
(for example that at the University of Glamorgan), it has been found
that there is a considerable demand for space for students to
participate in such group work, even late into the evenings and at
weekends. The learning resources centre was designed so that round
the periphery of the large central open area (housing books and
study-tables) a series of glass-fronted 'seminar' rooms was provided.
These can be used by groups of students spontaneously or, in busy
times, booked in advance and reserved for planned groupwork.
Similar rooms were used for banks of computers and printers and
for educational resources such as interactive video stations, so that
the sounds arising from such equipment would not cause disturbance to those wishing to work in silence elsewhere.

It was also decided to make specified parts of the main resource
centre areas 'silent' and other parts 'fairly quiet' – in other words, in the
latter parts, learners were encouraged to work together in twos, threes
or fours, but to make their discussions sufficiently 'restrained' so as not
to disturb neighbouring groups of students. The 'fairly quiet' areas
were positioned among the book stacks in such a way that sounds did
not stray to the silent areas in other parts of the building.

Photocopying facilities

It is increasingly common for learning resources centres to contain such facilities, allowing learners to make instant copies of relevant extracts from books and journals and helping to minimize the need to remove important reference sources from the centre. Even with eight or so photocopiers in the learning resources centre at the University of Glamorgan (operated by tokens obtainable from adjacent cash-accepting machines or from the Students' Union), there is normally a queue during daytime hours.

Feedback and evaluation

As with all learning situations, feedback obtained from both students and staff regarding their problems and experiences relating to resources centres can be of considerable value in determining where and how improvements need to be made. We saw in the previous chapter that on-going evolution based on such feedback should be a feature of *all* components of an instructional system, and it is probably true to say that this is particularly important in the case of a resources centre, especially if it plays a key role in the work of the pupils or students who use it.

Chapter 10

Computers in Education and Training

INTRODUCTION

It may be thought that the use of computers in education and training is connected with the model of 'technology *in* education and training' that we mentioned in Chapter 1, but the use of computers is now so firmly established throughout all sectors of education and training that it can equally be claimed that they are also 'technology *of* education and training'. Computers and their applications are encountered from primary school to university and throughout the training world. Indeed, the generation in schools now are far quicker to learn how to use computer applications than most of the educators or trainers who have worked with computers for many years. This is not unrelated to the fact that computerized video games constitute a mass leisure market for the young (and also some not-so-young!), so familiarity with computers and electronics has largely overcome (in the younger generation) the attitudinal fears which beset their predecessors.

One reason for the massive expansion of the uses of computers is that the costs (unlike any other costs in education or training) have actually fallen by a considerable amount in real terms. It is normal for lecturers or trainers to have microcomputers or word-processors on their desks (or in their briefcases) with memory and processing capacities greater than it would have been possible to house in a whole room only two decades ago.

It is no longer possible in a book of this size to give more than a 'taste' of the range and diversity of the uses that electronic equipment and computers are serving in education and training. Nor does it serve a useful purpose to go into the history of computers (for example the development of early 'analogue' machines bristling with glowing thermionic valves, then the introduction of 'digital' machines and the development of a range of complex and specialized programming languages). Gone are the days when every user of computers was expected to know how they worked. Only a tiny proportion of the people who use computers now write computer programs themselves. Computer programming is a specialist subject, and readers wishing for more information are advised to consult the massive literature to be found on the subject. For educators and trainers, computers are now as much 'tools of the trade' as are overhead projectors or video players, and the key requirement is how to *use* such tools rather than how to build them or design their programs. Therefore, in this chapter, our purpose is simply to provide some illustrations of ways in which computers are used as tools by educators and trainers.

WHAT CAN COMPUTERS DO?

Looking at computers from first principles, their main capabilities include the following; they can:

- store vast amounts of information (data)
- analyse it at great speed
- search it at great speed and supply the results of such searches very quickly
- be made to churn out requested information in a variety of ways
  - as text and graphics on television monitor screens
  - as moving images on television monitor screens
  - as sound through loudspeakers or headphones
  - as charts, graphs, tables, histograms
  - as 'hard copy' through printers and copiers
  - as magnetically-stored information on computer discs
  - through cables and telephone links to other computers
- respond to requests from users
- control other electrical and mechanical equipment
- be used to access other information-storage media, such as videodiscs, compact discs, databanks
- be used to provide simulations of situations and conditions which would be far too dangerous to work with directly (for example, processes in the core of nuclear reactors).

The above list presents only a tiny fraction of the things computers can do – but of course they can not do any of these things without being programmed to do them. Ultimately, the quality of the applications of computers in education and training depends on the skill of program designers.

HOW DO PEOPLE INTERACT WITH COMPUTERS?

Studies of the 'human-computer interface' are now so important that they have their own acronym (HCI) amidst the large vocabulary of acronyms which surrounds computer-based training (CBT), computer-assisted learning (CAL) and computer-managed instruction (CMI). However, again taking a simplified look at how people interact with computers, the most common means include:

- keyboards (for typing in commands and data)
- the mouse (controlling the position of a 'cursor' on the monitor screen and, by 'clicking', instructing the computer to take specified actions from menus shown on the screen)
- touch-sensitive screens, using a pen or even a finger
- light-sensitive screens, using a light pen
- joysticks and joypads (as used on home video games and simulations)
- infra-red remote controllers (such as used in home video recorders, television sets and sound reproduction equipment such as compact-disc players).

HOW CAN COMPUTERS HELP PEOPLE TO LEARN?

We ended Chapter 1 by looking at the natural processes by which people learn in terms of four overlapping stages:

- *wanting* to learn – motivation, enthusiasm, interest and so on
- *doing* – having a go, trying things out, experimenting, practice, learning from mistakes
- *feedback* – finding out whether it was right or wrong, good or bad and so on
- *digesting* – making sense of the learning experience and of the feedback, taking stock, gaining a sense of 'ownership' of what has been learned.

In many respects, the success of the use of computers in education and training can be attributed to the close match that well-designed computer-based learning resources have to these natural ways of learning. Let us follow the arguments through in a little more detail.

'Wanting'

Computer-based learning systems such as interactive video can be highly attractive to use, with colourful and impressive images on the screen, interesting sounds and graphics, fascinating tasks to try and the knowledge that there will be immediate feedback from the system every time one interacts with it (for example, selecting an option from a series, or keying in an instruction). In other words, people *enjoy* working with such learning resources (in fact it is often a problem separating users from the equipment when it is time to close the building). It is not surprising, therefore, that the 'wanting' stage of the learning process is catered for by many kinds of computer-based learning resources.

'Doing'

Computer-based learning in any of its forms is essentially 'learning by doing'. There would be little point having an interactive video workstation simply playing a 30-minute video straight through; a simple video player would suffice for that. The essence of all computer-based training resources is giving people decisions to make, or options to select, or data to enter or interpret and so on. 'Learning by doing' is far more effective than learning by watching, or learning by listening. In addition, most computer-based learning resources are used in the relative 'comfort of privacy'. This means that it matters little if one 'does it wrong'. Indeed, most learners using computer-based learning packages are interested to see how the package will respond to them if they deliberately select wrong options or enter in 'silly' data. So the 'learning by doing' is done in a way where making mistakes is non-threatening – there is not a teacher or trainer looking over one's shoulder disapproving of such 'mistakes', whether genuine or deliberate.

'Feedback'

This is probably the strongest link in the chain with computer-based learning. The feedback which learners receive after making an action (entering data, selecting an option, giving an instruction, making a request – the list is endless) is *virtually instant* feedback. The 'response' from the learning package will appear on the screen, (or will be printed out, or will be heard through headphones) very quickly indeed compared to traditional education or training situations. Learners therefore receive feedback while they remember exactly what they are getting feedback about.

'Digesting'

One problem with computer-based learning packages is that it is not always possible for learners to have continuous access to them (for example, interactive video packages are too expensive for each learner to take one home). However, because in a well-designed computer-based package, learners have a great deal of control over the way they 'navigate' the package, there is often considerable opportunity for them to go backwards and forwards through the package at will, repeating parts of the package until it all makes sense to them.

MAINFRAME COMPUTERS AND TERMINALS

Most large educational institutions, and many companies in commerce and industry, have centralized computer systems, linking to terminals throughout their premises. This is similar in principle to banks and building societies who arrange computerized remote updating to cash-dispenser machines all over the country, allowing customers not only to withdraw cash and check balances, but to order statements or chequebooks and (in some cases) to obtain a printout of the last few transactions they made.

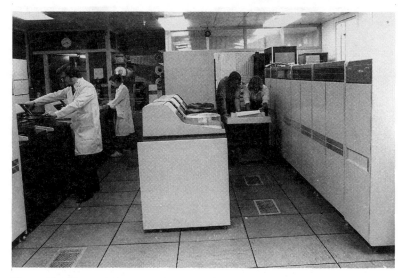

Figure 10.1 **Part of the central processing unit and back-up memory of a typical mainframe computer**

Large mainframe computers have massive amounts of memory capacity for the storage of data, which can be entered and retrieved at the terminals, each of which consist of a keyboard and a monitor screen. The mainframe computer also houses the central processing unit for the system, where data is analysed using a wide variety of software packages stored centrally. Figure 10.1 shows a typical mainframe computer – though there is not much to be seen since such devices are essentially collections of boxes and cabinets housing the hardware and software.

Usually, the keyboards linked to the main computer are not simply terminals, but microcomputers in their own right. These allow calculations and data handling to be done locally, contact being made with the main computer only when requiring some of the programming software stored there, or to store or retrieve data from the central information store. In educational institutions, it is common to find rooms filled with terminals so that all the members of a class can interact simultaneously with a mainframe computer or file server. Figure 10.2 shows a typical microcomputer work station in use. Terminals are often linked to their own printers, allowing users to obtain printouts of the results of information processed by the computer. Alternatively, the mainframe computer itself can be instructed from a remote terminal to provide a printout which can be mailed to, or collected by, the user.

Figure 10.2 **A typical microcomputer work station in use**

COMPUTERS AS SUBSTITUTE TUTORS

When computers are used as 'substitute tutors', they are pro-grammed to pose questions to learners and then to give feedback responses to the answers keyed in by learners. The questions can be 'direct answer', where learners key in the appropriate words making up the answers. The computer is programmed to recognize the correct answer (or a near-miss at spelling the correct answer!) and to respond accordingly to learners. The computer can also be programmed to recognize anticipated 'wrong' answers and to respond to learners in terms of what may have been the cause of their entering such answers. The computer can also be programmed to keep track of the progress of individual learners, and to provide learners or tutors with an analysis of such progress and a diagnosis of any particular difficulties such learners seem to be having.

An example of part of a 'tutor mode' computer-assisted learning package is shown in Figure 10.3.

In practice, only a small part of the information in this example would appear on the screen at any given time, but the ability to generate a printout of the whole interaction allows learners to reflect on what they have learned while interacting with the package – particularly wrong answers they gave and what they learned from doing this.

One of the most common 'substitute tutor' formats involves the use of multiple-choice questions. We have already explored some of the

You are required to investigate experimentally the chemical equilibrium of the system: $Fe^{3+} + SCN \rightleftharpoons FeNCS^2$ in order to discover how the equilibrium constant varies as a function of the ionic strength.
You need a method which is both sensitive and discriminating. Which method(s) do you suggest?

I'm sorry, but I haven't a clue

You first need to consider the physical properties of the individual species, or of the system as a whole, which you might use.
What feature do all the species involved have in common?

They are all ionic

Good!
So what method or methods might you choose which makes use of this property?

Conductivity methods

Yes — a conductance method.
Is a conductance method sensitive? (Very, Fairly, Not Very, Not at All)

Very

No. A conductance method is only fairly sensitive.
Is it a discriminating method?

Yes

Conductance methods are only really discriminating when applied to H^+ ions: for all other ions, the readings are rather similar.
Do you want to consider this method further?

No

What other method(s) might be more discriminating and sensitive?

Possibly a colourimetric method

Good. Are colourimetric methods sensitive?

and so on

Figure 10.3 **Extract from a 'tutor' mode CAL dialogue**

advantages and disadvantages of this form of question (or item) in Chapter 6. However, multiple-choice questions have distinct advantages as ingredients in computer-based education and training programmes. They can be used in the simplest computer-based packages, with the questions being presented on-screen and learners either keying in an option at the keyboard by typing in A, B, C and so on, or by using a mouse (or cursor control keys) to move the cursor to one of a number of labelled 'boxes' on the screen, then clicking the mouse (or pressing the 'enter' key on the keyboard). The computer will then produce a response on-screen to the option that was selected by the learner. The same principle applies to much more sophisticated applications, including interactive video packages, where the 'response' may be much more than some text on the screen; for example, it could be a video sequence illustrating the result of that option being chosen.

Advantages of using multiple-choice formats in computer-based education and training include the following:

- they involve learners in the process of decision-making – necessarily an active form of thinking and learning
- there is no need to restrict the number of options to four (often used in multiple-choice written tests) as the computer can be programmed to provide responses to as many options as are useful
- when learners have selected a correct option, they can instantly be provided with a feedback response confirming that they have chosen correctly and leading towards the next set of options
- when learners select an incorrect option, they can instantly be provided with a feedback response indicating exactly what is wrong with the option they chose and, if necessary, giving some further information to help them tackle the question again
- the use of multiple-choice questions does not need to be restricted to 'right' or 'wrong' questions; it is just as easy to present a series of options where some are better than others, (for example, proposed actions in a management case study) with each response providing feedback on the strengths and weaknesses of each of the options
- learners *enjoy* multiple-choice questions when working 'in the comfort of privacy' when it does not matter if they pick incorrect options and when they know they will receive rapid feedback on their choices
- 'high-flying' learners need not be slowed down by information they do not require; such information can be contained in the responses to incorrect options and therefore will only be used by the less-experienced or less-able learners who select incorrect options
- the computer can be programmed to record and analyse the choices made by individual learners and even to give them a diagnostic printout from time to time, summarizing the parts of the program they have mastered and the parts that caused them difficulties.

Computer-marked Tests and Assignments

A further use of computer-stored multiple-choice questions is to provide multiple-choice tests. These are of considerable use in distance learning, and have been used extensively in Britain by the National Extension College and Open University. A computer-marked assignment may, for example, consist of a bank of ten four-option multiple-choice questions, with learners selecting the correct (or preferred) option in each case and sending their choices by post to the host organization. Cards have been designed on which learners can pencil in their choices and which can be 'optically read' by machine, thus saving anyone having to carry out the tedious task of entering thousands of such choices into the computer. The feedback responses to each chosen option can then be printed by the computer, which can also add prepared comments about the overall performance on the test. This adds up to a 'letter' produced by the computer (very quickly) to individual learners, commenting specifically on the choices they made for each of the questions in the test. For 'routine' questions (for example, involving lower-cognitive objectives) this sort of use of computers can help save human resources for the more important task of giving detailed feedback on tutor-marked assignments addressing higher-level questions and objectives.

Of course, the same sort of test can be used 'in person' in colleges and training centres, with learners sitting at the computer keyboard and entering in their choices of options, then receiving their scores and feedback directly at the end of the test.

The 'Simulated Laboratory' Mode

In this mode, the computer plays the part of a learning resource rather than an instructional device. Practical situations can be modelled by the computer, allowing learners to select the values of variables, (for example, temperature, pressure, or concentration in chemical engineering plant processes), then arranging that the computer calculates and displays the effect of changing such variables. Similarly, in economics, a variable such as the level of income tax can be changed by learners, with rapid feedback on the effects it may have on a wide variety of financial factors in a country. Simulated practical situations are used in many disciplines and industries, including medicine, engineering, geography, mathematics, physical sciences, military training and management training. Examples of the sorts of situation which point towards the use of computer simulations include:

- where a conventional practical demonstration is extremely difficult or impossible (for example, manipulating a country's gross domestic product, or exploring how nuclear reactors function when variables are altered)
- where the apparatus or machinery being simulated is not readily available, or is too bulky, or expensive, for classroom or laboratory demonstration (for example, when training personnel in off-shore drilling techniques)
- when a conventional real situation would take an impossibly long

time to investigate (for example, experiments in population dynamics or genetics)

■ where it is beneficial for learners to 'get the feel' of a topic by 'playing with the variables' and seeing when disasters would happen (for example, landing a 'damaged' aircraft using only one engine).

Figure 10.4 shows a sample printout for a laboratory-simulation computer-assisted learning package which allows learners to explore the effects of temperature and pressure on the proportion

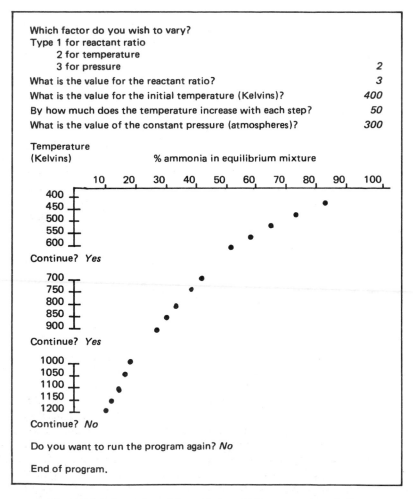

Figure 10.4 **Sample printout from a 'laboratory simulation' mode CAL exercise**

of ammonia in a manufacturing process. In practice, most such packages would give immediate graphical displays on-screen, but the production of a printout as well enables learners to do further interpretation of the data provided by the computer after they leave the simulation package.

Computer Conferencing and Electronic Mail

In *Producing Teaching Materials* (Ellington and Race, 1993) there is a detailed case study of the uses by students and staff in a college of computer conferencing and electronic mail. Electronic mail allows particular messages to be sent from one terminal to another (and from one site to another round the world, using telephone lines), with the message being coded so that it can only be received by the holder of a particular username. When the recipient logs on to the computer system, a message shows whether any new mail messages have been received, and a few keyboard entries allow each of the new messages to be seen in turn. With computer conferencing (which also works as easily globally as locally), messages are 'public' in that anyone participating in the conference can see all the entries and can add new entries or replies to existing ones. A major advantage of both electronic mail and computer conferencing in education and training is that participants can use them at times and places (provided there are terminals) of their own choosing, and can download interesting items to printout form for further dissemination where this is useful. Computer conferencing and electronic mail constitute a powerful and versatile medium for educators and trainers to maintain contact with learners, both in their own organizations and far away (for example, students on work placement). Such computer applications allow individual feedback between tutors and learners, even when it may be difficult or impossible to arrange face-to-face meetings.

Computers as databases and data managers

For some years now, laser-readable videodiscs have been used to store large amounts of information which can be quickly tracked down by a linked computer and displayed on screen. Such discs store the data for interactive video learning packages, where the principles of decision-based learner activities are linked to moving-image, sound and digitized graphics displays on-screen. With the widespread use of compact discs (CD) in home music-reproduction systems, there is a rapidly growing educational and training industry in CD-ROM (compact disc, read only memory) where compact discs have vast amounts of information stored on them digitally. Whole books, dictionaries and encyclopaedias are now widely available on such discs (commonly called 'Electronic Books'), and computer software allows very rapid searching of such databases for specific information requested by users of such systems. Interactive compact disc systems are presently being targeted at the domestic leisure market, and a wide range of educational and training packages are emerging in this format. A Compact Disc Interactive (CD-I) system presently costs little more than a good domestic sound-reproduction system (and also reproduces music CDs as well as a plethora of interactive computer games).

Hypermedia

It is fair to claim at the time of writing the third edition of this book that more is being published about Hypermedia than any other topic in the vast field of educational and training computing. The characteristics of Hypermedia include the ability to create and use education and training interactive programmes without any knowledge of computer programming, and 'drop-down' on-screen menus to help both in the design of software and the use of learning packages. The best known example of Hypermedia is 'Hypercard', introduced on Apple Macintosh machines during the 1980s. However, the term 'Hypermedia' is now being extended to an ever-growing range of ways of using computers to access other media such as videodisc, compact disc and so on.

With Hypercard, it is possible for a relative novice to learn to compose interactive educational software quite quickly. However, the escalation of the production of such software has meant that the standards of presentation have increased dramatically. Professionally produced educational software uses high resolution graphics, a full range of colours and all sorts of on-screen effects which make amateur productions look decidedly old-fashioned. We advise readers who wish to get directly involved with Hypermedia to consult the literature referred to in the Bibliography – or better still, to find a professional or firm who can demonstrate to them just how powerful these media can be.

Compact Disc Interactive

Most readers will think of compact disc technology as something they have on their domestic hi-fi sound equipment. From around 1950 to the early 1980s, vinyl gramophone records were the most common music medium, with 'long play' records capable of holding 40 minutes per side of recorded sound (though it was much more common for side-lengths to be 25 minutes or so, and as low as 15 minutes in the field of popular music). LPs were known for their 'snap, crackle and pop' – an array of background surface noise which pervaded quiet passages of music. They were also known for their 'clicks' and the ease with which they could be scratched by rough handling. When compact discs came onto the scene, it was at first thought that they would be unlikely to catch on, as the market for recorded vinyl discs and for cassette tapes was so established.

However, in 1993, very few vinyl discs are manufactured, and compact discs are rapidly overtaking cassette tapes in music shops. Already, compact 'mini-discs' are being introduced, which can be used to store many other kinds of data in digital form. Digital audio tape systems are also coming onto the domestic market, using tape cassettes of the same size as for ordinary analogue cassette players, but with the information on them coded digitally. With these, it is possible (though not always legal!) to copy digitally recorded information without loss of quality and to make direct recordings digitally. Digital audio tape is not restricted to the recording of audio sound, however, and other information (text, graphics and so on) can be recorded and copied with ease.

The compact disc uses digitally stored information, which is read using a low-power laser, then transformed into sound with no discernible loss of quality in either the recording or the playback stage. 'Snap, crackle and pop' were abolished at a stroke, and compact discs are so robust they can be handled quite carelessly and still produce perfect sound quality. For music reproduction, it is now common to find compact discs containing well over 70 minutes of recorded sound. What is more, the 'tracks' can be digitally selected and you can programme your playback equipment for which tracks to select and in which order.

Compact disc technology has, however, potential far beyond domestic audio reproduction. In 1992, the first training and educational programmes to use the medium of compact disc were launched in Britain following successful introduction of the technology in the United States in 1991. Philips Interactive Media Systems launched the technology into the UK consumer market.

CD-I integrated digital video, digital audio, graphics and text onto a 5" optical disc. A CD-I player is similar in size and technology to an ordinary domestic CD player (and can play ordinary CDs as well). The CD-I machine is connected to a television set, through which it delivers sound and pictures, controlled by the user of the CD-I educational software being used. Visual scenarios can feature colourful graphic images, animated sequences and full motion video; using a computer keyboard (or mouse, or light pen), the user interacts with information on the screen. For example, users can select from alternative choices to questions or situations posed on the screen, then immediately receive constructive feedback on the implications of their choices. In other words, the pathway through which the training package is delivered is completely responsive to each individual user's choices, needs and wishes.

It is thought that this technology is set to become the 'next generation' medium for training and education, and also for the distribution of entertainment and information. The technology is backed by the world's largest suppliers of consumer electronics: Philips, Sony and Matsushita, JVC and Panasonic, all of whom have adopted an agreed international standard, making global compatibility a reality.

CD-I technology is quite inexpensive, with a CD-I player including colour TV or monitor ranging (in 1992) from £800–£1600. The system can use 16 simultaneous soundtracks. This means that, for example, the sound commentary in a training programme can be recorded in several languages and, provided translated versions of accompanying workbooks and assignments are made, a good training resource from one country can be directly used in several other countries. The technology is particularly user-friendly, and it is claimed that it even appeals to computerphobes. Most of the control is exercised with either a mouse, or with a remote-control very similar to those which are endemic in homes already, for televisions and videorecorders.

SPIN UK (a Philips subsidiary company – see contact addresses in the Bibliography) is the UK's first producer of CD-I education and training software. It claims that during the remainder of the 1990s CD-I is likely to become as commonplace in the office and the school as CD audio already is in homes. Among the advantages claimed for CD-I are that it is easily transportable from room to room (ie, can be used anywhere where there is a suitable TV set), and that there is no need to waste time training learners how to use the equipment. The first four CD-I packages launched in the UK by SPIN UK are:

- The Complete Manager (a training package approved by the Management Charter Initiative, and supported by the National Council for Vocational Qualifications [NCVQ], which includes guidance and assessment towards a BTEC Certificate in Management);
- Developing Competence through Coaching, Mentoring and Assessing;
- Welcome to Work (an induction training package);
- No Need to Shout (an assertiveness training package).

An ever-increasing flow of such training packages is planned.

Photo-CD

'Photo-CD' or 'Picture-CD' is yet another adaptation of compact disc technology, but this time involving discs on which photographs, pictures and so on can be recorded digitally. The technology is being developed jointly by Kodak and Philips. At the same time as taking a normal 35mm colour film for prints or slides, it is now possible to order the images to be recorded onto such a compact disc. Each disc can hold between 100 and 125 digitized images. They are stored on the disc in a 'master' format, ie retaining all the quality of the original source. They can be copied from the disc 'faultlessly' as many times as may be wished, and downgraded to a lower-resolution form suitable for displaying on a normal television screen, in which case as many as 800 images can be stored on a single disc. All the normal features of compact disc technology apply; for example, a given image (or a planned sequence of images) can be selected through an infrared remote controller and the images played in the order desired (and timed accordingly if wished). Text can be added to the images, or parts of a selected image can be 'zoomed into', indexes can be compiled, and the user can create soundtrack material to accompany the displays.

A Photo-CD setup will play ordinary audio compact discs as well, and various CD-I systems will be wholly compatible with Photo-CD. It is anticipated that the Photo-CD facility will be incorporated into many of the better domestic sound systems, at only marginally extra cost. Photo-CD is already being used in medicine, data storage, training manuals and mail-order catalogue development, and could be an attractive way for holiday companies to display their locations, or even for supermarkets to promote visually their special offers of the week. We can imagine Photo-CD developing to play stimulating and useful roles in education and training, for example:

- allowing colour illustrations of high quality and high resolution to be projected on to lecture-room screens, with 'instant' access to chosen images, rather than the 'backwards–forwards' searching of slide magazines or carousels;
- allowing zoom-in or zoom-out to be done 'live' during presentations, rather than having to show separate slides showing different magnifications;
- allowing the sequence of images to be re-selected as easily as changing the planned track-sequence for an audio compact disc, rather than tedious loading of magazines or carousels.

When equipment for playing Photo-CD becomes present in most homes, distance-learning organizations such as the Open University in the UK may well find it cost-effective to mass-produce Photo-CDs containing still-image illustrations relating to course materials, again with the possibility of learners altering the magnification of the displayed images at will, and possibly even 'interacting' with the images (for example, 'clicking' an icon, pinpointing a defect, identifying a component, and so on) and receiving feedback from information programmed on to the compact disc.

CONCLUSIONS

In all areas of everyday life, computerized equipment has become increasingly used. Some examples include:

- bar-code scanning at supermarket checkouts and itemized receipts
- bills and bank statements, cash dispensers and so on

- programmable video recorders
- remote controlled domestic entertainment equipment
- video games
- digital telephone equipment.

The list is endless! It is therefore not surprising that computer-based learning resources and teaching aids are increasingly common in education and training. The younger generations have no fear of computers. They are not afraid that they will break them – unlike some of their older counterparts. Computer-based resources are likely to become as common as once was chalk in classrooms and training rooms. The variety of computer-based resources already defies sensible description in a single chapter in a book like this. Nevertheless, we hope that our intention of reminding you of the broad picture of computer-based training has been achieved. We have also included an extended Bibliography covering recent publications in the wide field of computer-based training and added a list of some of the most relevant journals where the most recent developments in the field are expounded. Interested readers are referred to these.

Chapter 11

A Glimpse into the Future

INTRODUCTION

In Chapter 1, we briefly examined the history of educational technology, showing how it has developed and matured in the last few decades. In this, the final chapter of our book, we will attempt to look into the future, trying to make informed guesses as to how the current trends in educational technology will be affecting education and training at the start of the the twenty-first century. We also hope that this final chapter will enable us to pull together the various topics that have been examined in the earlier parts of this book and help readers to develop their own perspectives of the many things that are encompassed by the term 'educational technology'

CURRENT TRENDS IN EDUCATIONAL TECHNOLOGY

We believe that there are a number of important underlying trends in the roles of educational technology in education and training. In fact, we have identified no less than twelve such trends, and we will devote the rest of this chapter to speculation on how these trends may change the face of education and training (or at least some features of the face) in the next 10 or 20 years. Some of these trends are of the 'technology *of* education variety, and include:

1. A continuation of the firm (if sometimes slow) shift towards learner-centredness, rather than teacher-dominated or trainer-led provision.
2. A continuing increase in the use of individualized learning materials, rather than traditional face-to-face teaching-learning situations.
3. An increasing realization that there is much more to education and training than the teaching of facts and principles; in other words, that the processes of learning are even more important than the content of syllabuses.
4. A growing appreciation of the importance of competences which relate to life as a whole rather than particular job

specifications, including interpersonal skills, leadership skills, creative thinking and problem-solving skills.

5. A continuation of the various moves to clarify and specify the nature of intended learning outcomes, such as the formulation of competence descriptors and performance criteria (often based on objectives).

6. Growing awareness of the advantages of learning by working in groups (with and without teachers or trainers present) and of the dangers of the isolation which can accompany individualized learning (and the 'isolation' which, in a different way, pervades mass instruction systems).

7. An increasing realization of the artificiality of traditional assessment methods (such as three-hour written examinations) as vehicles for measuring many of the competences which it is intended to develop through education and training.

Other trends are of the 'technology *in* education variety, and include:

8. A continuation of the rapid escalation in information technology and computer-aided systems.

9. The participation of a much greater proportion of the education and training communities in the design and use of computerized equipment and programs.

10. Increasing expectations from learners regarding the provision and round-the-clock availability of stimulating multi-media learning resources.

11. Increasing expectations from learners that teachers and trainers will make fuller use of educational technology support devices to increase the effectiveness of their courses and programmes.

12. Rapidly escalating familiarity of learners with sophisticated media, including interactive laser-disc hardware and software, due to similar technology being in many homes as part of home-entertainment systems (often with parallel educational software such as electronic books and databases).

For the remainder of this chapter, we would like to expand on the possibilities (and the dangers) which could result from the continuation and development of each of these trends. However, we are well aware that it is usually unwise to speculate – and we invite readers who dislike such speculation to close our book now (as the list of 12 trends is in itself a summary of much of our book).

1. *A continuation of the firm (if sometimes slow) shift towards learner-centredness, rather than teacher-dominated or trainer-led provision.*
We believe that a distinct *lack* of learner-centredness in the past has been responsible for many people escaping from education at an early stage and staying as far away from education and training as they could for the rest of their careers. In the model of learning that we introduced at the end of Chapter 1, one of the key stages was

'wanting' to learn. Already, there is abundant evidence that many people are returning to learning in mid-career (and even after retirement) to learner-centred programmes such as those offered by the Open University.

It is also well known that comparatively more learning takes place during the first four or five years of life than during any other such period. One characteristic of 'early' learning is the natural inquisitiveness of the human mind and the pleasure children gain as they acquire new competences (and new knowledge). Sadly, the education systems often seem to subdue this natural enthusiasm to learn, not least due to the insistence that certain things must be learned. Perhaps the secret that the most gifted teachers possess is the ability to enable young children to *want* to learn the things that in this world they are going to *need* to learn.

The trend towards learner-centredness will continue, we feel, but at a cost. For example, teachers and trainers who are accustomed to traditional approaches may feel uncomfortable, unvalued and unskilled in the arts of learner-centred provision.

2. *A continuing increase in the use of individualized learning materials, rather than traditional face-to-face teaching-learning situations.*
Open- and flexible-learning materials are already widely used in distance-learning programmes. The quality of such materials has increased dramatically over the last two decades, not least because of the use of educational technology principles and resources in their design and formulation. However, such materials are still most often used by individuals, alone, and often at a distance from an educational or training establishment. We feel that in the next few years, such materials will be used additionally in the following ways:

- as learning resources for group-based learning, without tutor or trainer presence. It is relatively easy to 'translate' a good flexible learning package designed for individual use, to one designed for group use, for example by adding group exercises and activities and providing feedback comments for members of the groups to reflect on after undertaking such activities
- as learning resources for group-based learning in the presence of tutors or trainers. This allows all the benefits of peer-group feedback and 'learning from each other' to continue, but has the additional advantage of the extra 'resource' – that of the experienced, skilled tutor or trainer. Our primary concern with this use of flexible-learning materials does not relate to the quality of the materials themselves, but to the difficulties of some tutors or trainers in making the adjustment to being a 'resource' rather than a leader
- as alternative learning pathways in college-based or training-centre-based courses. We accept that there will always be learners who prefer face-to-face contact with tutors and trainers and

who even enjoy sitting in formal lectures. However, when parallel learning resource provision exists, why not allow the learners who *don't* like formal teaching-learning situations to manage the learning in their own way? Provided that either pathway links fairly to the assessments that the learners face in due course, we see no difficulty with allowing learners this sort of choice.

3. *An increasing realization that there is much more to education and training than the teaching of facts and principles; in other words that the processes of learning are even more important than the content of syllabuses.*

This realization seems to grow rather too slowly in the minds of those who have ultimate control of education provision in the UK! However, employers are keen to take on employees who will be highly competent, not just highly knowledgeable. When we think of the multitude of things we have learned in our time which were never of use to us, and of the many skills we did not have the opportunity to learn during our education and training, and which we had to pick up as best we could by trial and error in later life, our hope is that the next 20 years will see a further progression away from content-dominated education.

4. *A growing appreciation of the importance of competences which relate to life as a whole rather than particular job specifications, including interpersonal skills, leadership skills, creative thinking and problem-solving skills.*

This appreciation already exists in the world of employment. In fact, more attention to such skills would not only create a more flexible workforce, it would create a better society. Skills like these can not be 'taught' in the traditional sense of the word. They can, however, be 'facilitated'. They are high-level skills, and are best learned by 'doing' and (particularly) through 'feedback', yet so often they only have lip-service paid to them in education provision. Not so in training. Similar skills constitute the backbone of 'customer care' training, 'dealing with the public' training, management training and so on. The world of education has a lot to learn from the world of training here. A useful first step (which is already happening in many places) is the credit-rating by universities of the programmes provided in the world of training; this is already helping to bridge the (unnecessary and unfortunate) gap between education and training. Educational technology has long been another bridge across this gap, and should continue to bring the two sectors closer together.

5. *A continuation of the various moves to clarify and specify the nature of intended learning outcomes, such as the formulation of competence descriptors and performance criteria (often based on objectives).*

When people know exactly what in due course they are expected to be able to do, they are usually well on their way towards being able to deliver the goods. Competence descriptors are now providing a much clearer picture of exactly what people should aim to become able to demonstrate. In particular, more attention is being given to describing the *evidence* which reflects the achievement of specified competences. In many ways, this attention to giving a picture of the 'evidence' is the most useful dimension of the 'competence revolution'. It also allows learners to recognize the value of competences they already have developed, in terms of the evidence they can already supply to demonstrate their achievements.

We hope that the next 20 years may see a swing away from becoming 'rule-bound' in matters such as the expressions of objectives and competence descriptors and that the aim will be clarity to learners rather than 'to impress academics, moderators and policymakers'.

6. *Growing awareness of the advantages of learning by working in groups (with and without teachers or trainers present) and of the dangers of the isolation which can accompany individualized learning (and the 'isolation' which, in a different way, pervades mass instruction systems).*

We have at several times in this book emphasized the importance of feedback to learners as an essential step in successful learning processes. While 'expert-witness' feedback of the sort that trainers and tutors can give has indisputable value to learners, there is no doubt that the feedback that learners can give each other is also of great value. In particular, when group work is built in to either massinstruction or individualized learning programmes, it can allow learners to get *much more* feedback than they may have been able to get from trainers or tutors. Another advantage of peer-group feedback is that it is often better received than feedback from a 'figure of authority', in that learners can be much less defensive when receiving feedback from each other. The processes of giving and receiving peer-group feedback are useful in their own right, helping to develop interpersonal and communication skills. We anticipate a steady growth in the use of group work to complement mass instruction programmes, as well as to supplement individualized learning programmes.

7. *An increasing realization of the artificiality of traditional assessment methods (such as three-hour written examinations) as vehicles for measuring many of the competences which it is intended to develop through education and training.*

In our chapter on Assessment, we raised serious concerns not only about the validity and reliability of assessment devices and processes, but also about what some of these actually assessed (or failed to assess). For example, written examinations tend to measure people's ability to succeed at answering exam questions in writing against the clock – not really a very important competence in the real world. Examinations may well test whether candidates have particular knowledge and information at their fingertips 'on the day', but in the real world it is usually much more useful to be able to *find* the requisite information quickly rather than to know it, and more important still to be able to *use* it to solve problems, and so on.

The swing towards competence descriptors moves the emphasis away from what people happen to know on a particular morning, towards what evidence they can provide for their ability over a period of time. While admitting that traditional examinations are relatively easy to design and administer, we feel that the next 20 years will see a steady swing towards the use of self- and peer-assessment, where one of the main purposes of assessment is to provide useful learning experiences, and feedback.

The above overlapping speculations relate to how we see the 'technology *of* education' trends developing over the next decade or two. We are well aware that several factors can cause acceleration or deceleration of any of these trends, including:

- government thinking (and spending) on education and training
- global economic factors
- employment prospects and the likelihood of people needing to retrain
- the style in which universities and colleges are led and managed
- changes in attitudes and expectations of learners, particularly mature learners
- attitudes of teachers and trainers to changes in what is expected of them.

However, the other trends we mentioned, those of the 'technology *in* education' variety, are much less dependent on the vagaries we have just listed. Let us continue this chapter by speculating how these trends may progress in the next 10 or 20 years.

8. *A continuation of the rapid escalation in information technology and computer-aided systems.*

The development of information technology has been described as being 'explosive' in the 1980s and 1990s. Few educators or trainers of 20 years ago could have imagined the sophistication and impact of present-day educational technology resources and techniques, so we feel it would be unwise to try to guess what the next 20 years may bring. However, we have noticed that while the sophistication and impact of educational technology has been increasing so quickly, the cost in real terms both of the hardware and software has been falling dramatically. Similarly, the physical size of computers, control equipment and databases has decreased, increasing their portability and ease of use. Most important of all, the mass production of equipment such as video recorders and recently CD-I systems is bringing them into the homes of many more people than could have been imagined a few years ago. The fact that children are being brought up in a world where they use computer-based equipment both at school and at home and for both work and play purposes, means that familiarity with the technology side of 'educational technology' is increasing exponentially.

Some years ago, many people were seriously concerned at the potential damage of the extended hours for which children were exposed to broadcast television. Many people now feel, however, that such exposure has its own natural cut-off – in other words, the television set becomes merely part of the 'wallpaper' while children think about other things as they both work and play. We feel bold enough to speculate that similar effects will overtake computer games and other leisure high-technology equipment. In other words, after a while, the marvel of new developments will become taken for granted. When this happens, the high-technology equipment now being introduced into education and training will cease to be a novelty, making it easier to see beyond the technology to the content of educational programs and the processes by which learning takes place.

9. *The participation of a much greater proportion of the education and training communities in the design and use of computerized equipment and programs.*

This should result in part from the familiarity we mentioned in point 8 above. At present, it tends to be the 'technical enthusiast' who becomes involved in the design of computer-based programmes or interactive video software. However, the availability of authoring languages enables educators or trainers with only a basic knowledge of how the 'new technology' works, to design educational programs which exploit the technology. We believe that, just as now, almost every tutor or trainer knows how to use an overhead projector and to design transparencies for projection, in the next few years more and more 'ordinary' members of the education and training professions will play a part in designing learning resource materials using relatively sophisticated equipment. This, coupled with increasing learner-centredness in the design of the content of programmes, should help the education and training communities to think in terms of effective learning, rather than in terms of how they teach or train.

10. *Increasing expectations from learners regarding the provision and round-the-clock availability of stimulating multi-media learning resources.*

Many educational organizations already have learning resource centres available to learners for extended hours. With increased student numbers, some universities are already extending the teaching day, timetabling some lectures during the evenings. In part-time education, evening classes are of course anything but a new development. Training organizations provide more intensive short courses than they once did and somewhat fewer extended courses. These short courses often use workshop formats (learner-centred), and it is not unusual for them to be timetabled from 9 in the morning to 9 at night (with more informal work in the bar thereafter!). We envisage the 'teaching' day being extended and more weekend classes provided in colleges and universities. This has implications regarding the conditions of employment of teaching and training staff of course, and there may well be some obstacles on the path to greater flexibility. The increased expectation of *quality* of learning support materials seems inevitable. Just as learners in the UK are accustomed to highly exacting standards regarding the technical and editorial quality of broadcast television, expectations will demand that training videos demonstrate similar standards. With multimedia packages, learners' expectations will continue to rise. Once they have worked with an excellent, stimulating package, they will be very critical of anything less good.

11. *Increasing expectations from learners that teachers and trainers will make fuller use of educational technology support devices to increase the effectiveness of their courses and programmes.*

Some years ago, when much teaching and training was face-to-face and didactic, with learners writing down what was being said to them or shown to them, *any* use of educational technology was a welcome relief. In future, we think learners will be far less willing to try to write down everything that goes on in lectures or training sessions, but will expect as a matter of course to be given the content in print and to spend the time in such sessions *exploring* the content, or *discussing* the implications, or *practising* techniques and so on. A one-page handwritten handout with the main headings on it will be frowned upon. Learners will expect to be given an interactive handout of several pages, which they can use actively during the session and which will be a permanent learning resource for them thereafter. Such handouts will be expected to contain any tables of data, pictures, flowcharts, models and so on that are projected during the course of a session, rather than learners being expected to sketch them for themselves.

12. *Rapidly escalating familiarity of learners with sophisticated media, including interactive laser-disc hardware and software, due to similar technology being in many homes as part of home-entertainment systems (often with parallel educational software such as electronic books and databases).*

We think this will result in a much greater willingness on the part of learners to accept responsibility for extending their learning at home. Electronic books may be loaned in the same way as libraries loan textbooks, with multiple copies available for class use. Groups of learners will require the facility to book the use of equipment and resources, so that they can study them collaboratively under their own initiative. With mature learners, other members of their families will take more interest in the content of programmes of study when they see home entertainment systems being used as study aids. (Already, Open University materials are often read by spouses and children, and Open University broadcasts are watched by millions of people who are not students of the University.) In other words, learning will become less of a separate activity done in a separate place (for example a college) and more a part of the fabric of normal life. Already, visionaries talk of creating a 'learning society'; educational technology will play a vital part in bringing this to fruition.

PRE-SCHOOL, PRIMARY, SECONDARY, TERTIARY AND CONTINUING EDUCATION AND TRAINING

We no longer feel it necessary to offer many speculations on how each of these sectors will evolve in the next 20 years, nor do we think it wise. We will, however, offer some general comments about the picture as a whole. We feel that the importance of 'staff development' for educators and trainers will be understood better than it is at present. No longer will a one-off training course or educational programme equip trainers or teachers for a lifetime of service. The move towards learner-centredness will continue in all sectors. Pre-school and primary education are already very learner-centred, with learning demonstrably along the lines of the 'wanting', 'doing', 'feedback' and 'digesting' model we have discussed. There is already considerable emphasis on group learning and individualized learning running hand-in-hand in these sectors. Secondary education may be the sector most difficult to move from the comparatively traditional approaches often used therein. Much depends on the relative emphasis that is placed in future on syllabus content versus learning and teaching processes. We hope that the use of competence descriptors will help make secondary learning more understandable to learners and more relevant to the world they are destined to be part of. We believe that the boundaries between tertiary education and continuing education will continue to fade, as the model in which education was a one-off process that equipped people for life disappears.

We also believe that the boundaries between education and training will tend to melt away to a considerable extent. All of these boundaries between sectors and organizations are, after all, irrelevant if the overriding consideration is *learning*. Helping people to learn is the common factor. Perhaps in 20 years time the definition of 'educational technology' will be far easier than it is today. It may no longer be necessary to think of the 'technology *of* education and training' or the 'technology *in* education and training'. It may be simple and accurate to define educational technology along the lines of:

> ways and means of enabling people to learn effectively, and helping them to put their learning into practice.

FINAL WORD

This book bears witness to the accelerating growth of educational and training technology. Though the growth of the 'technology *in* education and training, dimension is highly visible, the growth of the 'technology *of* education and training' dimension is probably even more pervading. Increasingly, the whole of educational technology is taking more account of how people learn – whether in crowds, small groups, or as individuals. All this has far-reaching consequences for practitioners in education and training. There has been a rapid growth in the range and diversity of techniques, resources and approaches which practitioners are required to employ. This has wide-ranging implications for the staff development requirements of educators and trainers.

Gone are the days when a one-off pre-service training course in teaching and learning techniques could serve practitioners for a career in education or training. Staff development is needed on a massive scale to ensure that practitioners are able to put the advances of educational technology into use in their work. Such staff development needs to move far beyond the skills required to give traditional lectures or classroom presentations. Staff development for educators and trainers needs to be much more than merely keeping up to date with the advances in their subject disciplines; it needs to focus not only on the design of learning resource materials, but also on the processes whereby successful learning occurs.

Individualized learning, in all forms, is already one of the most important ways in which educational technology helps learning to take place. Increasing emphasis now needs to be given to group learning and interpersonal skills development. Faced with an array of learning resources and learning environments, learners themselves need to be helped to develop their entire approach to learning. We hope that this book will go some way towards helping teachers and trainers to increase their skills in the many aspects of educational technology that they will use in their everyday work. We hope that, through them, this book will also help to make learning more successful and more enjoyable for the next generations of learners.

Glossary of Terms used in Educational Technology

PREFACE

This glossary includes most of the terms we used in the last edition of this book, with the addition of new terms which have crept into the technology of education and training since that time. We decided to leave in some of the older terms which are used less often nowadays, since even though they may not have been used in the chapters of the present book, readers will still find them in many older books and papers of interest. Words in italics are cross-references.

A

Ability profile a chart or diagram which provides a graphical representation of learners' scores in respect of a number of separately-assessed aptitudes and abilities, thus giving a balanced picture of their overall competences.

Access a term used in discussions of the opportunities that an educational or training system offers regarding entry into the system. In recent years many such systems have reduced their formal entry requirements (exam qualifications, etc) so as to offer *wider access*, ie, entry opportunities for a much wider range of applicants than was traditionally the case. Estimation of the entrant's *ability to benefit* is increasingly being taken into account, regardless of qualifications.

Accessory materials a US term for any teaching materials that are used to supplement basic textbooks, eg audiotapes, tape-slide programmes, video materials, computer-based learning packages, etc.

Accreditation of prior achievement, experience, learning granting formal recognition of the achievement, experience or education of learners or trainees, prior to admission to a course or training programme. This is done by giving appropriate remission from part of the normal work of the course or programme; see also *credit accumulation and transfer*.

Achievement test a test designed to measure people's knowledge, skills, understanding, etc, in a given area at a particular time, as opposed to their potential for learning.

Acoustic coupler a device that enables a remote terminal to be connected to a computer via an ordinary telephone link by using a *modem* to convert the digital signal into an analogue signal and then converting it back into digital form after transmission.

Action research processes of learning-by-doing (including learning by making mistakes when this can be done safely) in a real-life situation (factory, office, business) or in a simulated environment of the same sort.

Active, activity learning learning which involves active participation on the part of the learner, ie, 'learning by doing'.

Adaptability the ability of learners or trainees to handle change and respond to uncertainty; one of the so-called *enterprise skills*.

Adjunctive programme a type of instructional programme which incorporates a set of questions which are presented to the learner at the end of a text (or section of a text) in order to determine what has been learned.

Advance cue, signal synonyms for *synchronizing signal*.

Advance, advanced organizer an overview of new material which is presented before teaching (or exposing a learner to) the material in order to prepare the learner's cognitive structure. Objectives and competence descriptors can be valuable components of advanced organizers.

Affective (adjective) relating to attitudes, feelings or values; see also *affective domain*.

Affective domain one of the three broad sets into which Bloom and his colleagues classify learning objectives, containing all those connected with attitudes, feelings and values (see Chapter 3).

Agricultural/botanical approach (to evaluation) a scientific approach to evaluation that involves measuring the extent to which specific objectives are achieved by an instructional system under controlled conditions; contrast with *social/anthropological approach*.

Aims the desired outcomes of an exercise, programme, etc expressed in fairly general terms; cf *objectives* (see Chapter 3).

Algorithm a series of instructions or procedural steps that can be used to solve problems of a given type, reach decisions in a given area, etc.

Analog(ue) a term applied to something that is continuously proportional to some variable or to a device or system that handles or processes material in analog(ue) form (eg analog record players or cassette recorders); cf *digital*.

Analysis a *cognitive* process which involves breaking down an idea, system, process, etc into its constituent parts and examining the relationships between those parts; level 4 of Bloom's *cognitive domain* (see Chapter 3).

Analytic(al) method of marking a method of marking essays, projects, etc based on a separate assessment of specific aspects or features; cf *impression method of marking*.

Animation creation of an illusion of movement in a visual display by use of special effects.

Application a *cognitive* process in which a learner, given a new problem, will be able to make use of the appropriate theories, principles, facts, etc needed to tackle it; level 3 of Bloom's *cognitive domain* (see Chapter 3).

Applications software *computer programs* (or suites of programs) that are designed to carry out specific jobs for the user of the computer; cf *system software*.

Artificial intelligence (AI) simulation of the characteristics and cognitive functions of the human brain using 'intelligent' computer systems such as the *fifth-generation computers* currently being developed.

Aspect ratio the numerical ratio of the horizontal length of a picture, screen, etc to its height.

Assessment grid a table or grid used in the *analytical method of marking* in order to help the marker assess specific aspects of an essay, project, etc independently. Equally useful in self-assessment and peer-assessment (see examples in Chapter 7).

Atomist a person whose preferred learning style is *atomistic learning*; cf *holist*.

Atomistic learning a *learning style* in which ideas are developed piece by piece, with the result that sequences of pieces can be repeated without the learner necessarily having a clear understanding of the whole.

Attention span the time during which a learner can give his full attention to a topic, programme, etc (see Chapter 4).

Attitude scale a linear instrument designed to assess people's attitudes to a specific issue, phenomenon, etc by determining their positions on some form of rating scale.

Audible advance a term applied to a synchronized sound/vision presentation with an audible *synchronizing signal* which indicates when the next frame should be shown.

Audio relating to sound, or to the sound aspects of a system, signal, programme, etc.

Audio signal an electronic signal, either in *analogue* or *digital* form, representing a specific sound and capable of being used to reproduce that sound; cf *video signal*.

Audio tutorial (AT) an *individualized learning* system based on the use of audiotapes, generally in conjunction with other types of learning materials to which the learner is directed by the recorded commentary.

Audiovisual specifically, a term used to describe instructional materials or systems which use both sound and vision; more generally, a term used to describe all educational communications media.

Author(ing) language a *programming language* (such as MICROTEXT) designed to enable people with little or no conventional programming skills to write *computer-aided learning* materials. See also *authoring system*.

Authoring system the system which which an *author(ing) language* is designed to be used, consisting of a suitable *work station* together with all the necessary *software*.

Autonomous learner a learner who controls the selection and content of the learning materials and also has control over the pace of the learning process (see Chapter 2).

Autonomy of learning the degree to which learners have control over their own learning, for example: choice of modes of learning, attendance patterns; see also *flexible learning*.

Auto-threading a facility in a film projector, tape recorder or similar device whereby the film or tape is threaded into the machine automatically. (Now largely replaced by the use of cassettes, where auto-threading still takes place, but without being seen).

B

Backing store an extension to the *main store* of a computer, generally physically distinct from it.

Back projection projection of an image on to the back of a translucent screen for viewing from the opposite side.

Backward branching a type of *branching* in programmed instruction in which learners are sent back to repeat items which they have not yet mastered; also known as *washback*.

Barrel distortion distortion of a projected image whereby straight lines parallel to the edges of the field curve inwards at their ends; cf *pincushion distortion*.

Batch mode, processing, system a method of using a computer in which all the data relating to a given task (or set of tasks) are fed into the computer at one time and processed to give a specific output (or set of outputs) based on this.

Battery any group of tests, scales, etc that are normally administered consecutively over a short period, the results being used to give an overall picture of performance, ability, attitude, etc in the area of interest.

Behavioural objective a precise statement indicating the performance expected of a learner (in terms of specific skills) as a result of exposure to given instructional material; see also *Magerian objective*.

Behavioural(-ist) psychology the school of psychology which holds that all behaviour of an organism can be explained in terms of the *stimulus-response mechanism*; also known as behaviourism.

Bit an abbreviation for binary digit. One bit represents the smallest amount of information that can be held in a computer store or carried by a communication channel. The two binary digits are 0 and 1.

Black box a term (originating from the name of Professor Black, an early worker in the field of systems theory) for an electronic device whose internal mechanism is hidden from (or is irrelevant to) the user, or, more generally, any system whose input and output are much more important than its internal mode of operation.

Bloom's taxonomies a set of taxonomies of learning objectives, compiled by the American psychologist B S Bloom and his co-workers, in which all such objectives are classified into three broad groups, or domains – the *cognitive*, *affective* and *psychomotor* domains. (See Chapter 3).

Booting (a) a computer term for transferring a *program* from a disk (usually a floppy disk) to the computer's *working memory* and running the program; (b) also used in computing to denote the use of an extremely simple process to initiate a more complex one.

Brainstorming a technique for generating ideas, solving problems, etc whereby members of a group are encouraged to originate ideas, no matter how wild or apparently unrelated to the topic under discussion and then to consider their potential. The term 'brainstorming' is also now used for a similar process used by people working alone, for example to generate a range of ideas to select from when writing an essay or report.

Branch see *branching program, branching programme*.

Branching program a *computer program* that incorporates *branches*, ie points at which alternative courses of action are possible.

Branching programme a *programmed learning* sequence that incorporates *branches*, ie points at which the learners are directed to alternative items depending on their responses to the items just tackled (see Chapter 1).

Briefing an introductory session for the participants in a game, simulation or other exercise that is used to describe the background to the exercise, assign roles, etc.

Broadcast videotex(t) *videotex(t)* in which a limited number of pages of information are incorporated into ordinary television transmissions and can be 'called up' by owners of receivers that incorporate the necessary decoding facilities; the British CEEFAX and ORACLE systems are typical examples.

Bulletin board (a) a panel of cork, wood or other soft material to which pictures, notices and other display materials may be pinned: (b) a form of *electronic mail* system whereby computer users can pool and/or exchange information via a suitable *network*, or via the public telephone system.

Bulk eraser a device (incorporating a powerful electromagnet) that can erase the signals recorded on an entire reel or cassette of *magnetic tape* at one time, without the need to unwind the tape.

Bulletin typewriter a manual or electronic typewriter which produces very large print, suitable for *OHP transparencies*; also known as a *primary typewriter*.

Buzz session a short period in a lesson or exercise in which small groups of people (buzz groups) intensively discuss a given topic.

By-passing missing out part of an instructional programme because of successful performance of earlier parts, successful performance in a diagnostic test, etc. See also *forward branching, skip branching.*

Byte in computing and data processing, a group of adjacent *bits* (usually eight) that together form a larger unit, such as the code for a letter, number etc.

C

Cablecasting dissemination of information via cables, as in *cable television.*

Cable television a television system in which the signal is distributed to subscribers via cable rather than by broadcasting; cable systems can carry a much larger number of channels than broadcast systems, and (in some cases) also enable users to communicate with the distribution centre; see also *switched-star system, tree-and-branch system.*

Cafeteria plan see *course unit plan.*

Camcorder the new generation of portable video recorders, usually powered by rechargeable batteries and taking video cassette cartridges of one sort or another; see *VHS, VHS-C, Super VHS-C, 8mm, Hi-8.*

Capacitance, capacitive videodisc a *videodisc* which depends on the variation of the electrical capacitance between the disk and the sensor to read the information stored; cf *contact videodisc, optical videodisc* (optical videodiscs are by far more common now).

Caption generator an electronic device for creating alphanumerical captions using a keyboard and feeding them directly into a *video signal.*

Carrel a small enclosed space in a library, resource centre, language laboratory, etc designed for individual or private study. See also *dry carrel, wet carrel.*

Cartridge a type of *cassette* carrying a closed loop of audiotape, videotape or film that does not require re-winding.

Case study an in-depth examination of a real-life or simulated situation carried out in order to illustrate special and/or general characteristics.

Cassette a closed container of film or magnetic tape designed for loading and unloading into a suitable projector, reader or recorder without prior threading.

CD-I (Compact Disc Interactive) systems using compact discs containing audio, graphics and video information, combined with interactive programs, allowing users to interact with the software using infrared remote controllers, joysticks, or light pens. The software available includes management training packages and games and simulations.

CD-ROM (Compact Disc Read-Only Memory) a term applied to compact discs containing electronic information or databases which can be text files (for example dictionaries, electronic books), graphics images or motion sequences.

Ceiling and floor effects reduction of the usefulness or effectiveness of a test or other form of assessment due to the upper and lower limits of performance (the ceiling and floor) being too close together.

Central processor, processing unit (CPU) the main part of a computer system, comprising the main store, arithmetic unit and control unit, or (in the case of some modern computers) simply the arithmetic and control units.

Chaining a mode of learning in which the learner connects two or more previously-learned *stimulus-response bonds* into a linked sequence.

Changeover cue another name for a *synchronizing signal*.

Characterization an *affective* process that involves the organization of values into a total and consistent philosophy; the highest level (level 5) of Bloom's *affective domain* (see Chapter 3).

Check list a predetermined list of items to be looked for or asked about, eg during observation of a process or in an interview.

Class analysis chart a chart on which the relative performances of the members of a class of pupils or students are displayed in graphical form.

Class interval the range of scores between the upper and lower boundaries of a class or score in a test or other assessment.

Clip a term used to describe a short excerpt from a motion picture film or videotape, especially when it is used in a different context (eg in a lesson, or as part of a larger presentation).

Clip art ready-to-use illustrations that can be transferred on to artwork, overhead transparencies, etc from plastic sheets. The term 'clip art' is also now used to describe computer software, whereby graphics, pictures and diagrams can be 'lifted' and 'pasted' into desk-top publishing files.

Closed access a practice whereby users are not normally given direct access to the stock of a library or resources centre or to parts thereof, such access being restricted to the staff of the library or centre (see Chapter 9).

Closed-circuit television (CCTV) a television system which limits distribution of the signal to those receivers or monitors which are directly connected to the origination point by coaxial cable, optical fibre or microwave link; see also *cable television*.

Closed question an examination or test question in which a unique answer is required and where there is no scope for divergent thinking, evaluation, explanation, etc.

Cloze procedure a language development technique that involves learners in trying to understand passages from which words have been deleted at regular intervals (typically every sixth or seventh word) or from which certain parts of speech have been deleted. See also *Cloze test*.

Cloze test a standard test for assessing the *readability* of textual material based on the use of the *Cloze procedure*.

Cognition a generic term for the rational processes of perception, discovery, recognition, imagining, judging, memorizing, learning and thinking through which an individual obtains knowledge and conceptual understanding.

Cognitive domain one of the three broad sets into which Bloom and his co-workers classify learning objectives, containing all those associated with the acquisition of knowledge or knowledge-related skills (see Chapter 3).

Cognitive psychology a school of psychology that holds that learning comes about as a result of the restructuring of perceptions and thoughts *within* individuals, thus enabling them to perceive new relationships and solve new problems.

Cognitive skill a skill associated with the acquisition, application or manipulation of knowledge, relating to *cognition* or the *cognitive domain*.

Cognitive style an alternative name for *learning style* or *thinking style*.

Cohort a group (or set of groups) of individuals chosen for investigation, analysis, etc on the grounds of a particular criterion, eg the year in which they entered a course.

Collator a machine (or section of a machine) which uses a series of boxes or shelves to sort or order sheets, cards, etc automatically, eg in reprography or data processing.

Compact cassette the most commonly used type of audiotape *cassette* containing tape 4mm wide and having separate supply and take-up spools.

Compact disc a disc on which information (audio, video, or text) is recorded in *digital* form; such discs are only 5" in diameter (hence the name) and are played in a similar way to an *optical videodisc*, using a laser to read the signal.

Compact Disc Interactive see *CD-I*.

Compact slide a 2" × 2" *slide*, as opposed to a *lantern slide*.

Compatibility (of learning resources) the suitability of one learning resource as it relates to other learning resources in terms of content, format, target, population, etc.

Competence a broad term used to describe the range of abilities that people can demonstrate. Competences are often expressed in the form of 'can do' statements, such as 'can work effectively as a member of a team' (see the examples in Chapter 3).

Competence-based progression a form of individualized, self-instructional learning in which learners are not allowed to progress to the next stage of the learning programme until they have demonstrated complete mastery of the current stage.

Competence descriptor the terminology with which competences are described, for example descriptions of the *evidence* necessary for learners to demonstrate that they have developed and displayed identified competences, skills or abilities; see also *range statement*.

Competence objectives behavioural objectives expressed in terms of work-related activities; see also *competence, competence descriptor, competence statement*.

Competence statement an expression of the performance that can be demonstrated by a learner who has achieved a particular competence, ability or skill.

Compiler a special *computer program* that enables user programs written in a particular *high-level (programming) language* to be handled by a particular make or model of computer by translating the program into the appropriate *machine code*.

Completion item a test *item* in which an incomplete statement, calculation, figure, etc has to be finished by the person taking the test, usually by supplying a missing word, symbol, number, section etc.

Comprehension a *cognitive* process whereby an individual understands a particular idea, set of knowledge, etc without necessarily being able to relate it to other material or appreciate its wider implications; level 2 of Bloom's *cognitive domain* (see Chapter 3).

Compressed speech recorded speech that is processed so as to increase the number of words per minute without any increase in pitch or distortion.

Computer any device, usually electronic, which is able to accept information, apply some processing procedure to it, and supply the resulting information in a form suitable to the user; see also *mainframe computer, minicomputer, microcomputer,* and also *first-, second-, third-, fourth-* and *fifth-generation computer.*

Computer-aided (assisted) assessment, examination, test an assessment, examination or test that is constructed and/or administered and/or marked with the aid of a computer.

Computer-aided (assisted) instruction (CAI) use of a computer as an integral part of an instructional system, the learner generally engaging in two-way interaction with the computer via a terminal (see Chapter 10).

Computer-aided (assisted) learning (CAL) learning with the aid of a computer through *computer-aided instruction,* computer simulations, etc.

Computer conferencing linking of microcomputers (or terminals on mainframe computers) so that any number of users can add entries to text files, or reply to entries already in the files. Users of computer conferencing can send messages over telephone lines to any part of the word using, for example, JANET (Joint Academic Network). The computer software is normally programmed to show users 'unseen' messages (ie, messages and entries they have not yet read) in order when they log in to the conference. Computer conferencing is increasingly being used by staff and students in higher education and by company personnel in industry, particularly in companies with several sites in a country, or with global operations.

Computer graphics the generation and/or display of graphic materials by computers, either on a *video display unit* or as *hard copy* produced by an electronic or mechanical plotter.

Computer-managed instruction (CMI) the use of a computer in a managerial or supervisory role, the computer prescribing work schedules, carrying out assessment etc.

Computer-managed learning (CML) a term used virtually synonymously with *computer-managed instruction.*

Computer-marked assignment a technique (pioneered by the UK Open University) whereby a computer is used to mark assignments completed by students at home; the student fills in his responses on special sheets which can be read by the computer, which guarantees a feedback letter to each learner.

Computer program the coded instructions that are given to a computer in order to enable it to carry out a specific set of actions.

Computer store any computer sub-system or *peripheral* in which data can be stored in a form in which it can be read by the computer. See also *backing store, main store.*

Computer terminal an electronic device which permits communication between a user/learner and a computer; see also *data tablet, graphics terminal, intelligent terminal, keyboard terminal, remote terminal, smart terminal.*

Computerized item bank an *item bank* which is held in a computer store and can be accessed via a computer terminal.

Concept cards information-carrying cards included in *resource materials* to stimulate awareness of key concepts in a particular topic or subject.

Concept film, tape a short sequence, recorded on film or tape, which gives an illustration or demonstration of a single concept or idea.

Concrete materials physical objects (eg models) or *realia* used in teaching.

Conditioning manipulation or *reinforcement* of behaviour in an individual.

Confidence testing a method for discriminating between levels of partial knowledge relating to the content of a test item in which learners indicate their respective degrees of confidence in the answers they choose.

Conflation the fusing together of two sets of scores to give a single overall mark, eg combining a *continuous assessment* score with a *terminal assessment* score.

Console a generic name for a piece of equipment (often desk-like and non-moveable) carrying the control panels, monitoring equipment, etc needed to control a computer, television studio, etc.

Constant angular velocity (CAV) a *videodisc, digital optical disk* or *compact disc* replay mode in which the disc(k) spins at a constant number of revolutions per second; cf *constant linear velocity (CLV)*.

Constant linear velocity (CLV) a *videodisc, compact disc* or *digital optical disk* replay mode in which the information is read at constant linear speed along a continuous spiral track similar to that on an ordinary gramophone record; cf *constant angular velocity (CAV)*.

Contact videodisc a type of *videodisc* on which the signal is read by electrical means using a stylus that is in actual contact with the surface of the disk; cf *optical videodisc, capacitance, capacitive videodisc*.

Content-centred a term applied to a *game, simulation* or other exercise whose educational objectives relate mainly to the subject matter on which the exercise is based; cf *process-centred*.

Continuous assessment on-going assessment of learners throughout a course of instruction or section thereof; cf *terminal assessment*.

Contract-based learning, teaching, training learning, teaching or training in which an agreed contract of learning expectation or objectives is drawn up between the learner and the tutor, a contract which the learner is expected to fulfil for assessment purposes.

Control track (a) on an audiotape, a *track* carrying instructions on operations to be carried out during running; (b) on a videotape, a *track* used to carry synchronization and similar information.

Controlled discussion a discussion in which learners may raise questions or make relevant comments, but whose general direction is under the control of the teacher, tutor or instructor (see Chapter 6); cf *free group discussion*.

Convergent thinking a rational, systematic approach to problem-solving, normally leading to the single correct, best, most conventional, or most logical solution; cf *divergent thinking*.

Conversational language natural language used to communicate on-line with a computer; see also *conversational mode*.

Conversational mode on-line dialogue between a computer and a user.

Copyright the right to reproduce or to authorize reproduction or performance of a literary, dramatic, musical or artistic work.

Core course (a) a teaching course in which a skeleton framework of ideas and teaching activities is provided and in which the individual teachers are able to add their own methods, ideas, etc; (b) a course that has to be taken as part of the *core curriculum* of a school, college, etc.

Core curriculum (a) key elements or subjects in the curriculum operated by a school, college, etc that are taken by all pupils or students; (b) basic elements in a course that have to be taken by all students, regardless of their selection of optional modules, materials, etc.

Core module, subject a *module* or subject that forms part of the *core curriculum* of a course.

Correction for chance, guessing reduction of the total in a test score according to a standard correction formula that is designed to allow for correct answers made by the candidate purely as a result of guessing.

Correspondence course a form of *distance learning* course that relies mainly on the postal service to provide a link between the individual learner and the person or organization running the course.

Counselling (a) advice and support given to participants during a *game*, *simulation* or similar exercise; (b) guidance given to pupils or students regarding their courses, future careers, etc.

Course unit plan a type of modular course that enables a student to build up credits by taking a series of optional courses, which may have different credit values depending on their relative length, importance and difficulty; also known (in the USA) as the *cafeteria plan*, and (in the UK) as the *pathway scheme*.

Courseware (a) a term that is becoming increasingly widely used as a synonym for instructional *software*, in the broadest sense of the word; (b) the actual instructional material, including both the content and the instructional technique, that is incorporated in a computer-based instruction system, as opposed to the *software*, which is taken to refer to the *computer program* that controls the computer's operation.

Credit accumulation a process whereby learners or trainees can acquire portions of qualifications over a period of time, often from a variety of different programmes; see also *credit accumulation and transfer systems (or schemes) CATS*.

Credit accumulation and transfer systems (schemes) (CATS) formalized systems of *credit accumulation* and *credit transfer* operated within a region or a country.

Credit transfer acceptance and recognition of an award or credit obtained for one purpose, or in one organization or institution, as part-credit towards another award or qualification in another organization or institution; see also *credit accumulation, credit accumulation and transfer systems (schemes) (CATS)*.

Criterion a characteristic or measurement with which other characteristics or measurements are compared.

Criterion frame in *programmed learning*, another name for a *test frame*.

Criterion-referenced assessment assessment designed to determine an individual's achievement with reference to predetermined, clearly-defined performance standards (see Chapter 7); cf *norm-referenced assessment*.

Cross-fade to fade out the image from one slide projector at the same time as the image from a second projector (focused on the same screen) is faded in; a technique used to present slide or tape-slide programmes without any 'gaps' between successive slides. The technique is also common in video editing processes.

Cross-media approach a methodology based on the principle that a variety of audiovisual media and experiences, correlated with other instructional materials, overlap and reinforce the value of one another.

Cue (a) a command or signal for a previously-specified event to take place; (b) in *programmed learning*, another name for a *prompt*.

Curriculum the subject areas or sections covered within a specified course of study.

Curriculum design, development the process of planning, validating, implementing and evaluating new curricula, etc.

Customized instruction instruction that is designed to meet the specific needs of individual learners, as in *programmed instruction*.

Cyclorama (cyc) a continuous curtain or back cloth suspended around the periphery of a film or television studio or stage.

D

Data base (database) a collection of data, bibliographic information, etc held on file and available for extraction or reference, usually via a computer terminal.

Data compression a technique whereby information is stored in a computer's *memory* in 'shorthand' form, thus using less memory capacity than would normally be required.

Data tablet a device whereby graphic material can be inputted into a computer by 'writing' on its (electromagnetically-sensitive) surface using a *light pen* or other form of electronic stylus; also known as a *graphics tablet*.

Daylight projection a projection system that produces an image bright enough to be seen without darkening the room.

Daylight screen a projection screen so constructed that clear images from a slide or other projector are visible in an undarkened room.

Debriefing review and discussion of the processes and outcomes of a *game*, *simulation* or similar exercise.

Decoy another term for a *distractor* in multiple-choice testing.

Dedicated a term applied to a computer, machine, system, etc that is set apart for special use.

Deductive method a method of teaching, study or argument which proceeds from general or universally-applicable principles to particular applications of these principles and shows the validity of the conclusions.

Deep processing a type of study method in which a learner reads material in order to gain deep understanding of the material being studied; cf *surface processing*.

Delivery system (a) in teaching, training, individualized learning, etc, a combination of medium and method of usage that is employed to present instructional information to a learner; (b) in *distance learning*, the method by which distribution of instructional materials to learners is organized.

Desktop publishing producing multiple copies of paper-based materials in one's own office or work situation using the methods of *electronic publishing*.

Developmental testing testing of a course, programme, exercise, system, etc carried out while it is actually being developed in order to identify and eliminate weaknesses.

Diagnosis the process of determining the existing capabilities and competences of learners by analysing their performance of a hierarchy of essential tasks in a specific subject, with the object of facilitating their learning by assigning appropriate remedial or advanced learning tasks.

Didactic method a method of instruction that emphasizes rules, principles, standards of conduct and authoritarian guidelines, usually conveyed directly to the learner by someone else.

Differential weighting assigning different weights (marks) to different options in a multiple-choice question in order to give some reward for partly correct answers.

Difficulty index another name for *facility value*.

Difficulty score a score that indicates the highest level of difficulty achieved by an individual in the assessment of a particular skill, quality, etc.

Digital a term applied to an information processing, storage or transfer system in which the signal is translated into binary code before processing, storage or transmission, or to the signal handled by such a system; cf *analog(ue)*.

Digital audio tape a recently introduced high-quality sound recording system in which the audio signal is recorded on audiotape in *digital* rather than *analogue* form. Domestic cassette recorders are now available which can play cassette-tapes of both formats (though of course the high-quality sound is only available from digital recordings).

Digital optical disk (DOD) a disk designed for the recording, storage and retrieval of *digital* information, using laser optics; see also *EDOD, OROM, WOOD*.

Digitizer a device for converting a graphical image into a *digital* signal capable of being handled by a digital computer.

Diorama three-dimensional representation of a scene, usually created by placing objects, figures, etc in front of a two-dimensional painted background.

Direct access (a) a situation where users of a library, resources centre, computer, etc have unrestricted access to all (or part) of the stock, or to the system; (b) in computing, another term for random access, as in *random access memory*.

Directed observation guided observation provided for the purpose of improving the study, understanding and evaluation of that which is observed.

Directed private study individualized instruction, normally carried out at home, that is built into a course which also uses other methods such as face-to-face instruction.

Directed reading a type of *directed private study* that involves reading specific books or sections thereof.

Discovery area a portion of an *open classroom* which is provided with reading, audiovisual and manipulative materials relating to one particular interest, activity or subject.

Discovery learning a method of instruction that attempts to teach principles or general concepts by providing learners with a set of relevant experiences from which it is hoped they will arrive at the principles of concepts by the process of induction; see also *inductive method*.

Discrimination index a measure of the ability of a *multiple-choice item* to discriminate between students of high and low ability; it is equal to the difference between the *facility values* for the top and bottom thirds of the candidates (see Chapter 7).

Disk drive a computer *peripheral* using data which can be read into or out of a *hard disk* or *floppy disk*.

Dissolve a gradual transition between two visual images in which one fades out as the other fades in.

Distance learning learning carried out by learners who are geographically remote from the body or person organizing the instruction (see Chapter 5).

Distractor an incorrect option in a *multiple-choice item* (see Chapter 7).

Divergent thinking a creative approach to solving problems and tackling tasks which produces a range of original solutions, procedures, etc.

Dot matrix printer a low-quality *printer* in which each character is made up of a series of dots; cf *letter-quality printer, laser printer*.

Double-frame a term used to describe a *filmstrip* where the horizontal axis of the pictures is parallel to the length of the film; also known as *full frame*.

Down a term to describe a computer or other system which is out of action due to malfunction, etc.

Down-time the period (absolute or fractional) for which a learning resource (usually a device or system) is out of action due to breakdown, routine servicing, etc; cf *up-time.*

Drill an ordered, repetitive learning activity intended to help develop or fix a specific skill or aspect of knowledge.

Dry carrel a 'bare' carrel which has no electrical connections and is fitted with no special equipment, being intended for study of paper-based materials only; cf *wet carrel.*

Dubbing (a) combining two or more *audio signals* into a composite recording; (b) transferring an *audio signal* from one medium or machine to another; (c) making a copy of a tape; (d) in film production, recording new dialogue to be substituted for the original.

Dumb terminal a *computer terminal* with no independent data processing capability; cf *intelligent terminal, smart terminal.*

E

Earphones another name for *headphones.*

Easement a legal process whereby a copyright holder grants limited performance, reproduction, publication or other rights to another person, body, etc while retaining ownership of the actual copyright.

Editing (a) selecting and re-arranging recorded audio and/or video signals or film into a new continuity by manual or electronic means; see also *electronic editing, mechanical editing*; (b) removing unwanted material from and/or inserting new material into a document, file, computer file, etc prior to storage, publication or use.

EDOD *e*rasable *d*igital *o*ptical *d*isk; a type of *digital optical disk* that is being developed as a possible replacement for magnetic disks.

Educational age (EA) another name for *mental age.*

Educational technology (a) the development, application and evaluation of systems, techniques and aids to improve the process of human learning; (b) the application of scientific knowledge about learning, and the conditions of learning, to improve the effectiveness and efficiency of teaching and training. In the absence of scientifically established principles, educational technology implements techniques of empirical testing to improve learning situations; (c) a systematic way of designing, implementing and evaluating the total process of learning and teaching in terms of specific objectives, based on research in human learning and communication and employing a combination of human and non-human resources to bring about more effective instruction (see Chapter 1).

Egrul(e) an *inductive method* of instruction in which the learner is led through a series of examples (the 'eg's) before having to formulate the 'rule' that explains them or ties them together; cf *ruleg.*

Eidophor a type of television projector which first produces an intense primary image by electronic means and then projects this by means of a system of lenses similar to those in a film projector.

Eight mm (8mm) (a) videotape cassette format designed for the newer forms of camcorders, giving higher picture and sound quality than VHS or VHS-C, and using improved recording processes and higher-quality videotapes than the above; (b) a standard size of motion picture film.

Eight-track a term applied to an audiotape (usually in a cartridge) with eight separate tracks of sound recorded on it; the term may also apply to the players and recorders used with such audiotapes.

Electronic blackboard or writing board a type of *digitizer* on whose display surface material can be written or drawn, such that the material can be electronically transmitted and reproduced on a similar device (or set of similar devices) elsewhere.

Electronic books compact discs readable by lasers (similar to domestic audio compact discs) but containing text information and graphics images. Applications include dictionaries, encyclopaedias, literature, catalogues, databases and so on.

Electronic classroom a classroom (such as a *language laboratory*) in which instruction can be given to and feedback received from individual learners by electronic means, usually via individual *carrels* connected to a master *console* operated by the teacher or instructor.

Electronic editing a form of audiotape or videotape *editing* in which the signal from one recorder is re-recorded on another machine.

Electronic flipchart Similar in size and shape to a flipchart, but allowing electronic photocopying of what is written on its surfaces. Normally, the surfaces are in the form of a write-on flexible white markerboard, and when one or both sides are written on, the images can be reduced in size and printed out on paper (eg A4 size). The same sort of pens are used as for whiteboards and the surfaces are erased with a soft damp cloth (or spirit-moistened cloth if necessary).

Electronic mail communications medium whereby messages are transmitted to computer terminals from one user to another (or several others). Such systems often display 'new messages' automatically when individual users 'log on' to the system. Where terminals are coupled to a printer, messages can be printed out in 'hard copy' if required. Electronic mail can be sent to remote sites down telephone lines, and internationally using the Joint Academic Network (JANET).

Electronic publishing the reproduction and distribution of documents using the electronic media or *new information technology* rather than by conventional printing and publishing methods; see also *desktop publishing*.

Electrostatic copying a reprographic process that first produces an electro-statically-charged image of the original material on a plate or drum and then uses this to transfer pigment particles to the copy paper; also known as *xerography*.

Elliptic questioning a method of question writing (widely used in *programmed learning*) whereby a learner is not asked questions directly but is left to complete statements by adding missing words.

E-mail see *electronic mail*.

Enactive learning a term (first used by Olson and Bruner) to denote learning through direct experience as opposed to learning via *media* of some sort (*mediated learning*).

End spurt in learning, a final increase in effort made at the end of a period or sequence of work.

Enhancement materials instructional materials which are used to extend understanding of basic course material in specific areas.

Enterprise the willingness and ability of individuals to take a pro-active, self-determining and flexible approach to influencing and shaping their own futures; see also *enterprise skills*.

Enterprise skills a genetic term for skills involving initiative, drive, self-determination, flexibility, exerting influence, entrepreneurial skills, etc. In other words, skills connected with displaying *enterprise* characteristics.

Entry behaviour the set of skills which learners possess at the time they enter or begin a course or sequence of instruction.

Entry level performance a set of statements specifying the prior skills and concepts necessary for undertaking a particular learning task, sequence of instruction, course, etc.

Entry skills another term for *entry behaviour*.

Episcope a name for an *opaque projector* that is commonly used in the UK.

EPROM *e*rasable *p*rogrammable *r*ead- *o*nly *m*emory; a *PROM* (programmable read-only memory) from which the encoded *program* can be erased, thus allowing the device to be re-programmed; cf *read-only memory (ROM)*.

Erase head the *head* in a tape recorder which removes any previous recording from the tape prior to new material being recorded.

Error score the difference between individuals' *raw scores* in a test or assessment and their *true scores*.

Essay test, examination a test or examination that involves writing essays of a given length on one or more topics (see Chapter 7).

Evaluation (a) a *cognitive* process which involves making judgements about the value of ideas, works, solutions, methods, materials, etc for some specific purpose; the highest level (level 6) of Bloom's *cognitive domain* (see Chapter 3); (b) a series of activities designed to measure the effectiveness or value of a course, instructional programme, exercise, etc (see Chapter 8).

Evaluation instrument any of the means by which one obtains information for the purpose of *evaluation*, eg questionnaires, rating scales.

Experiential learning learning which is based on participants' reactions to the activities experienced during an exercise, ie, a combination of 'learning by doing' and feedback to learners.

Expert system (a) a computer system which is programmed with all the knowledge that is currently available in a particular specialized field and is capable of making 'intelligent' evaluations in the field; (b) sometimes used as a synonym for an *artificial intelligence* system or intelligent learning system. Also known as a *knowledge-based system*.

Expert witness method a group instruction technique in which students question or cross-examine one or more experts in a particular field.

Expository display a display which presents information only; cf *inquisitory display*.

Expository organizer a preliminary lesson in which learners are introduced to material that is completely new and unfamiliar to them by using principles and concepts with which they are already familiar to form a 'cognitive bridge' to the new material; see also *advance(d) organizer*.

Expository teaching methods teaching methods that are based on exposition, ie presentation of material to a class in a lesson, lecture, etc.

F

Facilitator a group-discussion leader whose primary function is to act as a catalyst in stimulating discussion rather than providing information.

Facility index, value the fraction (expressed as a decimal) of candidates choosing the correct answer or *key* in a multiple-choice question (see Chapter 7).

Facsimile transmission (fax) an electronic system whereby an exact copy of a document can be produced at a distance, in *hard copy* form, usually down telephone lines.

Feedback (a) the information received by learners immediately after each of their responses during a sequence of programmed instruction which indicates the correctness (or otherwise) of the response; (b) communication of responses to a teacher by learners, as in a *feedback classroom.*

Feedback classroom a special classroom where student positions are electronically or electrically connected to the teacher's desk so that responses to multiple-choice questions or similar items can be monitored by the teacher.

Feltboard a flat display surface covered with felt, flannel or similar material on to which pictures, symbols or shapes backed with the same or similar material will adhere; also called a *flannel board* or *flannel-graph.*

Fibrevision a cable television distribution system that employs optical fibres to carry the signals; such systems can carry many more channels than conventional systems; see also *switched-star system.*

Field test, trial the assessment of a near-final system (eg an instructional exercise or programme) in an appropriate realistic setting prior to full-scale production and/or use.

Fifth-generation computer a term applied to the new type of *computers* currently being developed to act as *expert systems*; cf *first-, second-, third-, fourth-generation computer.*

Film clip a short sequence of motion picture film used as an insert in a presentation to illustrate a specific point.

Film gauge the width of a motion picture or photographic film; the most commonly used gauges are 8mm, 16mm, 35mm and 70mm.

Filmstrip a strip of 35mm film carrying a sequence of positive photographic images intended for projection (or viewing) as still pictures.

Firmware a term applied to a *computer program* that is recorded in a storage medium from which it cannot be accidentally erased, or to an electronic device containing such a program, eg a *ROM, PROM* or *EPROM*; cf *software.*

First-generation computer a term applied to any *computer* based on the technology of electronic valves (vacuum tubes); all the early computers built during the late 1940s and 1950s were of this type; cf *second-, third-, fourth-, fifth-generation computer.*

Fishbowl session a group-discussion technique whereby a number of the class sit in an inner circle and hold a discussion while the remaining members sit around the outside and observe the interaction.

Fixed-response item a type of objective test *item* which provides all the options from which a testee must select correct responses; cf *free-response item.*

Flannelboard, flannelgraph alternative names for a *feltboard.*

Flashcard a card or other opaque material carrying words, pictures or other information designed to be displayed briefly, usually by hand, during a programme of instruction.

Flesch formula a standard formula that is used to give a quantitative measure of the *readability* of textual material based on the number of syllables in a typical sample of 100 words and the number of sentences (including any incomplete sentence) in the sample.

Flexible learning a term increasingly being used to describe institution-based learning systems where learners have some *autonomy of learning* (see Chapter 5).

Flexistudy an individualized learning system in which students are provided with learning materials for home-based study, counselling, tutorial support and access to college facilities (see Chapter 5).

Flip chart a set of large sheets of paper attached to an easel unit so that they can be flipped over the top of the unit into or out of view as a presentation progresses (see Chapter 4); see also *electronic flipchart.*

Floppy disk a small flexible magnetically-coated disk (usually 8", 5¼", 3½" or 3" in diameter) used as a medium for storing data in *digital* form; cf *hard disk.*

Fog index a numerical indicator of the *readability* of a text.

Follow-up activities additional and/or enrichment activities that are used to build upon the work of a lesson, the content of a programme, etc.

Font originally a set of printer's type of uniform style and size; now extended to denote a particular alphanumeric character set available within a system such as a *video display unit, word processor* or *desk-top publishing system.*

Forced-choice item another term for a *fixed-response item.*

Formal prompt (cue) in *behavioural psychology* or instructional design, a *prompt (cue)* which provides information about the form of the expected response; cf *thematic prompt (cue).*

Formative evaluation evaluation of instructional programmes or materials while they are still in some stage of development (see Chapter 8).

Forward branching in programmed learning, *branching* in which the learner is sent forward by several frames if he makes a correct response; also known as *washhead.*

Foundation course (studies) a course designed to provide a basis for more advanced or more extended studies.

Foundation training in occupational training, the organized learning of the basic skills appropriate for a specified occupation or related range of occupations.

Fourth-generation computer a term applied to a *computer* based on the technology of integrated circuits; such computers, which started to be built in the late 1970s, are much more compact than earlier computers and also have much greater calculating powers than earlier machines of comparable price; cf *first-, second-, third-, fifth-generation computer.*

Fractal compression a type of *image compression,* based on fractal theory, that enables extremely high compression ratios to be achieved, thus greatly reducing the amount of *memory* needed to store a given image; used in *electronic books.*

Frame (a) each separate presentation of a small basic unit of material, eg an individual picture in a series of pictures such as a motion picture film or filmstrip; (b) one of the discrete stages into which a *programmed learning* sequence is broken down, i.e. a *step.*

Frame game a type of *game* or *simulation* which is structured in such a way that a variety of roles, ideas and relationships may be inserted as and when required or appropriate.

Free group discussion a group discussion in which the specific topics covered and the direction that the discussion takes are largely controlled by the learners (see Chapter 6); cf *controlled discussion.*

Free-response item a test *item* in which responses can be made freely, provided that they satisfy set criteria, eg as in a *completion item;* cf *fixed-response item.*

Frieze a long wallchart on which scenes are built up by pupils.

Front-end processor a separate processing system (such as an analog-to-digital converter or microcomputer) that is used to pre-process signals or data before they are fed into a computer.

Front projection projection of an image on to the front of an opaque screen, for viewing from the same side as the projector; cf *back projection*.

Full-frame another term for *double-frame*, as applied to a *filmstrip*.

Full-track a term applied to an audiotape with a single recording track covering almost the whole width of the tape.

G

Gain score the measured amount of favourable change in an individual of some trait or variable due to treatment or instruction.

Game in an instructional context, any exercise that involves competition (either between participants or against the game system) and rules (arbitrary constraints within which the participants have to operate).

Gate frame in *programmed instruction*, a *frame* in a *branching programme* that poses a key question, the answer to which determines the next frame to which the user is routed.

Gate-keeper function the 'qualifying' function of an examination or assessment that has to be passed in order to progress to further instruction.

Gateway course a course that is taken with the specific object of attaining the qualifying standard for another course such as a first or higher degree.

General purpose language a computer *programming language* whose use is not restricted to a single type of computer or to a small range of computers; examples are BASIC, COBOL, FORTRAN and PASCAL.

Generic skills skills that are fundamental to a class of activities and are transferable from one job or activity to others.

Ghost (a) an 'after image' that remains on a chalkboard, whiteboard, etc after material has been rubbed or wiped off; (b) a secondary image on a television screen, due to faulty transmission or reception.

Goal-free evaluation *evaluation* in which the evaluator examines the actual effects of a programme without prior consideration of the programme goals.

Goal specification the detailed description of the desired results of an action or programme prior to the action or programme.

Graded difficulty a term applied to a series of tasks that are made progressively more difficult in order to extend a learner's capabilities gradually; a technique commonly used in *programmed learning*.

Grading on the curve a grading system in which grades or marks are allocated to the students in a class or large group so that they conform to the *normal distribution*; a form of *norm-referenced assessment* (see Chapter 7).

Graphical plotter an electro-mechanical device that can draw graphs, diagrams, etc on the basis of signals supplied by a computer.

Graphics tablet another name for a *data tablet*.

Graphics terminal a *computer terminal* on which graphical materials may be created, altered, displayed, etc.

Group dynamics the methods by which a group of people function as a collective whole.

Group learning *learning* that takes place through some form of interactive small-group activity, eg in a *game* or *simulation* (see Chapter 6).

Group pacing a type of programmed group instruction in which all the members of the group progress in lockstep (that is, all doing the same tasks at the same time).

Guided discovery learning a form of *discovery learning* in which the activities of the learner are partly structured or pre-determined by the teacher.

H

Half-frame another term for *single-frame*, as applied to a *filmstrip*.

Half-track a term applied to an audiotape with two separate recording tracks on it, each approximately half the width of the tape.

Halo effect in assessment, bias resulting from the assessor being influenced by favourable traits or behaviour on the part of the person being assessed.

Haptic (learner) a term applied to a learner who, in a visual sense, analyses the visual presentation of material into discrete elements; the visual version of an *atomist* or *serialist*; cf *visual learner*.

Hard copy information printed, typed or otherwise reproduced on paper, as opposed to information temporarily displayed on a screen, held in a store, coded on tape, etc (known as *soft copy*).

Hard disk a large, rigid disk (or stacked system of disks) on which digital data can be stored in magnetic form; such disks can carry much more data than *floppy disks*.

Hardware a generic term for the equipment used in instruction, computing, etc; cf *software*.

Hawthorne effect in learning, where improvement apparently brought about by the use of a new technique is wholly or partly due to the increased interest and motivation produced by the use of the technique rather than to the intrinsic properties of the technique itself.

Head (a) a component of a tape recorder, compact disc player, video-disc player, computer peripheral, etc whereby a signal can be read into or out of the system or existing signals erased; (b) the system that carries the characters in a daisy wheel printer, golf ball printer or similar device.

Headphones two small audio transducers connected to a headband for individual listening to audio sources; also known as *earphones*.

Hectograph (gelatin) duplication a once commonly-used type of *spirit duplicating* process in which copies of writing, drawing, etc are made from a pre-prepared gelatin surface to which the original image has been transferred.

Helical scanning a video recording technique in which the tape is wrapped helically round a fixed drum while the recording head rotates within a slot in the side of the tube, thus producing a diagonal scan across the tape as it moves through the machine.

Heuristic a term used to describe the method of instruction or problem-solving that involves using successive evaluations of trial and error in an attempt to arrive at a final result; see also *discovery learning*.

Hi-8 a tape cassette format for use in camcorders. It is more compact than VHS or VHS-C cassettes, with more advanced recording characteristics and higher quality videotape, producing better picture quality and, particularly, better sound quality.

Hidden curriculum the informal and subtle ways in which a school, college or similar establishment mirrors and supports the accepted values of the social system or organization that runs it; see also *informal curriculum*.

Higher cognitive a term applied to educational objectives, learning skills, etc that fall in the upper part of the *cognitive domain (application, analysis, synthesis* and *evaluation)*; cf *lower cognitive* (see Chapter 3).

High-level (programming) language a computer programming language which provides a range of facilities and standard constructions designed to simplify the writing of computer programs.

Histogram a graphical representation of a frequency distribution in the form of a vertical bar chart.

Holist a term applied by Pask to a person who learns, remembers and recapitulates material as a whole; cf *serialist*.

Hologram a visual recording, produced using a laser, which presents the illusion of three dimensions, including parallax.

Home experiment kit a package supplied or sold to students so that they can perform practical experiments at home, eg as part of a *distance learning* course.

Home study (a) course-related work carried out by pupils or students at home in their own time; (b) study carried out at home, eg as part of a *distance learning* course, *correspondence course*, etc.

Hook-and-loop board a display board covered with a nylon (or nylon-type) surface containing a large number of tiny loops on to which materials backed with tape strips carrying tiny hooks will adhere firmly.

Horizontal transfer (of learning) a form of *transfer of learning* in which no new higher-order skills are learned, but in which existing skills are applied to a new task (or set of tasks) of similar level of difficulty; also known as *lateral transfer*.

Humanistic psychology a school of psychology that emphasizes the concepts of 'self' and 'person' and the study of 'humanness' in an integrated or holistic manner as opposed to an analytical or psychometric style (see Chapter 1).

Hypercard a versatile software package developed by Macintosh Computers, which (for example) allows interactive computer-based learning programmes using text and graphics to be developed by educators and trainers without any specific knowledge of computer programming.

Hypermedia a general term for the new generation of interactive computer-based multimedia systems, originating from Macintosh 'Hypercard'. The term 'Hypermedia' also now includes such developments as CD-ROM, electronic books and CD-I.

Hypnopaedia literally 'education in sleep' (from the Greek); learning carried out while the learner is asleep, eg by playing audiotapes; also known as *sleep teaching*.

I

Ice breaker (a) an activity designed to establish rapport and generate a receptive atmosphere in a group of people who are about to take part in an exercise, course, etc; (b) a preliminary question or short paper taken by students before starting an examination in order to accustom them to the examination room environment and help overcome nervousness; it is not usually marked as part of the examination proper.

Icon in computing and desk-top publishing, a pictorial representation of a *menu* function, eg use of a picture of a pencil to indicate a drawing facility.

Illuminative evaluation another name for the *social/anthropological approach (to evaluation)*.

Image compression a type of *data compression* that enables graphic images to be stored in a computer's *memory* using less memory capacity than would normally be required; see also *fractal compression*.

Impression method of marking a technique of marking a composition, essay, etc purely on the basis of the overall impression it creates; cf *analytic(al) method of marking*.

Inaudible advance a term applied to a synchronized sound/vision presentation with an inaudible *synchronizing signal*.

In-basket (in-tray) technique a method of training or instruction in which an individual is called upon to play a specific role and must, in isolation, respond to a number of hypothetical situations as they arise.

Independent learning, study an instructional system in which learners, carrying on their studies without attending formal classes, consult periodically with instructors or tutors for direction and assistance (see Chapter 5).

Individualized instruction, teaching, learning the tailoring of instruction, teaching or learning to meet the needs of the individual learner rather than the learning group as a whole (see Chapter 5).

Inductive method a method of instruction that involves presenting learners with a sufficient number of specific examples to enable them to arrive at a definite rule, principle or fact embracing the examples; see also *egrul(e)* and cf *didactic method, deductive method*.

Informal curriculum material learned informally by association with fellow pupils, students or trainees; see also *hidden curriculum*.

Information technology the technology associated with the creation, storage, selection, transformation and distribution of information of all kinds; see also *new information technology*.

Inlay an image inserted or incorporated in another image as, for example, in television production.

Inquisitory display a display which asks a question; cf *expository display*.

Instant lettering rub-down adhesive letters which can be transferred from plastic or paper carrier sheets on to artwork.

Intelligence quotient (IQ) the ratio (multiplied by 100) of an individual's *mental age*, as measured by intelligence tests, to his or her chronological age.

Intelligent terminal a *computer terminal* which can be used to perform some local data processing without the assistance of a central processor.

Interactive a term used to describe an exercise which involves participants in communicating with one another in some way; see also *interactive mode*.

Interactive courseware development a technique whereby a teacher plans, writes and evaluates a computer-based course or instructional programme using a computer terminal.

Interactive mode a method of using a *computer* whereby the user carries out an *on-line* dialogue with the computer via a suitable terminal.

Interactive video a hybrid individualized learning system in which a *videodisc* recorder is linked to a *computer* (see Chapter 4).

Interactive videotex(t) *videotex(t)* in which the user is connected to a computer *data base* by cable (usually a telephone line) and can therefore interact directly with the data base; the British PRESTEL system is a typical example.

Interdisciplinary a term used to describe an exercise, programme, course, etc that draws its material from a number of different subject areas and illustrates the links and relationships that exist between them.

Interpersonal skills skills used in relating to and dealing with other people.

Inventory test (a) a general term for personality tests and questionnaires designed to assess or identify attitudes, traits or personality characteristics; (b) a stock-taking test used to determine the level of prior knowledge or later achievement in short components of a course of instruction; see also *pre-test* and *post-test*.

ISDN International Standard Data Networking – the high-capacity telephone line system used to provide *videophone* links.

Item (a) in assessment, a single component or question in a test; (b) in programmed learning, another name for a *frame* or *step*.

Item bank a bank of multiple-choice *items* from which multiple-choice tests can be made up by selecting suitable items.

Item difficulty gradient the extent to which items in a test or examination are arranged in order of increasing difficulty (a common practice in objective tests).

Item editing, trial testing, validation see *shredding*.

J

Job aid any form of 'aide memoire' designed to facilitate either the learning or the performance of a task.

Job competence the set of skills needed to carry out a particular job effectively, comprising task-related skills, task-management skills and the skills associated with dealing with the job environment.

Joypad a 'disc' which performs the same functions as a *joystick*.

Joystick a lever with two degrees of freedom that is used to control a cursor, 'write' on a *video display unit*, or in video games.

K

k (a) in conventional scientific usage, an abbreviation for kilo; used as a prefix to denote multiplication by 100, as in kW; (b) in computing, an abbreviation for 2^{10} (ie 1024, not 1000 as is sometimes mistakenly supposed); used as the standard unit in which capacity of computer *memory* is measured, 1k of memory corresponding to a storage capacity of 1024 *bytes*.

Keller Plan a type of individualized learning strategy based on the self-paced study of (mainly) written material backed up by tutoring and monitored by means of mastery tests at the end of each unit (see Chapters 2 and 5).

Key the correct answer to a *multiple-choice item* (see Chapter 7).

Keyboard terminal a computer terminal that incorporates a keyboard similar to that on a typewriter.

Keypad a small hand-held keyboard of the type used to call up pages of a videotex(t) system.

Keystoning the production of a trapezoid (out-of-square) image on a projection screen due to the fact that the screen is not perpendicular to the axis of projection.

Knowledge a cognitive process which involves the remembering of facts, ideas, etc without necessarily understanding them or being able to make use of or manipulate them; the lowest level (level 1) of Bloom's *cognitive domain* (see Chapter 3).

Knowledge-based system another name for an *expert system*.

L

Laboratory mode CAL *computer-assisted learning* in which the computer acts as a 'substitute laboratory', using which the learner can carry out simulated experiments (see Chapter 10); cf *tutor-mode CAL*.

Landscape (format) a term used to describe the format of a page, book, document, drawing, photograph, etc with an *aspect ratio* greater than 1:1; cf *portrait (format)*.

Language laboratory a room equipped for language instruction in which tape recorders, projectors, record players and other devices are used singly or in combination in order to present material, provide feedback, etc (see Chapter 5).

Laser printer a high-quality *printer* system that uses a laser to produce the characters on the copy paper.

Laservision a generic term for video systems that make use of *videodiscs* from which the recorded information is read using a laser.

Lateral thinking a term (first used by de Bono) that describes the process of solving a problem by indirect or interactive methods rather than by adopting a logical, direct approach.

Lateral transfer another name for *horizontal transfer*.

Leaderless group a group of learners who are required to carry out some activity on their own without any member of the teaching staff being present to act as leader; such a group may, however, choose a leader from within itself.

Lead-lecture a lecture designed to present material and information for later discussion or given in preparation for participative work.

Learner-based (-controlled, -managed) education education in which the individual learner has considerable influence over what is taught, how it is taught, the pace of instruction, etc (see Chapter 2).

Learning (a) in *behavioural psychology*, a change in the stable relationship between (i) a *stimulus* that an individual organism perceives and (ii) a *response* that the organism makes, either covertly or overtly; (b) a relatively permanent change in *behaviour* that results from past experience, produced either inadvertently or deliberately.

Learning (aids) laboratory an alternative name for a *resources centre*.

Learning block a flaw or weakness in an individual's cognitive function that causes difficulty in mastering a particular item, subject, group of subjects, etc.

Learning-by-appointment system a system in which learners can obtain access to teachers, instructors, self-instructional materials, hardware, etc as and when they need them by making appropriate appointments or booking arrangements.

Learning contract see *contract-based learning, teaching, training*.

Learning curve a graphic representation of the rate of progress of a learner (or group of learners) produced by plotting some appropriate measurable variable against time.

Learning resources all the *resources* which may be used by a learner (in isolation or in combination with other learners) to facilitate learning.

Learning resources centre an alternative name for a *resources centre*.

Learning style the preferred mode of problem-solving, thinking or learning that is employed by an individual; sometimes called *cognitive style*.

Lesson plan an outline of the important points of a lesson arranged in the order in which they are to be presented to the learners by the teacher.

Lesson unit a discrete individual lesson designed to form part of a larger course or sequence of lessons.

Lettering device, system any system designed for use in adding lettering to graphic or other materials.

Letter-quality printer a *printer* that produces output of similar quality to a standard typewriter; such printers generally employ golf ball or daisy wheel printing heads, and generally print on to single sheets of paper.

Life skills a generic term for the various *enterprise skills* and other *process skills* needed to cope effectively with the outside world.

Light box a back-illuminated translucent surface used for viewing and working with transparent graphic and photographic materials.

Light-emitting diode (LED) a solid-state electronic component which emits light when an electric current is passed through it; used to display data, as on/off indicators, etc.

Light pen a pen-like implement that may be moved across the face of a computer *data tablet* or light-sensitive monitor screen in order to enter new data or alter existing data.

Likert scale an *attitude scale* involving the use of a list of statements to which an individual has to respond, normally from a range of degrees of agreement/disagreement (see Chapter 8).

Linear programme a type of instructional programme in which no *branching* occurs (see Chapter 1).

Line printer a printer mechanism that produces a *hard copy* printout from a computer, word processor, etc one line at a time.

Liquid crystal display (LCD) a data display technique that produces visible characters as opaque liquid crystals by application of suitable electric fields.

Listening centre an audio distribution device to which several sets of headphones can be connected in order to enable more than one learner to hear an audio programme at the same time.

Listening group an organized group that meets to hear an audio presentation of some sort (eg a radio broadcast or audiotape) as part of an instructional programme.

Listing a computing term for a line-by-line *readout* or *printout* of a *computer program* (or section thereof), a set of data, etc.

Long-term memory that part of the human *memory* in which material is stored on a long-term or permanent basis as opposed to a short-term, temporary basis; cf *short-term memory*.

Loop film a length of motion picture film joined as an endless band to facilitate continuously-repeated projection; usually contained in a *cartridge*.

Lower cognitive a term applied to educational objectives, learning skills, etc that fall in the lower part of the *cognitive domain* (*knowledge* and *comprehension*); cf *higher cognitive* (see Chapter 3).

Low-level (programming) language a computer *programming language* (such as *machine code*) which requires the programmer to specify his program in minute detail, but also gives access to the more intimate facilities of the hardware.

M

Machine code a *low-level (programming) language* in which the instructions that cause a particular computer to operate are written.

Magazine (a) a container for slides, a filmstrip, a film, etc for use in conjunction with a projector; (b) a light-proof container for use with a camera, processor, etc.

Magerian objective a *behavioural objective* which indicates what the learner should be able to do, under what conditions, and at what level of competence (see Chapter 3).

Magnetic board a flat sheet of ferromagnetic material (or steel) to which objects may be stuck with magnets for display purposes (see Chapter 4).

Magnetic chalkboard, markerboard a chalkboard (markerboard) made of ferromagnetic material so that it can also serve as a magnetic board, thus combining the advantages of the two types of board (see Chapter 4).

Magnetic film a type of motion picture film that uses a *magnetic soundtrack*.

Magnetic soundtrack a strip of magnetic oxide along one edge of a motion picture film used to carry the sound signal.

Magnetic tape (a) magnetic oxide-coated tape on which audio or video signals or data can be recorded; (b) heavy magnetized tape used for attaching light materials to a magnetic board or preparing displays for use on such boards.

Mainframe computer a large, 'fixed' computer facility (see Chapter 10); see also *minicomputer* and *microcomputer*.

Main store the rapid-access memory system incorporated in the *central processing unit* of a *computer*.

Manipulative materials learning resources such as model-making kits, educational toys and tools that are actually handled and manipulated by the person using them.

Manual (a) (noun) a detailed and comprehensive guide to practice, use, manufacture or service, usually in book or booklet form; (b) (adjective) a term applied to an exercise such as educational game that does not involve the use of an internal or external computer or data processor.

Markerboard a smooth light-coloured surface on which display material may be written or drawn using crayons, felt pens or other easily erased materials (see Chapter 4).

Marking scales scales that are established by examining bodies, schools, etc in order to guide examiners in marking examination papers (see Chapter 7).

Marking scheme any system that is used for evaluating and reporting achievement in a learner's work.

Master a copy or, in some cases, the original of a document, tape, film, etc from which further copies (or extracts) can be made.

Mastery learning the theory that mastery of a topic, subject, field, etc is (in principle) possible for *all* individuals provided that the appropriate amount of teaching time and the optimum quality of instruction are given to each student.

Mastery model the model for correct, error-free or minimally-acceptable performance of a task or set of tasks.

Matching item a type of objective test *item* which requires the testee to pair one word, object, symbol, etc with an associated response.

Mathmagenic information additional or augmenting information that is provided in order to facilitate learning, eg use of devices such as *prompts*, questions in text, *feedback* and *algorithms*.

Matt(e) screen a projection screen with a flat, even surface and dull finish which provides an even brilliance at all viewing angles.

Mechanical editing a general term for the various editing methods used with audiotapes or motion picture films that involve cutting them up and physically joining the pieces into the required continuity; cf *electronic editing*.

Mediated learning a term (first used by Olson and Bruner) to denote learning via media of some sort as opposed to learning through direct experience (*enactive learning*).

Mediated observation observation of a situation carried out using some type

of audiovisual medium (eg film or television) rather than direct observation.
Memory (a) the part of the mind/brain system in which impressions, facts, etc are stored; see also *long-term memory, short-term memory*; (b) in computing and data processing, a generic term for any system in which data can be stored in *digital* form.

Mental age an estimate of the intellectual development of individuals given in terms of the chronological age of the average population to which they are equivalent in intellectual terms.

Menu a list of options presented by a computer to a user, usually via a *video display unit.*

Microcomputer a small desk-top computer based on microcircuit technology; see also *mainframe computer* and *minicomputer.*

Microcopy a copy of printed or other material so reduced in size in comparison with the original that it cannot be read without the aid of a suitable magnifying device.

Microfiche a transparent sheet of photographic film bearing a matrix of *micro-images* (usually pages of text) together with an eye-legible title strip.

Microfiche reader a projector by means of which an eye-readable image of one or more pages of a *microfiche* can be produced for individual or group study.

Microfilm a roll or strip of photographic film carrying a series of *micro-images.*

Microfilm reader a projector by means of which an eye-readable image of one or more frames of a *microfilm* can be produced for individual or group study.

Microform a general term for any medium used to record *micro-images.*

Micro-image an image, obtained by means of an optical device, so reduced in size in comparison with the original that it cannot be read or studied with the naked eye; see also *microfiche, microfilm, micro-opaque.*

Micro-opaque a matrix of *micro-images* recorded on an opaque medium such as a card or sheet of photographic paper.

Microphone a device which converts sounds into electrical signals, usually for feeding into an amplifying, mixing or sound recording system of some sort.

Microphone characteristic the directional properties of a microphone, usually given in terms of a polar response diagram that indicates its relative sensitivities in different directions.

Microprocessor a self-contained solid-state microcircuit unit that can be used to build more complicated devices such as computers and control systems.

Microprojector a device designed to enlarge and project microscopic transparencies such as microscope slides for viewing by large groups.

Microsleep a term for the type of attention break that learners undergo periodically during a lecture, talk etc that lasts longer than their *attention spans* (see Chapter 4).

Microteaching training of teachers, lecturers, etc in specific skills or sets of skills in a scaled-down teaching situation, often using video playback to let them see and criticize their own performance.

Mimeograph, mimeographing see *rotary stencil duplication.*

Mimeoscope another name for a *light box.*

Minicomputer a term occasionally used to denote a computer intermediate in size between a *mainframe computer* and a *microcomputer.*

Minidisk an extra-small *floppy disk* 3½" or 3" in diameter.

Mix in sound recording or television work, to combine two or more signals from different sources into a single signal.

Mobile a three-dimensional non-projected display composed of elements hung from a system of threads so that they can rotate and move about (see Chapter 4).

Modem in computing, a contraction of *modulator-demodulator* – a device that can be used to convert a *digital* signal into an *analogue* signal capable of being transmitted along an ordinary telephone line or to re-convert such an analogue signal back into digital form after transmission.

Moderator an internal or external examiner who checks the standard of marking and/or examining in a course or section thereof.

Module (a) an organized collection of learning experiences assembled in order to achieve a specified group of related objectives; (b) a self-contained section of a course or programme of instruction.

Modular course a flexible course that allows individual learners to select the course programme that best suits them from a structural hierarchy of *modules*, some of which are compulsory and some optional.

Modulator-demodulator see *modem*.

Modular examination an examination in which candidates can elect to take a number of optional elements of equal difficulty in related subjects, topics or areas.

Moirée pattern, fringes patterns produced when two separate sets of parallel lines are superimposed at a small angle to one another.

Monaural a term used to describe a sound recording or sound reproduction system with only a single sound channel.

Monitor (noun) (a) see (*television*) *monitor*; (b) a person who acts as a tutor, supervisor, or assessor in an individualized instruction system such as *Keller Plan*; (c) (verb) to listen to a sound signal as it is being recorded or played back or check a system for correct operation.

Monitoring carrying out an on-going assessment or appraisal of a system while it is in operation.

Monophonic a term used synonymously with *monaural*.

Mouse a means of interacting with a computer or desktop publishing system, consisting of a hand-operated device containing a rolling-ball, whose movements are translated into displacements of the on-screen cursor, as the mouse is pushed to and fro and from side to side on a suitable flat surface (not-too-polished desk top, mouse-pad, or tile). The device has one or more buttons by which commands are entered when the cursor is in the desired position on the screen.

MS-DOS (Microsoft-Disk Operating System) the name of a widely-used personal computer operating system, developed by the Microsoft company (the world's largest software company). The system runs on IBM (International Business Machines) computers and a wide range of 'compatible' computers.

Multi-access a term used to describe a computer system whereby several users or operators may, through multiple or remote terminals, each use the same computer facilities at the same time; see also *time-sharing*.

Multi-channel learning *learning* that involves the use of more than one perception channel, eg the simultaneous use of hearing and sight.

Multi-choice item, question see *multiple-choice item, question*.

Multi-image of a presentation, the simultaneous use of two or more separate images, usually projected.

Multi-media a term used to describe (a) collections or groups of documents in several media; (b) a work designed to be presented through the integrated use of more than one medium (eg a tape-slide programme).

Multi-media kit, package a package of materials in several media dealing with a specific topic or subject area and forming an integrated whole.

Multiple-choice item, question a type of objective test or questionnaire question in which the testee has to choose the correct answer from a number of alternatives supplied (see Chapter 7).

Multiple-choice test a form of *objective test* composed of several *multiple-choice items* (see Chapter 7).

Multiple-completion item another name for a *multiple-response item.*

Multiple marking examination, essay, project or other marking carried out independently by more than one person in order to arrive at a collective mark that is (it is to be hoped) free from subjective influence and thus has a greater *reliability* (see Chapter 7).

Multiple-response item an *item* in an objective test of the multiple-choice type in which two or more responses are correct.

Multiple-track a term used to describe (a) a recording tape that carries more than one recording track; (b) a set of programmed materials with more than one track through them, ie a *branching programme.*

Multi-screen a term used to describe a presentation that employs two or more screens for showing projected images simultaneously.

Multi-sensory learning (teaching) aids learning or teaching aids which utilize or bring into play more than one of the physical senses (eg video materials or tape-slide programmes).

N

National Vocational Qualifications (NVQ) in the UK, qualifications based on statements of *competence* clearly related to work and intended to facilitate entry into (or progression into) employment and further learning. Such qualifications are issued to individuals by a recognized awarding body.

Negative transfer (of learning) a reduction in the efficiency of learning because of earlier learning carried out in a different situation.

Negotiated learning a form of *contract-based learning* in which the details of the contract are negotiated between the learner and the tutor.

Network a general term for any *system* consisting of a number of physically separated but interconnected sub-systems, eg computers, word processors, radio or television stations, agencies, institutions, organizations, etc.

New information technology the application of 'new' electronic and other technology (computers, communication satellites, fibre optics, videorecording, etc) to the creation, storage, selection, transformation and distribution of information of all kinds.

No-failure programme a course or programme designed to avoid outright failure by a system of adjustment of tuition and learning materials and/or transfer to other courses.

Non-book (non-print) media *media* that carry or transmit information or instructions by non-typographic means, eg by sound, pictorial representations, projected images, etc.

Non-directive tutorial (group) a tutorial (group) in which students are encouraged to contribute views and questions spontaneously, with the tutor acting as a leader and guide, but not to the extent of dominating the group or firmly structuring the course of the discussion (see Chapter 6).

Non-functioning distractor a *distractor* which attracts less than 5 per cent of the responses to a *multiple-choice item*.

Non-projected visual aids, materials visual materials which do not require the use of a projector for their display; also called *self-display materials*.

Non-verbal communication the meaningful transfer of thought or emotion through methods other than words or speaking, eg using body language.

Norm the average performance or measure in a specified function of a specified homogeneous population.

Normal distribution (curve) a symmetrical bell-shaped distribution that has, or approximates to, the shape of a Gaussian distribution; many statistical measures (eg intelligence) are found to follow such a distribution.

Norm-referenced assessment assessment designed to determine individuals' achievement in comparison with the group or population to which they belong (see Chapter 7); cf *criterion-referenced assessment*.

O

Objective a desired outcome of an instructional process or programme expressed in highly-specific (generally behavioural) terms; cf *aims* (see Chapter 3).

Objective assessment, examination test an assessment, examination or test that can be marked with total *reliability* by anyone, including non-subject specialists, or (in some cases) by computer (see Chapter 7).

Objective item (question) an *item* (question) in an *objective assessment, examination* or *test*.

Observational learning learning that takes place through the observation of a model system; see also *discovery learning*.

Obsolescence time the length of time before a learning resource becomes so outdated that it is no longer of any use.

Occupational competence the ability to perform the activities within a specific occupation or function to the standards required in employment.

Occupational skills the various skills characteristic of activities in a set of related jobs, and which contribute towards *competence* in those jobs.

Occupational standards see *standards*.

Off-campus study education carried out outside the formal school/college/ university system, eg via *distance learning*.

Off-line a computing term applied to a terminal or peripheral that is not at the time in question under the control of the central processing unit, ie is switched off or operating quite separately from the main computer.

OHP transparency see *overhead transparency*.

Omnibus test a test which covers a range of different skills or mental operations in an extended sequence of *items*, but which produces a single overall score.

One-two-four snowball technique a *snowball group* technique in which the members are first asked to reflect individually on a question or stimulus, then to form pairs in order to compare thoughts, then finally to form groups of four in order to arrive at a consensus response.

On-line a computing term applied to a terminal or peripheral that is under the control of the central processing unit at the time in question; cf *off-line*.

Opaque projector the US name for a device designed to project images of opaque, flat objects on to a screen by using light scattered from the object; in the UK, such a device is generally referred to as an *episcope*.

Open access (a) a practice whereby users are given direct access to all or part of the stock of a library or resources centre (see Chapter 9); (b) a system whereby admission to a course is open to anyone who wishes to participate, regardless of qualifications or experience; (c) an informal *individualized learning* system in which a student can have access to the facilities of the host institution more or less at any time (see Chapter 5).

Open-book examination, test an examination or test in which students are allowed to bring into the examination room, or consult, any reference material they wish.

Open classroom a classroom environment based on the concepts of *open education*, generally incorporating a system of *discovery areas*.

Open education an approach to education that includes an emphasis on learning (rather than teaching), personal and affective growth, exploring and questioning, decision-making, and the role of the teacher as a partner and guide rather than as an authoritarian figure (see Chapter 2).

Open-ended a term applied to a question, test, examination, exercise, project, etc in which many acceptable answers or outcomes are possible rather than one single correct solution or result.

Open learning an instructional system in which many aspects of the learning process are under the control of the individual learner, who decides what, how and when to study, usually under some form of guidance (see Chapter 5).

Open plan a learning environment that is designed in an open, flexible manner rather than divided into traditional 'closed-door' classrooms, thus allowing a wide range of teaching and learning methods to be employed (traditional expository teaching, team teaching, group learning, individualized learning, etc).

Open reel a term applied to an unenclosed audiotape, videotape or film reel (as opposed to the enclosed reels contained in *cassettes* or *cartridges*) and to audio or video systems which employ such reels.

Operating, operation(al) costs the total recurring expenditure of funds associated with operating a learning resource after any initial purchase and installation costs have been met.

Operational objective another term for a *behavioural objective*.

Optical character recognition (OCR) a technique (device) whereby characters that are illegible to the (unaided) human eye may be read by optico-electronic means.

Optical soundtrack a *soundtrack* which has been recorded and/or printed on a motion picture film in the form of an optical band of varying density or width along one edge of the film.

Optical videodisc a type of *videodisc* in which the signal is read optically, usually using a laser; cf *capacitance videodisc*, *contact videodisc*. Optical videodiscs are by far the most common form of videodisc.

Oral examination examination by spoken word and answer, as opposed to a written examination; also known as a *viva voce* examination, or *viva*.

Organization an *affective* process that involves the conceptualization of values and ordered relationships between values; level 4 of Bloom's *affective domain* (see Chapter 3).

Orientation course a short course designed to introduce pupils or students to a subject, course, institution, etc.

OROM optical read-only memory – a type of *digital optical disk* that is used in the *constant angular velocity* mode; such disks have extremely large capacities.

Overhead projector (OHP) a device designed to project easily visible images from transparent materials (usually either A4 or 10" × 10" in size) on to an external screen in a completely lighted room (see Chapter 4).

Overhead (OHP) transparency a transparent sheet of material (usually either 'A4' or 10" × 10" in size) intended for use with an *overhead projector* or *light box* as a means of showing graphic, textual or other information.

Overlay a transparent sheet which registers over another sheet or transparency, giving additional or alternative information.

P

Pacing the act of indicating the speed to be achieved by an individual learner, group or class in carrying out a given programme of work; see also *self-pacing*.

Package (a) a collection of all the materials needed to organize, run or participate in an exercise, course or programme of some sort; (b) a computing term for a generalized *program* or set of programs designed to meet the needs of several users.

Paddle a manual control device used in conjunction with a computer, eg in video games and *interactive video*.

Page a *viewdata* term for a collection of information that can be called up by means of its page number.

Paper-and-pencil test, examination any test or examination which involves question papers, answer papers and writing instruments.

Parent page a term used in *viewdata (interactive videotex)* for the *routing page* immediately prior to the page containing the information that the user requires.

Participative simulation a *simulation* whose main purpose is to enable people to participate in some activity (or group of activities); cf *predictive simulation*.

Passive learning learning in which the learner has a purely passive role, receiving information from the instructor or from the materials being studied without taking any active part in the proceedings.

Pathway scheme see *course unit plan*.

Peer group a group of individuals having similar age, background, qualifications etc.

Peer (group) assessment a method of assessment that is based on the consensus opinion of a *peer group* on the respective contributions to the work of the group made by each individual.

Peer teaching, tutoring a technique in which the teaching (tutoring) of learners is not done by a teacher but by other learners, usually either older or of the same age, who have already met the learning objectives involved.

Performance criteria statements which specify the standards to which an activity has to be performed and for which evidence must be gathered; see also *competence descriptor*.

Performance indicator a measurable criterion that can be used to assess the effectiveness/efficiency of an educational or training programme, including unit cost, completion rate, value-added and so on.

Peripheral (equipment, unit) in computer parlance, a terminal or backing store device that is (or can be) connected to the central processing unit of a computer system.

Personalized instruction another name for *individualized instruction.*

Personalized system of instruction (PSI) a generic name given to *individualized instruction* systems of the *Keller Plan* type.

Photo-CD compact discs onto which photographic images (from film, prints or slides) can be recorded digitally. About 100 high-quality images can be recorded onto a single CD, or about 800 lower-resolution images suitable for playback through an ordinary television set. The order of the images can be chosen in the same way as tracks are selected on audio compact discs.

Pictogram a diagram in which items or objects are drawn in different sizes or quantities in order to represent actual sizes or quantities more forcefully.

Picture-CD see *Photo-CD.*

Pilot testing carrying out early trials of an exercise, programme, etc during its development; a type of *formative evaluation.*

Pincushion distortion distortion of a projected image whereby straight lines parallel to the edges of the field move outwards at their ends; cf *barrel distortion.*

Pixel the smallest picture element on a television or video display unit screen.

Platen the flat surface or platform in an *opaque projector* on which the material to be projected is placed.

Playback head a *head* in a tape recorder that is used to play back a signal recorded on the tape; in audiotape recorders, such heads are generally used only for playback purposes, but in videotape recorders they also generally double as *record heads.*

Plenary session a session involving all the participants in an exercise, programme, course, etc.

Plotter a visual display or computer output device where the values of one variable quantity are automatically plotted against those of another; see also *x–y plotter.*

Point system a system used in English-speaking countries to measure type size, one point being equivalent to 1/72 of an inch (0.351 mm); thus, type 1" high would be described as 72 point type.

Polarized animation simulation of movement in *overhead transparencies, slides* and other display materials by the use of variably-oriented polarized light transmitted through special materials.

Port a point at which access can be gained to the *central processing unit* of a *computer.*

Portability a term used to give an indication of the ease with which an educational or other device can be moved and its resistance to damage when being transported.

Portapack a portable television camera and videorecorder system operated by rechargeable batteries.

Portrait (format) a term used to describe the format of a page, book, document, drawing, photograph, etc with an *aspect ratio* less than 1:1; cf *landscape (format).*

Positive transfer (of learning) facilitation of learning brought about as a result of learning a previous task which contained similar elements.

Posterization reproducing a photographic or video image using only a few specific tones or flat colours, with most of the tonal gradation and detail suppressed.

Post-test a test carried out after the completion of a course or programme of instruction in order to determine the extent to which the learner has achieved the specified objectives; cf *pre-test.*

Pounce paper transfer a system of transferring an outline of an illustration from one surface to another (eg from paper to a chalkboard) by making small holes along the lines of the original; the pattern can then be transferred to another surface by dusting along the lines with chalk dust, powder, etc.

Power test a test in which the score or level of performance attained is more important than the time taken to achieve the score or level; cf *speed test.*

Practice frame in *programmed instruction,* a *frame* that provides practice in the material just presented; cf *teaching frame, test frame.*

Practice items trial items that are included in a test, examination or questionnaire in order to familiarize the subject with its form.

Pre-coded question a question in which the answer has to be chosen from a number of alternatives supplied, usually by ticking or otherwise marking one of them.

Predictive simulation a *simulation* whose main purpose is to predict future behaviour, performance, trends, etc; cf *participative simulation.*

Pre-knowledge relevant knowledge which a learner or participant should have before embarking on a programme, course, etc or taking part in an exercise.

Pre-recorded materials recorded materials (such as audiotapes or videotapes) where the recorded signal was present at the time of purchase or acquisition.

Presentation programmer an electronic system which controls the synchronization of sound reproduction and/or projection devices in multi-media or multi-device presentations (eg cross-fade tape-slide programmes).

Pre-test a test carried out prior to a course or programme of instruction in order to determine the *entry behaviour* of the learner(s); cf *post-test.*

Primary typewriter another name for a *bulletin typewriter.*

Printer (a) a generic name for a *peripheral* to a *computer, word processor,* etc that gives *hard copy* output; (b) a system for producing photographic prints (usually positive) from original film (usually negative).

Printout the *hard copy* output that a *computer* or *word processor* provides via a *line printer* or similar device.

Problem method a method of instruction in which learning is stimulated by the creation of challenging situations that demand solution.

Process-centred a term applied to a *game, simulation* or other exercise in which the subject matter is far less important than the activities that the exercise involves; cf *content-centred.*

Process skills skills which are demonstrated in the conduct of an activity rather than its outcome; cf *product skills.*

Product skills skills which lead to clearly-definable outcomes, eg, typing 40 words per minute; cf *process skills.*

Profile a type of assessment report which provides separate assessments for different attributes of the assessee, rather than an aggregation within a single grade or score or statement; extensively used in *workplace assessment* and increasingly being used in UK secondary education.

Profiling the system or processes whereby information is gathered and collated to comprise broad records of learners' or trainees' competences and achievements.

Prognostic test a type of diagnostic test that is used to predict the future performance of an individual in a specific task, course of study, etc.

Program a coded sequence of instructions whereby a programmer communicates with a computer; cf *programme.*

Programme an ordered sequence of learning or other activities; cf *program*.

Programmed instruction, learning a general term for instruction or learning that takes place in a systematic, highly-structured manner, generally in a step-by-step fashion with feedback taking place between steps (see Chapter 1).

Programmed text a set of programmed learning materials produced in the form of a printed text.

Programming language the code that a computer programmer uses to communicate with a computer; see also *high-level programming language, low-level programming language*.

Project method a method of instruction in which learners (individually or in groups) carry out projects, working largely free of supervision or control.

Projected (projection) television a television display system that produces a large projected picture on an external screen by optical or electronic means; see also *eidophor*.

Projected visual aids visual materials that require the use of a projector for their display.

PROM programmable read-only memory; a *read-only memory (ROM)* which can be programmed by the user provided that he or she has access to the necessary specialized equipment; see also *EPROM*.

Prompt in *behavioural psychology, programme instruction*, etc, a *stimulus* (eg a verbal or pictorial hint of some sort) that is added to another stimulus (eg a question) in order to make it more likely that a learner will give a correct *response*; see also *formal prompt, thematic prompt*.

Psychodrama the dramatic presentation of a personal conflict or crisis for diagnostic or therapeutic purposes, eg via *role play*; see also *sociodrama*.

Psychomotor associated with the co-ordination of mind and body in carrying out physical (motor) actions; see also *psychomotor domain*.

Psychomotor domain one of the three broad sets into which Bloom and his co-workers classify learning objectives, containing all those associated with the co-ordination of mind and body in carrying out physical (motor) actions.

Pygmalion effect the theory that a teacher's expectations of pupils' achievement can sometimes become a self-fulfilling prophecy in that pupils will perform to meet the teacher's preconceptions of them.

Q

Quadraphonic a term applied to a sound recording or sound reproduction system that makes use of four discrete but related sound tracks, channels or sources.

Quarter-track a synonym for *four-track*.

Qwerty keyboard a keyboard in which the alphanumerical and standard control keys are laid out in the same way as on a standard typewriter; the name is derived from the top left row of letters.

Quiz mode a *programmed learning* technique that involves providing learners with the correct response immediately after they have made a response to each item.

R

Radio listening group a group of people who meet in order to listen to and discuss educational radio broadcasts, usually with the help of related *study guides*.

Radio microphone a *microphone* connected to a small radio transmitter that can relay its signal back to the audio system with which it is being used without the need for connecting wires.

Radiovision an audiovisual instructional system which uses special film-strips, booklets, or other visual material linked with radio broadcasts.

Random Access Memory (RAM) a computing term for a fast random-access *store* of the type found in the *central processing units* of computers.

Random access slide projector a slide projector which can show slides in the magazine in any order rather than merely in the sequence in which they were loaded into the magazine.

Range statement used to describe the maximum and minimum levels of competence which it is intended that learners will develop during a programme of study or training, and to give details of the maximum and minimum levels of performance by which they will be able to demonstrate such competences.

Rank order a list of learners' scores, etc, given in order of merit, attainment or some other attribute(s).

Rating scale a numerical scale (generally with no more than five or six points) upon which aspects of an exercise, programme, course, etc can be scored as part of a diagnostic or evaluation process.

Raw score a score which has not (so far) been modified by mathematical operations.

Read to scan the information held in a particular location or set of locations in a *store* (read out or *readout*) or feed information into a particular location or set of locations from another source (read in).

Readability a measure of the appropriateness of reading material to the age or ability of the reader.

Reader a projection device used to produce an eye-readable image of a *microcopy* on a small screen, which may be either opaque or translucent.

Reader-printer a microcopy *reader* with additional built-in facilities for producing an eye-legible *hard copy* of any page or section required.

Readiness test a test designed to determine whether a would-be learner has the characteristics needed to cope satisfactorily with a particular course, programme of instruction, etc.

Reading age a measure of the reading ability of an individual in terms of the chronological age of the average population to which he is equivalent in reading ability.

Read-only memory (ROM) a computing term for a *store* from which information can be read as often as required, but, once entered, cannot normally be changed; cf *read/write memory*. See also *PROM, EPROM*.

Readout (a) the display of output from a *computer* or *word processor* in *soft copy* form, normally on the screen of a *video display unit*; cf *printout*; (b) see *read*.

Read/write head a *head* in a *computer terminal* or similar device that can be used both to *read* data out of, and *write* data into, the system.

Read/write memory a computing term for a *store* from which information can be read as often as required and can also be altered as and when necessary; cf *read-only memory*.

Realia real objects, as opposed to models, representations, etc.

Real time the actual time over which a game, simulation or other exercise operates, as opposed to any simulated time scale built into its structure; see also *real-time processing*.

Real-time processing computer processing of data as it arises, so that the information obtained can be of immediate use in analysing or controlling external events happening concurrently.

Rear projection see *back projection.*

Rearrangement test a test that involves arranging items in the correct order or pattern.

Recall test a type of *objective test* in which the subject is required to supply missing items of information (usually words, numbers or phrases) to complete statements.

Receiving an *affective* process that involves showing awareness of, and willingness to receive, certain stimuli such as the aesthetic properties of an object, system, etc; the lowest level (level 1) of Bloom's *affective domain.*

Recognition test a type of recall test in which a learner has to recognize objects, symbols, patterns, words, etc previously encountered or learned.

Record(ing) head a *head* in a tape recorder, data storage device, etc which is used to transfer an incoming signal on to the storage medium.

Recurrent education education that continues throughout an individual's life rather than terminating at the end of the formal education that precedes entry into employment.

Reel-to-reel a term describing a process or machine in which tape or film moves from one open reel or spool to a separate take-up reel or spool during processing, play-back or projection.

Refresher course a course that is designed to reinforce previously-learned skills, knowledge, etc which may have deteriorated through disuse or lapse of time.

Register (a) (verb) to place in exact position or alignment, eg when placing an *overlay* on an overhead transparency or drawing; (b) (noun) a computer *store* which holds information, addresses or instructions on a temporary basis, eg during a multi-stage calculation.

Reinforcement (a) in behavioural psychology, a process in which a *stimulus* presented immediately following a *response* increases the likelihood of the response being repeated when the same situation recurs; (b) the process of helping a learner to master new facts, principles, etc by repetition, rehearsal, demonstrating applications, etc.

Reliability (a) a measure of the consistency with which an item, test, examination, etc produces the same results under different but comparable conditions; (b) the capability of a device to function properly over a period of time.

Reliability co-efficient a statistical measure used to quantify the *reliability* of a test or between two forms of a test.

Remedial frame(s) a frame (or sequence of frames) in a *programmed learning* sequence that covers material previously covered in a programme, usually in order to help learners to master material that they did not succeed in mastering the first time (see Chapter 1).

Remedial instruction a specific unit (or system of units) of instruction based on comprehensive diagnostic findings and intended to overcome a particular learning deficiency (or set of learning deficiencies) in a student.

Remedial loop a loop in an instructional programme that employs *backward branching* whereby learners are made to repeat sections they failed to master or are exposed to other remedial material (see Chapter 1).

Remote control a mechanical or electronic facility that enables an operator to control a device such as a camera, projector, videoplayer or television set from a distance, or from another room or building.

Remote learning often used as a synonym for *distance learning* but increasingly being given a somewhat wider interpretation than the latter (see Chapter 5).

Remote terminal a computer terminal sited in a place convenient to a user rather than in the vicinity of a central processing unit; it may be anywhere from the next room to the other side of the world.

Resource a system, set of materials or situation that is deliberately created or set up in order to enable an individual student to learn (see Chapter 9).

Resource-based learning a highly-structured, individualized, student-centred learning system that makes full use of appropriate *resources*, both material and human, in creating an effective learning situation (see Chapter 9).

Resource materials (a) the basic components of a package used in an exercise, programme, course, etc; (b) a general term for *resources* and instructional materials used by learners or teachers.

Resource(s) centre a place – which can be anything from part of a room to a complex of buildings – that is set up specially for the purpose of housing and using a collection of *resources*, both in printed and in non-printed form (see Chapter 9).

Responding an *affective* process that involves showing an interest in an object, system, etc as opposed to merely being aware of it; level 2 of Bloom's *affective domain* (see Chapter 3).

Response (a) in *behavioural psychology,* any implicit or overt change in an organism's behaviour brought about by the application of a *stimulus*; (b) the behaviour a learner emits following an instructional *stimulus* (usually a question or request to perform some activity).

Response card, sheet a printed card or sheet used in an *objective test* as a vehicle for the person being tested to record his answers.

Response frame (a) a *frame* in an *interactive videotex(t)* system that requires a response from the user; (b) in *programmed instruction,* a *frame* which follows on from a *test frame* in a *branching programme,* providing either *reinforcement* or appropriate remedial material depending on whether the response was correct or incorrect.

Restricted response in instructional design, assessment, etc, a *response* which is constrained in some way (as, for example, in a *multiple-choice question*).

Retention test a test administered some time after the completion of a course or programme of instruction in order to determine the extent to which knowledge, skills, etc have been retained by the learner.

Review items items or frames in a *programmed learning* sequence that cause the learner to repeat or review material, usually for *reinforcement* purposes.

Role play a technique (used in *games* and *simulations*) in which participants act out the parts of other persons or categories of persons.

ROM see *read-only memory*.

Rosenthal effect another name for the *Pygmalion effect*.

Rotary stencil duplication a duplicating process in which a special perforated *master* (known as a mimeograph master or stencil) is first prepared and then attached to a rotary drum; the printing takes place by forcing ink through the holes in the master on to the copy paper; also known as *mimeographing*, or *stencil duplication*.

Rote learning a type of learning *drill* in which material is learned by simple repetition.

Routine in computing, a sequence of instructions designed to make a computer carry out a single process or set of related processes.

Routing page a *viewdata* term for a *page* whose function is to indicate a choice of other pages.

Rubric (a) instructions on an examination or test paper; (b) an introduction to a printed syllabus, course description or similar document.

Ruleg a didactic technique that involves first giving a general principle, formula, classification, etc (the 'rule') and then giving illustrative examples, instances, etc (the 'eg's); cf *egrul(e)*.

S

Sandwich course a course in which a learner or trainee alternates between periods of full-time study at a college, university, etc and periods of training and/or work experience in industry, commerce, teaching, etc.

Scale an ordered series of symbols or numbers by means of which a measure of some aspect(s) of a person's behaviour or some aspect(s) or attribute(s) of a system can be given; see also *rating scale*.

Scaling adjustment of examination or other marks so that they conform to an agreed standard or yardstick, thus allowing meaningful comparisons or inferences to be made; see also *grading on the curve*.

Scanner an *optical character recognition* system that enables typed or typeset text (and even pictures and graphical images) to be read directly into a computer from hard copy. Such text may subsequently be converted into a word-processing format and edited and adjusted.

Scenario background information relating to the setting of a *game, simulation* or other exercise.

Scene the basic unit of continuity sequence in a film or television production, planned for shooting as continuous, uninterrupted action.

Scrambled text, book a text (book) in which the sequence of pages does not follow logically and whose order of use is determined by the response of the reader to questions; a type of *branching programme*.

Script (a) the detailed scene-by-scene or frame-by-frame instructions for the production of film, television programme, tape-slide programme, etc; (b) the written answers produced by a person sitting an examination or test.

Scroll a continuous roll of transparent film designed for use with an *overhead projector*.

Scrolling adding a new line of information to an overhead projector display, video display unit screen, etc and accommodating it by moving the existing display upwards or downwards so that part of it disappears from the field of view.

Second-chance institution an institution that provides educational opportunity (particularly at post-school level) for people who did not receive such education at the normal age.

Second-generation computer a *computer* (of the type built during the 1960s) based on the technology of the discrete transistor; see also *first-, third-, fourth-, fifth-generation computer*.

Self-assessment assessment of progress, attainment of objectives, etc by the actual learner, generally by using some sort of questionnaire or criterion-referenced test.

Self-completion questionnaire a questionnaire that is completed by the recipient or interviewee rather than by the interviewer.

Self-display material another name for *non-projected visual aids*.

Self-help group a group of students on a *distance learning* or other course who get together in order to share ideas, problems and experience and generally help one another with the work of the course (see Chapter 6).

Self-help materials instructional materials or *resources* designed for use by individuals in order to help them carry out some specific task.

Self instruction an instructional technique which involves the use by learners of individualized instructional materials or *resources* that require minimal (or no) intervention on the part of the teacher (see Chapter 5).

Self-pacing a method where individual learners control the speed at which they carry out a given programme or course of work, eg the *Keller Plan* (see Chapter 5).

Self-study centre another name for a *resources centre*.

Self-study material(s) another name for *self-instructional material(s)*.

Semantic differential technique a diagnostic technique involving the use of pairs of antonyms joined by a *rating scale* (see Chapter 8).

Semantic prompt (cue) in *behavioural psychology* and instructional design, a *thematic prompt (cue)* that is based on the meaning of language; cf *syntactic prompt (cue)*.

Semester system division of the academic year into two equal *semesters*, each of roughly 15–18 weeks' duration, rather than into three terms.

Seminar (a) a small class organized in order to discuss a particular topic; (b) a conference of specialists in a particular field; (c) a short, intensive course on a particular subject or topic.

Sentence completion a type of *completion item* in which the learner has to complete a sentence by adding a missing word (or words).

Sequential access a term applied to any system in which a specific item or section can only be reached by running through the entire system up to the item or section required; cf *random access*.

Serial access another name for *sequential access*.

Serial learning learning to make a series of responses in the correct order, as in the manner of a *serialist*.

Serialist according to Pask, a person who learns, remembers and recapitulates a body of information in terms of string-like cognitive structures where items are related by simple data links; cf *holist*.

Setting *streaming* of pupils in different subjects according to their ability in each subject.

Short-answer question, item an examination or test question requiring only a short answer rather than an extended essay, discussion, proof, etc.

Short-term memory that part of the human *memory* in which material is stored on a short-term, temporary basis before either being forgotten or transferred to the *long-term memory*.

Shot (a) in film or television production, a *scene* or sequence that is photographed or recorded as one continuous piece of action; (b) a particular photograph taken with a still camera.

Shredding submitting possible *multiple-choice items* to a battery of diagnostic procedures in order to determine whether they are suitable for inclusion in a multiple-choice test or examination, ie a combination of item editing and item trial testing; see *validation*.

Simulation (a) in general, any operating representation of a real system or process (or part thereof); (b) an educational, training or research exercise that incorporates such features; see also *participative simulation, predictive simulation, simulation game* (see Chapter 6).

Simulation game an exercise that includes all the essential characteristics of both a *game* and a *simulation*.

Single-concept film loop (loop film) a *loop film* that illustrates a particular concept, idea, process, etc and can be shown or viewed at an appropriate point in an instructional programme.

Single-frame a term used to describe a *filmstrip* where the horizontal axis of the pictures is at right angles to the length of the film.

Single-track a term used to describe (a) a recording tape that carries only one recording track; (b) a set of *programmed learning* materials with only a single track through them, ie a *linear programme*.

Situational assessment assessment of a learner's ability to handle particular situations (often simulated) involving decision-making and other skills (see Chapter 7).

Skill ownership a skill is said to be 'owned' by an individual if it can be deployed in a variety of situations and contexts, including unfamiliar ones; see also *skill transfer*.

Skill transfer the phenomenon whereby an individual is more effective in a new or unfamiliar situation as a result of acquiring a particular skill or set of skills in another (earlier) situation or set of situations.

Skill(s) analysis a detailed analysis of a task, job or activity in terms of the basic skills involved; also known as task analysis.

Skip branching a type of *branching programme* in which not all the frames are necessarily worked on, depending on the progress of the learner.

Sleep teaching another name for *hypnopaedia*.

Slide a single positive image on transparent material (a slide transparency) held in a mount and designed for projection; see also *compact slide*, (see Chapter 4).

Slow motion the technique of slowing down a motion picture film by running the camera faster than normal and then showing the resulting film at normal speed; cf *slow play*.

Slow play the technique of slowing down a motion picture film or video-recording by operating the projector or playback machine slower than normal; cf *slow motion*.

Smart terminal a *computer terminal* which has a certain amount of inbuilt data processing ability, but not so much as an *intelligent terminal*.

Snap change a very rapid slide change between two projectors of a dual- or multi-projector system.

Snowball group a discussion group which moves or is guided through successive phases of idea sharing, with one idea leading on to another; see also *one-two-four snowball technique*.

Social/anthropological approach (to evaluation) a subjective approach to evaluation that is more concerned with studying the on-going process of education than with trying to measure specific outputs (see Chapter 8); also known as *illuminative evaluation*.

Social skills the skills needed when dealing with other people, both at work and in private life; see also *life skills* and *interpersonal skills*.

Sociodrama the use of *role play* as a means of providing experience of or seeking a solution to a social problem of some sort; see also *psychodrama*.

Soft copy computer output displayed on a *video display unit* or fed into a storage medium, as opposed to *hard copy*.

Soft keyboard a representation of a keyboard on the screen of a *video display* *unit* that can be used to input data into a computer by pointing a *light pen* at each required character in turn.

Software a general term for material which is used in conjunction with *hardware* (see Chapter 1), although its use is sometimes restricted to describe the programs that control computers; see also *courseware*.

Sound film a motion picture film with a self-contained optical or magnetic *soundtrack*.

Sound filmstrip a *filmstrip* accompanied by an audiorecording, usually a tape cassette.

Sound synchronizer a device linking an audiotape recorder to an automatic slide or filmstrip projector which causes the projector to advance by means of signals recorded on the audiotape.

Soundtrack the optical or magnetic strip on a *sound film* that carries the sound signal; see also *magnetic soundtrack, optical soundtrack*.

Speech compressor an electronic device capable of compressing or expanding an *audio signal* (usually human speech) without changing the pitch.

Speech synthesis the production of speech by artificial means, eg by using a computer to generate the component sounds.

Speed test a test in which the total number of items or questions answered is an important factor; cf *power test*.

Spirit duplicating a method of producing multiple copies of a document from a specially-prepared *master* carrying a reversed image by pressing the copy material, moistened with spirit, against the master.

Splice (a) to make a physical join between the ends of two sections of tape or film using cement or adhesive tape; (b) the resulting cemented or taped join.

Split screen (projection) projection or showing of two or more different images on different parts of the same screen.

Spot questions test test or examination questions requiring short, usually factual answers rather than more discussive, essay-style answers (see Chapter 7).

Spreadsheet in computing, a facility whereby a complete table (or set of tables) of data, information, etc can be presented, and where alteration of any one item causes any resulting changes in other items to be made automatically by the computer.

Sprite a small *computer graphics* element (such as a face) which can be controlled and moved as a unit.

Squeezezoom a device that enables the geometry of a video image to be manipulated for artistic or other effects.

S-R bond, connection, mechanism see *stimulus-response bond, mechanism*.

Stand-alone (capability) the capability of an item of equipment to function independently of any other equipment.

Standards/occupational standards training standards based on the needs of employment, which embody the skills, knowledge and the levels of performance related to workplace activities.

Start-up costs the total costs involved in launching a project, programme, etc, over and above any operating costs subsequently incurred.

Stem the introductory part of a *multiple-choice item* containing the information on the basis of which the candidate makes a choice of answer from the various options that follow (see Chapter 7).

Stencil duplication another name for *rotary stencil duplication*.

Step in *programmed learning*, one of the discrete stages into which the programme is broken down (see Chapter 1); also known as a *frame*.

Step size in *programmed learning*, the size of a *step* measured in terms of (a) the length of time needed to complete it, (b) the number of words; (c) the amount of information contained (see Chapter 1).

Stereograph a pair of slides or transparencies designed to produce a three-dimensional effect when viewed using a suitable projector or viewer.

Stereophonic a term used to describe a sound recording or sound reproduction system that employs two discrete but related soundtracks, channels or sources.

Stereoscope an optical device for viewing *stereographs*.

Still motion slide a stationary *slide* or transparency in which an illusion of motion is produced by use of polarized light, *moirée fringes* or some other technique.

Stimulus (a) in *behavioural psychology*, an external or internal force, burst of energy, or other signal that is supplied to an organism in an attempt to activate sensory receptors and internal data processing systems and hence elicit a *response*; (b) in learning theory, a signal, message, question, etc that is given to a learner in an attempt to elicit a desired *response*.

Stimulus-response (S-R) bond, connection, mechanism the link between a *stimulus* and the *response* that it elicits.

Stop motion the technique of exposing one frame of a motion picture film at a time in *time-lapse photography* or *animation* work.

Store a computer memory unit; see also *backing store, main store*.

Storyboard a series of sketches or pictures and any accompanying text used in the planning of an audiovisual programme.

Streaming dividing children of the same chronological age into separate classes on the basis of overall ability or ability in a particular subject; see also *setting*.

String in computing, data processing etc, a linear sequence of *bits*, characters or words recording a particular set of connected data.

Structural communication test a test in which the subject is presented with a grid containing a number of (correct) statements pertaining to a particular topic and has to select and arrange relevant pieces of information in response to questions on the topic (see Chapter 7).

Structured programming a systematic way of designing, building, validating and documenting *computer programs* which, if carried out correctly, leads to the production of error-free, efficient and reliable *software*.

Student-centred approach, learning, teaching an approach to instruction that concentrates on the needs of the individual student, and in which the teacher and the host institution play supportive rather than central roles (see Chapter 2).

Student-paced learning aids, materials learning aids (materials) that are designed in such a way as to allow individual students to work at their own natural pace (see Chapter 9).

Study guide a document that provides learners with instructions and/or guidance designed to help them cope with the work of a particular course, learning programme, etc, particularly if it is of the self-instructional type.

Study skills the set of skills that a learner needs to develop in order to study effectively.

Stylus (a) a 'needle' used to read the *audio signal* from the groove of a vinyl gramophone record; (b) a pen-like device used to input data into a *data tablet*, select material from a computer *menu*, etc; (c) a pointed scriber used in stencil preparation, graphics work, etc.

Subroutine in computing, a minor sequence of instructions that is often repeated, and which is held in a *store* so that it can be called up as and when required rather than entered in full every time it is used in a *program*.

Suite (a) a set of inter-related *computer programs* which can be run consecutively as a single job; (b) a related set of learning packages, instructional exercises, etc; (c) a set of rooms or equipment set aside for a particular purpose (eg an editing suite in a film or television studio).

Summative evaluation evaluation carried out at the conclusion of a project, activity, etc in order to provide data for product validation or to determine the overall effectiveness of a course or other activity.

Super 8 a type of 8mm motion picture film with a larger image than standard 8 (see Chapter 4).

Super VHS-C a system used on camcorders, using improved recording formats and higher-quality videotape than *VHS-C* recorders.

Surface processing a type of study method in which a learner scans material in order to acquire straightforward factual knowledge or an overview of the content, rather than an in-depth understanding of the latter; cf *deep processing*.

Switched-star system a high-capacity *cable television* distribution system currently being developed in the UK; subscribers are connected via optical fibre cables to local distribution centres, which are, in turn, linked to the main distribution centre.

Synchronizing signal, pulse an audible or inaudible signal or pulse (stored on an audiotape or sound disc) used as a component of a synchronized sound/vision presentation in order to cause the frame to be advanced manually or automatically.

Synchronizing unit an electronic device that enables a pulsed *tape-slide programme* to be played using an ordinary tape recorder and automatic slide projector.

Syndicate a small group of course students or participants in an exercise who are separated from the rest of the students or participants in order to undertake a specified task or investigation.

Syntactic prompt (cue) in instructional design, a *formal prompt (cue)* that is based on the nature of grammar or the structure of language; cf *semantic prompt (cue)*.

Synthesis a *cognitive* process which involves the rearranging of elements, parts, items, etc into a new and integrated whole; level 5 of Bloom's *cognitive domain*.

System the structure or organization of an orderly whole, clearly showing the interrelationship between the different parts (sub-systems) and between the parts and the whole (see Chapter 1).

System software *computer programs* (usually prepared and supplied by the manufacturer of a computer) that provide the link between user programs and the computer *hardware*, eg the programs that control the operation of the computer itself and *compilers* for the high-level programming languages that can be used with it.

Systems approach a term used to describe the systematic application of educational technology to an educational or training problem, starting with the input (*entry behaviour*) and output (*terminal behaviour*) and determining how best to progress from the former to the latter (see Chapter 1).

T

T-group a group in which the members study their own social interactions and try to improve their interpersonal and social skills.

Tablet arm a writing surface attached to, or built into, the arm of a chair in order to facilitate note-taking and similar activities.

Talking book a spoken text recorded either on audiotape or on a sound disc, eg for use with the visually handicapped.

Tape-slide programme, presentation an instructional programme or presentation in the form of a slide sequence accompanied by an audio-tape, the two being synchronized by means of audible or inaudible cues recorded on the tape.

Target population that proportion of the total learner population selected for exposure to a specific unit of instruction, instructional product, etc.

Task an activity which forms an observable and/or measurable unit of work, has a direct and immediate outcome, and contributes directly to the accomplishment of a goal or purpose.

Teacher's guide an explanatory handbook for teacher use produced to accompany a textbook or instructional package.

Teacher/institution centred approach the 'traditional' educational system in which instruction is almost entirely under the control of the host institution and teaching staff (see Chapter 2).

Teaching frame in *programmed instruction*, a *frame* that provides the users with new knowledge or helps them to re-structure knowledge already possessed; cf *practice frame, test frame.*

Teaching machine a term applied to the various mechanical and electromechanical devices that were developed during the 1960s and early 1970s as *delivery systems* for the *programmed learning* materials that were being developed at the time (see Chapter 1).

Team project a project carried out by a co-operative group, often as part of the work of a course (see Chapter 6).

Team teaching a teaching technique in which two or more teachers share responsibilities for a given instructional programme with the same group of learners.

Teazle board, teazlegraph alternative names for a *hook-and-loop board.*

Telebeam projector another name for a *television projector.*

Teleconference a conference arranged by connecting geographically-separated individuals or groups through the public telephone system, using either audio links only (an audioconference) or audio links plus slow-scan television pictures (a television conference).

Telelecture an arrangement which enables a speaker or lecturer to communicate with several classes in different locations simultaneously, using public telephone links.

Telephone instruction education or teaching in which practically all direct communication between the teacher and the student is carried out via the public telephone system; also known as telephone tutoring.

Telepresence a term for the direct participative experience of a simulated environment or situation made possible through the use of *virtual reality.*

(Television) monitor an electronic device which translates television signals into pictures on a cathode ray tube screen and sound; a *monitor* differs from a television receiver in that the input signal is unmodulated and the picture quality is higher; monitors are used mainly in television production and broadcasting, and as *video display units.*

Television projector an electronic device which projects television images on to a large screen, usually for viewing in large rooms or spaces and/or by large groups of people.

Telewriter a device which transmits hand-written or hand-drawn material over a telephone line for display or viewing elsewhere; see also *facsimile transmission (fax).*

Terminal (a) a device for sending and/or receiving information over a communications channel; (b) see *computer terminal;* (c) relating to the end of a course or programme.

Terminal assessment assessment that is carried out at the end of a course (or section thereof); cf *continuous assessment.*

Terminal behaviour the set of knowledge, skills, behaviours, etc that a learner is expected to have acquired by the end of a course or programme of instruction.

Terminal course a course in a subject which is not likely to be taught again during a student's subsequent studies.

Terminal frames *frames* that end or terminate a *programmed learning* sequence; such frames are often used to revise or summarize earlier material.

Test frame in *programmed instruction,* a *frame* (usually at the end of a sequence of *teaching frames* and *practice frames*) that tests the user's mastery of the material covered therein; also known as a *criterion frame.*

Thematic prompt (cue) in *behavioural psychology* or instructional design, a *prompt (cue)* which takes the form of the presentation or implying of meaningful associations that are likely to help the subject or learner to give the desired *response;* cf *formal prompt.*

Thermal copier a reprographic device that makes use of some type of thermographic process, ie makes use of heat for the formation of the image.

Third-generation computer a *computer* that uses microcircuits (complete electronic circuits, including networks of transistors and switches, contained in thin silicon chips) as its main components; such computers started to be built during the early 1970s; see also *first-, second-, fourth-, fifth-generation computer.*

Throw the distance from a projector to the projection screen with which it is used.

Time base corrector an electronic device for synchronizing the *frame* speed of a *video signal* (eg from a videotape) with that of the system into which it is being fed.

Time chart a type of chronological wallchart used in the teaching of history, geology, etc, divisions of time being represented by spaces of corresponding width and events being depicted in those spaces.

Time lapse photography a technique for visualizing normally invisibly slow processes by shooting one frame of a motion picture film at a time at prescribed intervals, and then showing the resulting sequence at normal speed.

Time-sharing a system whereby several users may, through *remote terminals,* each use the facilities of the same large computer at the same time so that each appears to have exclusive use of the computer.

Toner the black powder that is used to produce the dark image in electrostatic copying and laser printing.

Tool subject a subject (such as mathematics) through which key skills needed for use in studying other subjects are acquired.

Touch screen terminal a *terminal* with a screen via which information can be fed into a *computer* or similar device by touch, eg using a *soft keyboard*.

Track (a) that discrete area of a film, videotape or (usually) audiotape on which a particular signal is recorded; (b) a term used in *programmed learning* – see *multiple-track, single-track*.

Trackerball a ball-operated control that enables a cursor to be moved around a video screen.

Tractor-feed printer a *printer* that uses continuous stationery, the paper being pulled through the system by sprocket wheels.

Transceiver a *terminal* (such as a teleprinter) which can be used both to transmit and to receive information.

Transcribe to copy a recording or set of data from one storage system or medium to another.

Transducer (a) a device for converting electrical signals into mechanical vibrations or vice versa; (b) an *information technology* term for any device designed to convert signals from one medium to another.

Transfer (a) a term used in *behavioural psychology* to denote the effects of previous experience on later learning – see *horizontal, negative, vertical transfer (of learning)* (b) a term applied to film, lettering, images, etc that can be transferred from one sheet to another by pressure or other means – see *transfer film lettering, type*.

Transfer film transparent or translucent film with a pressure-sensitive adhesive back that can be used to add colour, shading, etc to overhead transparencies.

Transfer lettering, type a generic name for sheets of letters which can be transferred to other material by application of pressure (or some other process) during the preparation of graphic material, etc.

Transfer of learning see *transfer*.

Transferable skills skills (generally *product* or *process* skills) that can be deployed in different contexts from those in which they were originally acquired; see also *skill transfer*.

Translucent screen a type of screen with a translucent surface used in *back projection*.

Transverse scanning a video scanning system in which the head moves across the recording tape rather than along it as in *helical scanning*.

Tree-and-branch system a *cable television* distribution system in which subscribers are connected to the distribution centre by a branching system of coaxial cables.

True-false test an *objective test* in which the testee has to mark items as either 'true' or 'false'.

True score a score that has been corrected for errors, subjected to standardization, etc; cf *raw score*.

Tuning carrying out fine adjustments to a system in order to optimize its operation.

Turtle a small robot, shaped like a turtle, that is controlled via a *microcomputer*, eg in systems that use the LOGO *high-level programming language*.

Tutor-mode CAL a type of *computer-assisted learning* in which the computer interacts with the learner in a similar way to a live tutor, engaging in a dialogue whose course depends on the responses made by the learner; cf *laboratory mode CAL*.

Twinning stand a stand for mounting two automatic slide projectors one above the other for use in dual-projection displays.

U

Underware a term sometimes applied to those aspects of educational technology which underlie the use of *hardware* and *software*; but which cannot be placed in either category (see Chapter 1).

Unique answer question an examination or test question that has a single correct answer or solution, as opposed to an *open-ended* question.

Unit of competence in the UK, a primary subdivision of a *National Vocational Qualification* which may be recognized and certificated independently.

Unobtrusive assessment assessment based on observation that is carried out without the knowledge of the individual or group of people being assessed (see Chapter 7).

Unobtrusive measure an evaluation tool where the actual measurement process is not immediately apparent to, or is remote from, the individual or group being observed (see Chapter 8).

Up-time the time (absolute or fractional) during which a learning resource (usually a device or system) is fully available for use; cf *downtime*.

Use life the maximum amount of time (or number of times) for which a system can be used under normal conditions before deteriorating past the point of usefulness.

User friendly a term applied to a machine or system which is specifically designed so as to be as simple as possible to operate or use.

User-oriented language a computer *programming language* that is designed for use by ordinary computer users rather than by specialist computer staff; see also *high-level programming language*.

V

Validation determination of the effectiveness of instructional materials or systems by the use of appropriate *summative evaluation* techniques.

Validity the extent to which a test or other measuring instrument fulfils the purpose for which it is designed (see Chapter 7).

Valuing an *affective* process that involves accepting that an object, system, etc, has value; level 3 of Bloom's *affective domain*.

Variable speech a technique used in audio instruction whereby the listener can vary the rate at which spoken information is presented without altering the pitch or introducing distortion.

Velcro board a type of *hook-and-loop board*.

Vertical file materials items such as pamphlets, newspaper or magazine clippings, pictures, etc which, because of their form, can be stored in vertical files in drawers or filing cabinets for ready retrieval and reference.

Vertical transfer (of learning) a form of *transfer of learning* in which a low-order learned skill, concept or fact is put to use in a higher-order or more complex situation of which it is a component.

Vestibule course a course whose purpose is to prepare learners for another course or to introduce them to a particular subject, area or field.

VHS the most common kind of videocassettes, with playing times for domestic use including 30, 60, 90, 120, 180, 210 and 240 minutes at standard speed (and double these times at half speed). The older generation of camcorders take standard VHS cassettes, which can be replayed directly through any VHS videocassette player, or by playing them through the camera connected with suitable cables to a television set or monitor.

VHS-C a half-sized VHS cassette format designed for use in camcorders. The VHS-C cassette can be inserted in a cartridge enabling it to be played in any VHS videocassette player.

Video (a) (adjective) a term applied to all visual aspects of television signals, equipment, etc; (b) (noun) a loose term for a *videorecording* or for any machine that can be used to record and/or play back such recordings (videocassette recorders, videotape recorders, etc).

Video cartridge a *cartridge* containing *videotape.*

Videocassette a *cassette* containing *videotape.*

Videodisc a disc on which visual images, with or without sound, are electronically or optically recorded; see also *capacitance videodisc, contact videodisc, optical videodisc.*

Video display unit (VDU) a television-like computer terminal on which verbal, numerical or graphical information generated by the computer and user can be displayed.

Videophone a sophisticated video telephone system that enables users to see as well as hear one another; such systems require the users to be connected by special high-capacity *ISDN* telephone lines; see also *telepresence.*

Video signal an electronic signal, either in *analogue* or *digital* form, representing a visual scene and capable of being used to reproduce that scene; cf *audio signal.*

Videotape special magnetic tape on which encoded television signals are (or may be) recorded.

Videotex(t) a generic term for electronic systems that make computer-stored information available via video display units or television sets; see also *broadcast videotex, interactive videotex.*

Video typewriter another name for a *caption generator.*

Viewdata an alternative name for *interactive videotex(t).*

Virtual reality a computer-simulated environment with which users can interact as if they were actually in the environment. Used in a wide variety of contexts, from training aircraft pilots to adventure games in the increasing leisure market. See also *telepresence.*

Vision mixer an electronic control panel for combining separate *video signals* to form a synchronized composite signal; used in television production.

Visual display unit (VDU) another name for a *video display unit.*

Visual learner a learner who, in a visual sense, views a system as a whole rather than analysing it in terms of discrete elements; the visual version of a *holist*; cf *haptic (learner).*

Visual noun a term used to describe a basic element of visual material (eg a chart, *slide* or *loop film*) which can be used in a variety of instructional contexts.

Vocational qualification a qualification built on statements of *competence* specific to a particular occupation or range of occupations.

Vocoder a device used in *speech synthesis*; it produces speech that is semantically clear, but does not resemble 'natural' speech in tone quality, etc.

Voice over a narrative accompaniment to a film or television programme, heard without the speaker being seen.

Vu-foil, vu-graph US names for an *OHP transparency.*

W

Wallchart a relatively large opaque sheet exhibiting information in graphic or tabular form designed to be attached to a wall for display purposes.

Washahead another name for *forward branching*.

Washback another name for *backward branching*.

Weighting the assignment of differential values to test items, scores, etc in order to give them the required degree of relative importance.

Wet carrel a *carrel* that is fitted with one or more mains outlets, so that electrically-operated equipment can be used in it; cf *dry carrel*.

Whiteboard a marker board with a white surface.

Wider access see *access*.

Winchester disk a widely-used type of *hard disk*.

Window (a) in *computer graphics*, a specified area that is selected for enlargement, thus effectively defining a 'window' through which that particular part of the display can be viewed in more detail; (b) see *windowing*.

Windowing a facility available with some *microcomputer* systems whereby multiple *inlays (windows)* can be incorporated in existing screen displays, the user then being able to work on any chosen section of the display.

WOOD *w*rite *o*nce *o*ptical *d*isk; a type of *digital optical disk* on which a user can record data, but, once recorded, it cannot be erased or re-recorded.

Word processor a keyboard/microcomputer system that enables text to be composed, edited and filed; the text is held in the computer store and any part can be called up, visually displayed, printed in *hard copy* form, or fed into a different system at any time.

Work-based learning learning that takes place within the context of, or in connection with, an individual's workplace or work situation.

Workbook a text produced as a study or learning guide, usually containing exercises, problems, practice materials, etc.

Work card a re-usable card carrying instructions relating to a particular piece of work, and (usually) giving background information relating to same.

Working memory that part of the *memory* in the *central processing unit* of a digital computer that is actually available to the user at any given time, ie the part not taken up by the operating programs that are in use at the time.

Workplace assessment measurement of performance taking place in the workplace, together with the judgement of competence based on the evidence thus accumulated.

Worksheet a sheet carrying instructions, information, etc relating to part of (or some aspect of) the work of an exercise; such sheets often incorporate spaces where information, answers, results, etc have to be filled in.

Workshop a practical session designed to illustrate the underlying principle, logistics or mechanics of an exercise, programme, etc without necessarily working all the way through it.

Work station (a) in general, a place in a workshop, factory, office, teaching laboratory, language laboratory, etc where an individual works; (b) a *terminal* whereby an individual can gain access to the facilities of a *computer*, *word processor*, *data base*, *interactive video* system, etc, or to a combination of systems of this type.

Write to feed data into a computer *store*.

X

Xerography a widely-used name for *electrostatic copying*.

x–y plotter a *plotter* in which the two variables are respectively plotted along a horizontal x-axis and a vertical y-axis.

Z

Zap to erase material from a computer store.

Zig-zag book a *scrambled text* in which pages are divided into cut sections which can be turned forward or backward independently of one another.

Zoom (a) a visual effect in which it appears that a camera is moving rapidly towards or away from a subject; it is often achieved using a *zoom lens*; (b) a similar effect in *computer graphics*.

Zoom lens a projector or camera lens system with a continuously-variable focal length.

Bibliography

Readers wishing to study in greater depth topics covered in the various chapters of this book may find further detail in the following books and articles.

CHAPTER 1: THE NATURE OF EDUCATIONAL TECHNOLOGY

Beard, R M and Hartley, J (1984) *Teaching and Learning in Higher Education* (4th edition) Harper and Row, London.

Bourner, T and Race, P (1991) *How to Win as a Part-Time Student* Kogan Page, London.

Bruner, J S (1960) *The Process of Education* Harvard University Press, Cambridge, Mass.

Buzan, T (1979) *How to Study* Encyclopaedia Britannica, London

Ellington, H I and Race, P (1993) *Producing Teaching Materials* Kogan Page, London.

Elton, L R B (1977) 'Educational technology – today and tomorrow'. In Hills, P and Gilbert, J (eds) *Aspects of Educational Technology XI* Kogan Page, London.

Gagné R M (ed) (1987) *Instructional Technology: Foundations* Lawrence Erlbaum Associates, Hillsdale, New Jersey.

Gibbs, G (1981) *Teaching Students to Learn* Open University Press, Milton Keynes, UK.

Hartley, J and Davies, I K (1978) *Contributions to an Educational Technology 2* Kogan Page, London.

Osborne, C (ed) (1992) *International Yearbook of Educational and Training Technology* Kogan Page, London. (*Note:* in the previous edition of *A Handbook of Educational and Training Technology* we included a short list of key educational and training technology organizations and contacts. A much more comprehensive source is the *International Yearbook* and we now refer readers looking for names and addresses of educational technology organizations and contacts to this book).

Paul, R (1990) *Open Learning and Open Management – Leadership and Integrity in Distance Education* Kogan Page, London.

Race, P (1986) *How to Win as an Open Learner* NCET, Coventry, UK.

Race, P (1989) *The Open Learning Handbook* Kogan Page, London.

Race, P (1992) 53 *Interesting Ways to Write Open Learning Materials* TES, Bristol.

Race, P (1992) *500 Tips for Students* SCED/Blackwell, Oxford.
Race, P and Brown, S (1993) *500 Tips for Tutors* Kogan Page, London.
Ramsden, P (1987) *Improving Learning: A New Perspective* Kogan Page, London.
Richmond, W K (1970) *The Concept of Educational Technology* Weidenfeld and Nicolson, London.
Rogers, C (1983) *Freedom to Learn for the 80s* Merril, Columbus, Ohio.
Romizowski, A J (1988) *The Selection and Use of Instructional Media* Kogan Page, London.
Romizowski, A J (1988) *Designing Instructional Systems* Kogan Page, London.
Rowntree, D (1992) *Exploring Open and Distance Learning* Kogan Page, London.
Skinner, B F (1968) *The Technology of Teaching* Appleton–Century–Crofts, New York.

CHAPTER 2: BASIC EDUCATIONAL STRATEGIES

Boud, D (ed) (1988) *Developing Student Autonomy in Learning* Kogan Page, London.
Mager, R (1991) *Developing Attitude Toward Learning* Kogan Page, London.
Mager, R (1991) *Making Instruction Work* Kogan Page, London.
Mulligan, J and Griffin, C (1992) *Empowerment through Experiential Learning – Explorations of Good Practice* Kogan Page, London.
Newble, D and Cannon, R (1991) *A Handbook for Teachers in Universities and Colleges* Kogan Page, London.
Ramsden, P (1988) *Improving Learning – New Perspectives* Kogan Page, London.
Romiszowski, A J (1988) *Designing Instructional Systems* Kogan Page, London.
Saunders, D and Race, P (eds) (1992) *Developing and Measuring Competence – Aspects of Educational and Training Technology XXV* Kogan Page, London.
Stephenson, J and Weil, S (eds) (1992) *Quality in Learning* Kogan Page, London.
Tessmer, M and Harris, D (1992) *Analysing the Instructional Setting* Kogan Page, London.
Trulove, S (ed) (1992) *Handbook of Training and Development* Blackwell, Oxford.

CHAPTER 3: EDUCATIONAL OBJECTIVES AND COMPETENCE DESCRIPTORS

Bloom, B S (ed) (1972) *Taxonomy of Educational Objectives, Book 1: Cognitive Domain* Longman, London.
Bloom, BS, Krathwohl, D R and Masia, J F (1971) *Taxonomy of Educational Objectives, Book 2: Affective Domain* Longman, London.
Drysdale, D and Field, F (1991) *Training for Competence: a Handbook for Trainers and FE Teachers* Kogan Page, London.
Fletcher, S (1991) *Designing Competence-Based Training* Kogan Page, London.
Fletcher, S (1992) *Competence-Based Assessment Techniques* Kogan Page, London.
Mager, R (1991) *Preparing Instructional Objectives (2nd Edition)* Kogan Page, London.
Mager, R (1991) *Goal Analysis* Kogan Page, London.
Rowntree, D (1989) *Assessing Students – How Shall We Know Them? (Revised 2nd Edition)* Kogan Page, London.

Sanderson, G (1992) 'Objectives and Evaluation'. In Trulove, S (ed) *Handbook of Training and Development* Blackwell, Oxford.

Saunders, D and Race, P (eds) (1992) *Developing and Measuring Competence – Aspects of Educational and Training Technology XXV* Kogan Page, London.

CHAPTER 4: MASS INSTRUCTION TECHNIQUES

Brown, G A (1978) *Learning and Explaining* Methuen, London.

Cryer, P and Elton, L (1992) *Promoting Active Learning in Large Groups* CVCP Universities Staff Development Unit, Sheffield.

Ellington, H I (1987) *Some Hints on How to be an Effective Lecturer* CICED Publications, The Robert Gordon University, Aberdeen.

Ellington, H I and Race, P (1993) *Producing Teaching Materials* Kogan Page, London.

Gibbs, G, Habeshaw, S and Habeshaw, T (1989) *53 Interesting Things to Do in Your Lectures* TES, Bristol.

Gibbs, G, Habeshaw, S and Habeshaw, T (1992) *53 Interesting Ways to Teach Large Classes* TES, Bristol.

Gibbs, G and Jenkins, A (eds) *Teaching Large Classes in Higher Education* Kogan Page, London.

Weimar, M G (ed) (1987) *Teaching Large Classes Well* Jossey-Bass, London.

CHAPTER 5: INDIVIDUALIZED LEARNING TECHNIQUES

Bosworth, D P (1992) *Open Learning* Cassell, London.

Boud, D (ed) (1988) *Developing Student Autonomy in Learning* Kogan Page, London.

Ellington, H I and Lowis, A (1992) 'Converting a conventional taught course into distance learning form'. In *Developing and Measuring Competence* Saunders, D and Race, P, Kogan Page, London.

Ellington, H I and Race, P (1993) *Producing Teaching Materials* Kogan Page, London.

Hartley, J (1988) *Designing Instructional Text* Kogan Page, London.

Lockwood, F (1992) *Activities in Self- Instructional Text* Kogan Page, London.

Paul, R (1990) *Open Learning and Open Management – Leadership and Integrity in Distance Education* Kogan Page, London.

Race, P (1989) *The Open Learning Handbook* Kogan Page, London.

Race, P (1992) *53 Interesting Ways to Write Open Learning Materials* TES, Bristol.

Rowntree, D (1992) *Exploring Open and Distance Learning* Kogan Page, London.

CHAPTER 6: GROUP LEARNING TECHNIQUES

Abercrombie, M J L (1979) *Aims and Techniques of Group Teaching* SRHE Publications, Guildford.

Bennett, N and Dunne, E (1992) *Managing Classroom Groups* Simon and Schuster Education, Hemel Hempstead, UK.

Boocock, S S and Schild, E O (eds) (1968) *Simulation Games in Learning* Sage Publications, Beverly Hills, California.

Bourner, T and Barlow, J (1991) *The Student Induction Handbook – Practical Activities for Use with New Student Groups* Kogan Page, London.

Bourner, T, Martin, V and Race, P (1993) *Workshops that Work* McGraw-Hill, Maidenhead.

Burnard, P (1992) *Interpersonal Skills Training* Kogan Page, London.

Ellington, H I, Addinall, E and Percival, F (1981) *Games and Simulations in Science Education* Kogan Page, London.

Ellington, H I, Addinall, E and Percival, F (1982) *A Handbook of Game Design* Kogan Page, London.

Ellington, H I, Addinall, E and Percival, F (1984) *Case Studies in Game Design* Kogan Page, London.

Griffiths, S and Partington, P (1992) *Enabling Active Learning in Small Groups* CVCP Universities Staff Development Unit, Sheffield.

Habeshaw, S, Habeshaw, T and Gibbs, G (1989) *53 Interesting Things to Do in Your Seminars and Tutorials* TES, Bristol.

Jaques, D (1991) *Learning in Groups (2nd Edition)* Kogan Page, London.

Jones, K (1987) *Simulations – a Handbook for Teachers and Trainers* Kogan Page, London.

Jones, K (1992) *Icebreakers – a Sourcebook of Games, Exercises and Simulations* Kogan Page, London.

Kemp, R and Race, P (1992) *Promoting the Development of Personal and Professional Skills* CVCP Universities Staff Development Unit, Sheffield.

McGill, I and Beaty, L (1992) *Action Learning – A Practitioner's Guide* Kogan Page, London.

Parker, K and Kropp, R (1992) *Team-Building – A Sourcebook of Activities for Trainers* Kogan Page, London.

Percival, F and Saunders, D (1993) *The Simulation and Gaming Yearbook 1993* Kogan Page, London.

Tansey, P J and Unwin, D (1969) *Simulation and Gaming in Education* Methuen, London.

Taylor, J L and Walford, R (1978) *Learning and the Simulation Game* Open University Press, Milton Keynes.

Weil, S W and McGill, I (eds) (1989) *Making Sense of Experiential Learning* Open University, Milton Keynes.

CHAPTER 7: ASSESSMENT

Bell, C and Harris, D (1990) *Evaluating and Assessing for Learning* Kogan Page, London.

Boud, D (1986) *Implementing Student Self-Assessment* HERDSA, Sydney.

Brown, G and Pendlebury, M (1992) *Assessing Active Learning* CVCP Universities Staff Development Unit, Sheffield.

Brown, S and Dove, P (eds) (1990) *Reflections on Self and Peer Assessment – SCED Paper 63* SCED Publications, Birmingham.

Gibbs, G, Habeshaw, S and Habeshaw, T (1989) *53 Interesting Ways to Assess Your Students* TES, Bristol.

Gipps, C (ed) (1992) *Developing Assessment for the National Curriculum* Kogan Page, London.

Mager, R (1991) *Measuring Instructional Results* Kogan Page, London.

Parsloe, E (1992) *Coaching, Mentoring and Assessing* Kogan Page, London.

Rowntree, D (1989) *Assessing Students – How Shall We Know Them? (Revised 2nd Edition)* Kogan Page, London.

CHAPTER 8: EVALUATION

Becher, T (1981) 'Evaluation and educational technology'. In Percival, F and Ellington, H I (eds) *Aspects of Educational Technology XV* Kogan Page, London.

Bell, C (ed) (1990) *World Yearbook of Education 1990 – Assessment and Evaluation* Kogan Page, London.

Nixon, J (1992) *Evaluating the Whole Curriculum* Open University, Milton Keynes.

Norris, N (1990) *Understanding Educational Evaluation* Kogan Page, London.

O'Neil, M and Pennington, G (1992) *Evaluating Teaching and Courses from an Active Learning Perspective* CVCP Universities Staff Development Unit, Sheffield.

Parlett, M and Hamilton, D (1972) *Evaluation as Illumination: A new Approach to the Study of Innovatory Programmes* Occasional Paper 9, Centre for Research in Educational Studies, University of Edinburgh.

Popper, K R (1972) *The Logic of Scientific Discovery* Hutchinson, London.

Rowntree, D (1992) *Exploring Open and Distance Learning* Kogan Page, London.

Sanderson, G (1992) 'Objectives and Evaluation'. In Trulove, S (ed) *Handbook of Training and Development* Blackwell, Oxford.

Thorpe, M (1988) *Evaluating Open and Distance Learning* Longman, Harlow.

CHAPTER 9: RESOURCE CENTRES

Barker, A J and Cowan, J (1978) 'Cataloguing and Retrieval of Interrelated Resource Material' *British Journal of Educational Technology*, 9 (1) 59–70.

Boyce, L (1987) *Student-Centred Learning: Some Implications for Learning Resources Provision* Coombe Lodge Report 19 (9) 547–58.

Brewer, J G (1988) *Guidelines for Learning Resources in Colleges* Learning Resources Development Group, Francis, London.

Clarke, J (1982) *Resource-Based Learning for Higher and Continuing Education* Croom-Helm, London.

Ellington, H I and Race, P (1993) *Producing Teaching Materials* Kogan Page, London.

Evans, C (1987) *The Organization and Management of Library and Learning Services* Coombe Lodge Report, 19 (9) 567–75.

Tessmer, M and Harris, D (1992) *Analysing the Instructional Setting* Kogan Page, London.

CHAPTER 10: COMPUTERS IN EDUCATION AND TRAINING

Barker, J and Tucker, R N (1990) *The Interactive Learning Revolution: Multimedia in Education and Training* Kogan Page, London.

Barker, J (ed) (1993) *The Multimedia Classroom* Kogan Page, London.

Barker, P G (1987) *Author Languages for CAL* Kogan Page, London.

Barker, P G (1989a) *Multi-Media Computer Assisted Learning* Kogan Page, London.

Barker, P G (1989b) *Basic Principles of Human–Computer Interface Design* Century-Hutchinson, London.

Barker, P G and Manji, K (1989) 'Designing electronic books', *Journal of Artificial Intelligence in Education* 1(2), 31–42.

Barker, P G and Giller, S (1990) 'An electronic book for early learners – a CDROM design exercise' *The CTISS File Issue* 10, 13–18.

Barker, P G (1990a) 'Designing interactive learning systems', *Educational and Training Technology International*, 27(2) 125–45.

Barker, P G (1990b) 'Electronic Books', *Learning Resources Journal*, 6(3) 62–8.

Barker, P G (1990c) 'Automating the production of courseware'. In Farmer, B, Eastcott, D and Mantz, B (eds) *Aspects of Educational and Training Technology – Vol. XXIII: Making Systems Work* Kogan Page, London.

Barker, P G (1991) 'Interactive electronic books', *Interactive multi-media* 2(1) 11–28.

Barker, P G and Giller, S (1992) 'Electronic Books'. In Saunders, D and Race, P (eds) *Developing and Measuring Competence* Kogan Page, London.

Barrett, E (ed) (1989) *The Society of Text: Hypertext, Hypermedia and the Social Construction of Information* MIT Press, Cambridge, Mass.

Bates, A W (ed) (1985) *The Role of Technology in Distance Education* Croom-Helm, London.

Bostock, S J and Seifert, R V (1986) *Microcomputers in Adult Education* Croom-Helm, London.

Boyd-Barrett, O and Scanlon, E (eds) (1991) *Computers and Learning* Addison-Wesley/Open University, Milton Keynes, UK.

Britannica Software (1990) *Compton's Multi-Media Encyclopedia – User's Guide*, Britannica Software, San Francisco.

Burns, H, Parlett, J W and Redfield, C L (1991 *Intelligent Tutoring Systems – Evolutions in Design* Lawrence Erlbaum, New Jersey and London.

CD-I (Compact Disc Interactive); for information: Weil, Stephen, Sales and Marketing Manager, SPIN UK Ltd, Lombard House, 2 Purley Way, Croydon, CR0 3JP.

Dean, C and Whitlock, Q (1988) *A Handbook of Computer-Based Training (2nd Edition)* Kogan Page, London.

Flegg, D and McHale, J (1991) *Selecting and Using Training Aids* Kogan Page, London.

Gerver, E (1986) *Humanizing Technology: Computers in Community Use and Adult Education* Plenum, New York/London.

Grolier Inc (1988) *The New Grolier Electronic Encyclopedia – User's Guide and Compact Disk* Grolier Electronic Publishing, Sherman Turnpike, Danbury, USA.

Hall, R M (1992) 'Using computer conferencing to develop competence'. In Saunders, D and Race, P (eds) *Developing and Measuring Competence* Kogan Page, London.

Harrison, N (1990) *How to Design Effective Computer Based Training* McGraw-Hill, Maidenhead, UK.

Hawkridge, D (1983) *New Information Technology in Education* Croom-Helm, London.

Kist, J (1987) *Electronic Publishing* Croom-Helm, London.

Latcham, C, Williamson, J and Henderson-Lancett, L (1992) *Interactive Multimedia – Practice and Promise* Kogan Page, London.

Luther, A C (1989) *Digital Video in the PC Environment* McGraw Hill, New York.

Manji, K A (1990) *Pictorial Communication with Computers* PhD Dissertation, Teesside Polytechnic, Cleveland, UK.

Mason, R and Kay, A (eds) (1989) *Mindweave: Communication, Computers, and Distance Education* Pergamon, London.

Mast Learning Systems (1988) *Secrets of Study* Mast Learning Systems, 3 Wetherby Mews, London.

McAleese, R (ed) (1989) *Hypertext: Theory into Practice* Intellect, Oxford.

McAleese, R and Green, C (eds) (1990) *Hypertext: State of the Art* Intellect, Oxford.

Nielsen, J (1990) *Hypertext and Hypermedia* Academic Press, London.

Nimbus Information Systems (1989) *Music Catalog on CDROM* Wyastone Leys, Monmouth, UK.

Picciotto, M et al (1989) *Interactivity: Designing and Using Interactive Video* Kogan Page, London.

Question Mark Computing (1990) *Objective Testing on a Computer* Question Mark Computing, London.

Romiszowski, A J (1986) *Developing Auto-Instructional Materials from Programmed Texts to CAL and Interactive Video* Kogan Page, London.

Romiszowski, A J (1988) *The Selection and Use of Instructional Media* Kogan Page, London.

Roth, J P (ed) (1991) *Rewritable Optical Storage Technology* Meckler, Westport and London.

Roth, J P (ed) *Case Studies of Optical Storage Applications* Meckler, Westport and London.

Schneiderman, B and Kearsley, G (1989) *Hypertext Hands-On – a New Way of Organizing and Accessing Information* Addison-Wesley, Reading, Mass.

Steinberg, E R (1991) *Teaching Computers to Teach* Lawrence Erlbaum, New Jersey and London.

Terry, C (1984) *Using Microcomputers in Schools* Croom-Helm, London.

Weatherall, D J, Ledingham, J G G and Warrell, D A (1989) *Oxford Textbook of Medicine on Compact Disk, Second Edition* Oxford University Press, Oxford.

COMPUTERS IN EDUCATION AND TRAINING – A SELECTION OF RELEVANT JOURNALS

(Developments in computer-assisted learning and interactive multimedia are accelerating so quickly that most textbooks on the subject quickly become dated. We therefore refer readers to the following examples of journals and periodicals containing up-to-date discussion on these aspects of educational technology.)

Artificial Intelligence Review Blackwell Scientific Publications, Oxford, UK.

British Journal of Educational Technology National Council for Educational Technology, Coventry, UK.

Classroom Computer Learning Peter Li, Dayton, USA.

Computers and Education Pergamon, Oxford, UK.

Educational Technology Educational Technology Inc. New Jersey, USA.

Educational Media International Kogan Page, London.

Educational Technology Abstracts Carfax, Abingdon, UK.

Hypermedia Taylor Graham, London.
Intelligent Tutoring Media Learned Information Ltd, Oxford, UK.
International Journal of Computers in Adult Education and Training Kogan Page, London.
International Journal of Instructional Media New York, USA.
Journal of Artificial Intelligence in Education Charlottesville, USA.
Journal of Computer Assisted Learning Blackwell Scientific Publications, Oxford.
Journal of Educational Multimedia and Hypermedia Charlottesville, USA.
Journal of Educational Research Washington, USA.
Journal of Information Systems Blackwell Scientific Publications, Oxford.
Journal of Information Technology Kogan Page, London.
Media and Methods Philadelphia, USA.
Multimedia and Videodisc Monitor Falls Church, USA.
Videodisc Newsletter British Universities Film and Video Council, London.

Keyword Index

(Where topics have been dealt with in depth, **bold type** indicates the page on which discussion of respective topics begins.)

administration of resource centres 171
affective domain 55, 108
agricultural approach to evaluation 153
aims 47
analysis 55
anthropological approach to evaluation 153
application 55
assessment **121–47**, 197
assessment criteria 138, **140–47**
assessment methods **127–47**
attention spans 66
attitude 108, 169
audio aids 82
audiovisual media in mass instruction **71–83**

behavioural objectives **46–62**
blackboards 73
Bloom, B 53
branching programme 15
buzz sessions 109

CAL 99, **177–92**
can-do statements 59
case studies 113–17
CD 82
CD-I, **188–90**
chalk-and-talk 34
chalkboards 73
charts 75
class discussions 110–13
cognitive domain 53, 106

communications skills 107
compact disc interactive 82, **188–90**
compact disc players 82
competence 23, 46, **59–61**, 106, 139, 196
completion items 132
comprehension 55
computer conferencing 187
computers as substitute tutors **182–4**
computers, functions of 178
computers, simulated laboratory mode 185
computer-assisted learning 99, **177–92**, 198
computer marked tests 184
cost-effectiveness 161
course design 48
creative thinking 106
criterion- referenced assessment 124, 139
current trends in education and training **193–202**

databases and data managers 187
digesting 25, 135, 145, 180
directed study 92
discussions 110–13
distance learning 36, 90
domains of objectives **54–7**

educational broadcasting 69
educational facilities **163–76**
educational objectives **46–62**
educational strategies **28–45**
educational technology – definitions 9

educational technology – nature of 1
electronic mail 187
Elton model 10, 11
episcopes 80
error elimination 149
essay-type questions 128
evaluation 55, **148–62**
exams 127, 137
extended writing tests 127

fairness of assessment 124
feedback (learning from) 23, 135, 145, 180
feedback from learners **157–9**, 176
feedback from teachers 160
feelings 23
feltboards 73
film projectors 81
filmstrips 78
flexible learning 36, **88–90, 95**
Flexistudy 89
flipcharts 76
free comments evaluation 157

games 113–17
group learning **18–20, 103–20**, 175, 195, 197
group projects 119
groups, self-help 120

handouts 77
hook and loop boards 74
hypermedia 188

individualized learning **12–20, 84–102**, 195
innovation, management of 21
institution-based systems 36, 85
interaction with computers 178
interactive video 101
interpersonal skills 107

Keller plan 43
knowledge 53

laboratory assessment 133
language laboratories 98
learners' expectations 199–200
learner-centredness 194
learning by doing 24, 135, 145, 179
learning and assessment **135–40**

learning cycles 25–6
learning design **47**, 196
learning experience 8, **22– 7**
learning resources **163–76**
lectures **64–7**
libraries **163–76**
Likert scales 155
linear programme 15

Mager, R F **51–3**
magnetic boards 74
mainframe computers 180
management of resource centres 169
markerboards 73
mass instruction 11, 13, 20, **63–83**
mediated feedback 117
mobiles 76
models 77
multiple-choice items 131

norm-referenced assessment 124

objectives **46–62**
objectives, advantages of 57
objectives, a fresh look at 58
objectives, rating scales 157
objectives, simpler classification of 57
objectives, types of 53
objectives, weaknesses of 58
objective tests 130
observation of instruction 159
OHP 79
opaque projectors 80
open learning 16
open learning packages 93–5
organizing 56
overhead projectors 79

patterns of communication 104
peer assessment **140–47**
performance criteria 60, 196
photo-CD 190
photocopying 176
planning resources centres 167
portfolios 61
Popperian approach to evaluation **149–52**
posters 76
practical activities 70
practical tests 133

problem solving questions 129
projects 119
project assessment 133
projectors, film 81
projectors, opaque 80
projectors, overhead 79
projected visual aids **77–81**

questionnaires 155, 157–8

range statements 60
realia 77
receiving 56
record players 82
reliability of assessment 123
remote learning 36, 38
responding 56
resource centres **163–76**
resource-based learning 165

scientific approach to evaluation 153
self-assessment **140–47**
self-instructional materials –
    audiovisual 96
self-instructional materials –
    computer-based 99
semantic differential scales 156
seminars 110–13
short notes questions 129
simulations 113–17
skills analysis 54
skills tests 134
slides 78
social approach to evaluation 153

space for learning 168
staff development 202
staffing of resource centres 168
student assessment 154
student questionnaires 155
student-centred approaches **34–44**
study skills 22
synthesis 55
systems approach 4, 6, 7

tape recorders 82
teacher-centred approaches **28–34**
teaching methods 33, 42, 117, 174
technology *in* education 2, 193
technology *of* education 3, 194
terminals 180
test construction 125
textbooks 92
textual materials 92–6
tutorials 110–113

unique-answer questions 132
unobtrusive assessment 134

validity of assessment 123
valuing 56
VCR 81
videocassettes 81
videodiscs 81
video presentations **67–9**
visual aids in mass instruction **72–81**

wallcharts 75
wanting (to learn) 24, 135, 145, 179
writing objectives 49